God Has Not Changed His Mind

His Pursuit of Image and Likeness

Cassy Gray

www.fardistancespublications.com

Published by Far Distances Publications
www.fardistancespublications.com

Printed on acid-free paper.

Far Distances Publications
2023

For Megan and Brandy

Table of Contents

Author's Note   i

Introduction   iii

REPENT

What Is a Worldview?   1

The Fall   9

The Long Road to Jabbok   17

The Necessity of Joseph   30

Failure in the Wilderness   42

The Insecurity of Saul   49

Nehemiah Takes a Stand   59

What About Me?   70

You Have One Teacher   77

IMAGE AND LIKENESS

The Heavenly Pattern   84

The Son of God   90

If I Tell You Earthly Things   97

Old Things Pass Away   104

Which Is Easier to Say…   110

The Closed Door   118

Tetelestai   125

The Power of an Empty Tomb   133

BELIEVE

Justification	138
The Trouble with Romans 7	144
Righteousness	152
Who You Are in Him	160
Who He Is in You	166
Either . . . Or . . .	174
The Narrow Way	181
It's Not About You	190
Tobiah in the Temple	198
Yeah, But . . .	209
On Earth as It Is in Heaven	216

Author's Note

I've had many good teachers throughout my Christian life who have helped me build the foundation I now stand on. I owe them a debt I can never repay. But from this group of teachers there are two who have truly impacted my understanding of the gospel. Their teachings, along with the revelations I received, have filled journal after journal until there wasn't room in my closet for any more journals. The things I wrote down in those journals were used to write this book.

I first read T. Austin Sparks in the early 1990s, but most of what he taught went right over my head. It wasn't until my crisis of faith in 2017 that I truly began to understand his teachings. T. Austin Sparks died in 1971, but all his books and teachings can be found at *www.austin-sparks.net* and are available free of charge. I can't thank the Lord enough for bringing his teachings into my life. So, if you're reading this book and thinking to yourself that a sentence here or there sounds like a proper Englishman and not an American from Cincinnati, those sentences probably belong to T. Austin Sparks.

The crisis of faith mentioned above lasted for seven months and during that time, I lived in utter despair of my true condition. One desperate night, I cried out to God for a teacher to show me what it meant to live by Christ's life, to see through His eyes, and to think as He thinks.

The next day, my YouTube feed was filled with one teacher—Dan Mohler. Just like T. Austin Sparks, much of what Dan taught went over my head. But my heart burned as I listened to sermon after sermon because I recognized the truth in what he taught. I listened to his teachings for days before the Lord turned on the light. Suddenly, Dan's understanding of the gospel was a thing I could grasp and live. His teachings changed my life for the better. I am eternally grateful for his ministry.

Just like with T. Austin-Sparks, Dan's teachings filled my journals. If you're blessed to listen to one of his sermons on YouTube and hear a familiar phrase or teaching that you've read in this book, give Dan the credit he deserves. I certainly do. He is a powerfully anointed teacher.

So right from the start, I want to thank T. Austin Sparks and Dan Mohler for the impact they've made on my life. This book couldn't be possible without them.

Introduction

The hardest part about writing this book was figuring out how to organize my thoughts. There were three main concepts I wanted to teach, but each concept was demanding to be written first. I wrote and abandoned draft after draft because the disorganization in my head showed up on every page I wrote. No one would be able to follow what I was trying to convey.

I grew discouraged. I believed I had something to say, but I didn't know how to say it. There was nothing I could do but wait until my thoughts settled down and allowed me to express them in a way that would be beneficial to the reader.

I began to think I had missed the Lord, and it wasn't His will for me to write the book. I gave up and put all the journals, notes, and drafts back in the closet. He would have to find someone else because I wasn't the one.

Two dear friends asked me how I was progressing on the manuscript. I told them I wasn't because I couldn't. Both expressed the same sentiment. The book needed to be written because people needed to hear the message. Then they told me to get to work.

I really wanted to get to work, but I still didn't know how to organize my thoughts. I told the Lord that if I was the one to write the book, He would have to help me make the three concepts behave and work together. Until they did, I was stymied. I left the book there with Him. I knew if He wanted me to write it, He would show me the way.

A few days later, I woke with a verse from the Gospel of Mark reverberating in my spirit. The verse held the key to the book. Suddenly, I could see exactly how it should be written. The three concepts became three parts. Everything I wanted to say easily fit into those three parts.

Part One, entitled *Repent*, has to do with the destructiveness of a believer's worldview. (Everyone has a worldview, which is defined as the way we perceive, react, and conduct ourselves in this present world.) This is why in His very first sermon, Jesus told us to repent, which means to change our thinking. It's imperative we see that our worldviews have become our jailers and keep us imprisoned in crippling patterns of thought that prevent us from walking in the fullness God would have for us.

In this section, I examine the lives of some Old Testament heroes and how God exposed the destructiveness of their worldviews. I also show how Christians' worldviews deceive them by teaching them to perceive life through self-centered lenses that keep them asking "What about me?" My constant demand for an answer to that question resulted in multiple wildfires being set in my life that threatened to consume me. I couldn't douse the flames because I was deficient in the necessary spiritual understanding required to do so. And upon this deficiency I foundered.

I could only put out the fires when I came to understand that I had only one teacher (Matthew 23:10). Only what Christ says matters. When I changed my thinking and believed what He said about me, I was set free. And you can be, too. The first step we must take to ensure His will is done on earth as it is in heaven is to repent.

Part two, entitled *Image and Likeness,* concentrates on Jesus as He lived out His life in the gospels. Genesis 1:26 reads, "Let us make man in our image and after our likeness. And let them have dominion…" I have heard many great sermons on dominion, but very few sermons on image and likeness. The good news is that God has not changed His mind about His purpose for our lives. He created us for His image and after His likeness, and He's still pursuing image and likeness today.

When God declared His great purpose for man, image and likeness wasn't vague or nebulous. He didn't sit back to see what type of image and likeness would develop in Adam and Eve organically and naturally as they worked and kept the garden. God's eternal counsel had already defined image and likeness before He created. Man was to bear the image and likeness of His Son.

The tragic result of the Fall was that man lost all sense of image and likeness. Throughout his long history, he hasn't hesitated to define what is good, right, and moral. He believes truth is subjective and malleable to fit any situation as long as it benefits him. That's the strength of the lie. Fallen man is oblivious that truth and goodness are objective and concrete and belong to God alone.

Jesus appeared along the banks of the Jordan to declare He didn't come to negotiate with man about God's will. He didn't come to debate it with those who thought they knew. He didn't come to compromise the Father's eternal purpose so we could live less than who God would have us to be. He came to embody God's will. He withstood temptations, other people's ambitions, and the priests' hostility and spoke the truth because we were in desperate need for someone to tell us the truth about who we were from the beginning.

Part three, entitled *Believe*, is the only way we will be set free from our worldviews and be stripped of everything the Fall and the flesh taught us. How many of us have been really taught the foundational things of Christianity? How many of us live free in the understanding of justification? How many of us truly believe we have been set free from sin's dominion and are no longer *just* sinners saved by grace forced to live in sin and weakness because we're still in the flesh? How many of us are standing, right now, before the Lord holy, blameless, and beyond reproach because our righteousness is perfect even on our worse days? How many of us have embraced the power of the doctrine of self-denial? How many of us are keeping score of all our weaknesses and failures and because we're keeping score, we believe the Lord is also?

The New Testament is a whole new way of living, and it begins with our thinking and the way we perceive the Lord, ourselves, and those around us. It is the renewing of our minds so we may discern what is of God and what is not.

This is His work in us. Our coming into spiritual maturity isn't as easy as we would like. It takes His light revealing just how unlike Christ we are to affect real transformation. As He conforms us to His Son, there will be tears, despair over our conditions, repentance, more light, more despair, and more tears. We have been enrolled in the school of Christ. But as we come to believe what He says over us instead of what we've been telling ourselves, we'll be reconstituted into His image and after His likeness. This is His promise to us from before the creation of the world. And God will not change His mind.

Now after John was arrested, Jesus came into Galilee, proclaiming the gospel of God, and saying, "The time is fulfilled, and the kingdom of God is at hand; repent and believe in the gospel."

Mark 1:14–15 ESV

Part 1
REPENT

Chapter 1
WHAT IS A WORLDVIEW?
The thief comes only to steal and kill and destroy.
John 10:10

FROM THE MOMENT I was saved, the Christian world taught me that the word *repent* means to be sorrowful for my sins, which were and always will be too many to count. This teaching laid upon me a heavy burden that I couldn't bear. I spent the majority of my Christian life just being sorry. Sorry for it all. There was always so much to be sorry for, so I repented and repented and repented. I cried tears of repentance but remained the person I had always been. And I was sorry for that too.

Then I heard a pastor teach that repentance isn't about sorrow but about changing your thinking. Could this possibly be true? Had I been laboring under a false teaching that did nothing but cause me heartbreak all my Christian life? To my amazement, I looked up the word *repent* in a Greek dictionary and discovered that it really does mean to think differently, to change the mind.

When Jesus came out of the wilderness (Mark 1:14–15), He preached repentance as the first step to believing the good news of the kingdom of God. Since changing my thinking was important to Him, I went to work to ensure this happened. But I quickly wore myself out trying to change the tenor of the self-talk that constantly went on inside my head.

My failure was devastating. If I couldn't even accomplish the first step, how could I ever do the second step and believe in the good news of the gospel? I did what I always did when confronted with failure. I retreated into my old understanding of repentance. I cried, told the Lord how sorry I was, and remained the person I had always been.

What Is a Worldview?

Finally, the Holy Spirit freed me from this work of the flesh by teaching me that Jesus wasn't saying to change every thought that bounced in and out of my mind. He was after something far more significant. He was after my worldview, for it was from my worldview that all my thoughts derived.

Our Worldview and How It Affects Us

Our worldview is the lens through which we perceive and react to life. Every compliment or criticism, every appreciation or slight, every approval or rejection impacted us. Our response to the situations we find ourselves in, whether good or bad, and the words spoken to us were used to create the wounds, scars, needs, desires, longings, and dreams that reside deep inside us. They became the motivation for who we are and what we do. They became our belief system, mindset, and how we think.

The *self* is at the core of our worldview, like a Tootsie Roll at the center of a Tootsie Pop. The *self* is the reason we found it necessary to develop a worldview in the first place. It is the *self* that receives all the blows of life, and it is the *self* that determines how we react in situations. Our *self* created our worldview to either shield it from further damage or hold it responsible for the harm inflicted upon it.

To illustrate the relationship between the *self* and the worldview, let's look at an insecure person. I'll call her Bonnie. For as long as Bonnie can remember, hurtful words have been spoken to her and about her. She has been called names. She has absorbed all the criticism, anger, impatience, and abuse that came her way. Her family, her friends, and perfect strangers have told her she was stupid and worthless, and she believes it. Her parents neglected her, so she believes she is unlovable. Bonnie is filled with self-loathing and frustration because she doesn't want to be insecure. She hates that she believes these things about herself. She doesn't want them to be true.

Now, if that's how Bonnie feels, why doesn't she break free from the names, the neglect, and the lies? It's because Bonnie's worldview constantly reinforces her opinion of herself. When she makes a mistake, her worldview accuses her of being stupid. When her good friend doesn't invite her to a party, her worldview accuses her of having a rotten personality that no one wants to be around. When she is sitting alone at night, her worldview accuses her of being unlovable. Her worldview blames her for the state of her life, and she accepts the blame because her worldview has conditioned her to think this way. She's trapped and can't find a way out of a life she doesn't want because her worldview won't allow her to do so. Her worldview is now her jailer.

The Man Born Blind

John 9:1–34 tells the story of the man born blind. He was sitting by the side of the road, begging for alms because his whole livelihood depended on the kindness of strangers. As people hurried by him, some would stop and give him a coin so he could eat that night. Most didn't even notice him, though. Then one Sabbath day, Jesus and His disciples walked by.

The disciples pointed the man out to Jesus. According to the law, this man was blind because of sin (Deuteronomy 28:28). They wanted to know who was to blame. Was the man being punished for his parents' sins? If not, what sins had he committed while still in the womb? Jesus' answer caught them by surprise. He said the man's blindness wasn't because of sin at all, but so the works of God could be displayed in him. Jesus mixed clay and spit together to make mud, smeared the mud on the man's eyes, and told him to wash in the Pool of Siloam. The man did and came back seeing.

And that's when all the trouble began. When the crowd learned that a miracle had occurred, they hurried the man to the Pharisees so the Pharisees could tell them how to think about what they just witnessed.

The Pharisees regarded themselves as the true teachers and shepherds of Israel. Their teachings were based on centuries of writings and traditions passed down through generations. Their authority came from their ability to rightly interpret the Scriptures and discern God's will for every situation. Their supreme confidence produced a rigid worldview in which they were always right and those who opposed them were always wrong.

Jesus of Nazareth was the latest in a long line of itinerant preachers who challenged the religious status quo the Pharisees strictly enforced, and they believed that while Jesus' miracles might fool the crowds, His miracles didn't fool them. God judged and punished sinners who broke the Sabbath (Exodus 31:15); He certainly didn't work through them. Previously, after Jesus healed the lame man by the pool of Bethesda (John 5:1–15), a small faction within the priests' ranks had suggested that perhaps their long-held beliefs were wrong. Jesus couldn't be a sinner because the types of miracles He performed could only be from God. The rest stubbornly refused to listen. If it were true that God could purposely work through someone who deliberately broke His law, then it could also be true that they didn't understand the law at all. That notion was inconceivable.

Since Jesus wasn't around to answer for His healing of the blind man, the Pharisees tried to discredit the man by proving he was a liar. They summoned his parents to ask them if he had been born blind. At face value, it would appear the Pharisees were honest brokers of truth. But they knew what they were doing when they called the man's parents before them.

The Pharisees had made it clear. If anyone declared Jesus was the Christ, the priests would throw that person out of the synagogue, which was more than being kicked out of a church. It was the complete and permanent exile from Jewish society. The person would become a pariah and have no choice but to uproot their life, go somewhere else, and pray that the news of their banishment wouldn't follow them and force them to leave their new home. It was a heavy price to pay, and the Pharisees knew it. So did the terrified couple, which was why they refused to answer. Their son was of legal age, they said, so the Pharisees should ask him.

The Pharisees brought the man before them and ordered him to give glory to God for his healing and not to Jesus, for He was a sinner. The man refused and said, "I don't know if He is a sinner. The one thing I do know is that I was blind but now I can see." They pressed the man to answer more and more questions. They wanted a detailed explanation of Jesus' actions to restore his sight. "Why do you want to know?" the man asked. "Unless you want to become His disciples too."

How dare he suggest such a thing! The Pharisees were Moses' disciples, for they knew God had spoken to Moses. As for Jesus, they didn't know from whence He had come.

Now, this was a staggering admission to make. These vaunted teachers were supposed to receive Messiah when He came to Israel. It was their number one job. Moses had given them all the signposts they needed to recognize Him. They, above all, should have known if opening the eyes of a man born blind was the work of God or not. Yet, before this beggar, they confessed that they knew nothing.

Can you imagine what this man must have felt at this moment, hearing the Pharisees confess they didn't know the difference between a sinner and a righteous man? The Pharisees' worldview that God could never forgive sinners had condemned him to the miserable life of a beggar. Their teachings also justified the actions of everyone who had walked by and mistreated him.

The man went on the offense. He took their teaching and used it to expose their utter blindness to the ways of God. "You are the ones who say God can't work through sinners," he reminded them. "You are the ones who say that God only listens to worshipers who do His will. But whether you like it or not, God listens to Jesus of Nazareth because no one has ever opened the eyes of someone born blind. Not even Moses."

How does one answer this? They couldn't, so they didn't. He had them. A simple beggar had exposed their blindness. The Pharisees took the only out they had left. They called him names and cast him out of the synagogue.

It was at this point that Jesus re-entered the story. Someone had told Him all the man had suffered at the Pharisees' hands. When Jesus found him, He asked if he believed in the Son of Man. "Who is he?" the man asked in response. "You have seen Him," Jesus told him. This man whom the Pharisees had judged and dismissed now received the greatest revelation of all: that Jesus is the Christ. "He is speaking to you right now," Jesus said. The man fell to his knees and worshiped.

In front of the man, His disciples, and the Pharisees, Jesus declared, "For judgment, I came into this world, that those who do not see may see, and those who see may become blind" (John 9:39). The Pharisees took umbrage at this statement. They asked Him if He was implying they were blind. Jesus responded, "If you were blind, you would have no guilt, but now that you say, 'We see,' your guilt remains" (v. 41).

The Pharisees' Blindness

John 10 explains why the Pharisees were blind. In the first five verses, Jesus described the working of a sheepfold. Those gathered about Him were familiar with sheepfolds, having been around them all their lives. What the Pharisees didn't understand was what a sheepfold had to do with them being blind.

5

Jesus declared He alone was the door of the sheepfold. There was no other door. Moses, the law, and the traditions passed down by the fathers were not doors. The Pharisees' condemnation of Jesus as a sinner and the miracles He performed as the works of Satan were the same as a thief or a robber breaking into the sheepfold. The Pharisees could only have one nefarious motive for doing so: they wanted to steal the sheep from their rightful owner. If the sheep were stolen and forced to live outside the shepherd's protection, the sheep would be killed and destroyed, which would be the inevitable outcome of the Pharisees' false teaching.

Not only had the Pharisees failed in their role as teachers, but they had also failed in their role as shepherds. A good shepherd lays down his life for the sheep because he cares for them. He doesn't flee when the wolf is sighted. A hireling is the one who runs. Even though the sheep's owner paid the hireling to shepherd the sheep, the hireling will always value his life more than the sheep's welfare. The Pharisees' insistence that they were good shepherds had been proven wrong by their continued hostility to Jesus. They were nothing more than hirelings who would rather see the sheep scattered and destroyed than lay down their power and position and receive Jesus as Messiah and King.

Homeschooled in the Wrong Home

No matter where it comes from, any teaching that lessens or denies what Jesus has said about Himself, the Father, the Spirit, who He is in us, and who we are in Him is the same as someone robbing us of our treasure. False teaching is never harmless. It has only one motive and is cunning in its operation against us. It steals from us, kills us, and destroys us.

Unfortunately, our worldview has been influenced and refined by the most potent false teacher and hireling known to man: this present world—a governmental system that answers only to Satan. This world has its value system, morality, and wisdom separate from God's. At its core, it is the enthronement of thwarted *self.* Satan rebelled against God because he wanted to share God's glory. His rebellion ended in total defeat, so he sought another avenue to gain what God had denied him. Satan entered the garden of Eden, deceived Adam and Eve, and took dominion over the earth.

He put God out of His place and became the god of this world (2 Corinthians 4:4).

Satan set up a government where he was on top and man was on the bottom. In between was a ranking of rulers, authorities, powers, and dominions tasked with ensuring man remained on the bottom. He infused this world with a duplicitous wisdom to convince us that it knows the way to life while leading us to death.

Worldly wisdom is directly responsible for our most deeply held truths. This false teacher taught us to fight for our rights to achieve what's best for us, even if we had to earn it at the expense of others. It made us willful and selfish so we could navigate and survive the hostile world it created. This world is hostile. It hates God and everything He has created, including us. Behind every good or bad lesson we learned was a wisdom opposed to God.

Think about it. From the moment we were born, Satan forced us to live in a system designed to punish us because we came from God. Simply put, we were homeschooled in the wrong home. So we wasted our lives searching for things that will never make us enough, bring the fullness we desire, make us worthy of love, and give us value. Those things will never come from the world because Satan didn't put the world system into place to provide us with those things but to keep them from us.

The Villainy of a Worldview

Unfortunately, your worldview didn't disappear the moment God saved you. It's still there, interpreting life for you. You might ask how that can be true now that you know Christ and have His Word. It's because your worldview is as much a part of you as the air in your lungs. It takes the work of the Holy Spirit to transform your worldview into the kingdom view God always intended you to have. Whether He works through a sudden burst of revelation or the gradual dawning of understanding, the Holy Spirit dwells in you to mature you into the full measure of sonship.

No matter how His truth and light come, He will always present you with two choices. You can choose the way of the man born blind after he realized the Pharisees did not understand God's ways to tell him who he was and how he should live. He threw off their teachings and the miserable life his worldview had imposed upon him. Or you can choose the way of the Pharisees. They decided to harden their hearts when confronted with the same truth and refused to believe the gospel.

It is necessary to understand the villainy of your worldview. Worldly wisdom has corrupted it, and your worldview can't be rehabilitated or reformed. It works against you to keep you enslaved in darkness and death. This corruption came as a result of Adam's fall. You can't escape it. All you can do is accept God's verdict on fallen man and repent of the worldview that came to all humanity. We'll discuss this in the next chapter.

Chapter 2
THE FALL

For you are dust, and to dust you shall return.

Genesis 3:19

WHEN GOD CREATED man in His image and after His likeness, image and likeness weren't vague or nebulous. He didn't sit back to see what type of image and likeness would develop in Adam organically and naturally as he went about working and keeping the garden. God's eternal counsel had already defined image and likeness before He created man. He created Adam and his descendants to bear the image and likeness of His Son. They were to be sons of God upon the earth and be limitless in their capacity to know God. The Father called all of humanity to share His Son's life so His eternal purpose could find its full expression in and through them.

Adam wasn't ignorant of his call to be in the Son's image and likeness. He knew God's will for his life just like he knew God's will regarding the fruit of the tree of the knowledge of good and evil. He knew what God expected of him and how to satisfy God's heart.

He was to live as the Son lives. The Son's position isn't on the periphery of life but central and supreme. *Central* is defined as of the greatest importance, and *supreme* is defined as the highest in authority. Jesus occupies the preeminent place in all the Father does. By making the Son the forever center of His work on earth, the Father gave Him the position of Lord, King, and Heir. He sums up His eternal purpose in His Son.

The Father has entrusted His glory to the Son and wanted to entrust His glory to Adam as Adam came to abide in the Son's life. But there could be no negotiation over what constituted image and likeness. And Adam knew

9

it. In fact, Adam knew everything God had said to him and about him, but knowing those things wasn't the same as choosing them when the choosing mattered.

The Loss of Image and Likeness

In Genesis 2, Moses wrote that God took the man He created and placed him in the garden of Eden to tend and keep it. He also planted two trees in the midst of the garden. One was the tree of life. The other was the tree of the knowledge of good and evil. He told Adam he could eat of every tree in the garden except one. He wasn't to eat the fruit of the tree of the knowledge of good and evil, for on the day he ate it, he would surely die. This commandment wasn't a trap but a choice. When the choice came, would Adam prove his fidelity to God or another?

In Genesis 3, the Bible introduces the other central figure of creation. Satan enters the garden to present a different source of life to Adam and Eve. He asked them a seemingly harmless question: "Did God actually say 'You shall not eat of any tree in the garden?'" (Genesis 3:1). But it wasn't benign. There was a fatal destiny bound up in the question. Eve responded and signaled her willingness to listen to whatever Satan had to say.

For Satan's deception to work, he had to change how they viewed the fruit. The Lord had made it known that the fruit of the knowledge of good and evil would only produce death. So Satan lied. He told them that the fruit wouldn't kill them. How could it? The fruit was the source of image and likeness apart from the Father. They didn't have to live dependent on God to secure the destiny God had proclaimed over them.

The offer was for personal freedom. Eat, and Adam and Eve would acquire the autonomy necessary to break away from God and the limits He unilaterally imposed on them. They would be able to determine what was good and what was evil, what was truth and what was a lie. More importantly, they would find that they now inherently and organically possessed the same qualities the Son had—life, preeminence, and dominion. This knowledge would make them equal to God. They would no longer need God to restrain their behavior with commandments and calling. In other words, they would be free of God's "meddling."

Satan took God's purpose for them and used it to goad them into acting in their self-interest. Adam and Eve would only find true dominion if they were courageous enough to supplant the Son's government by establishing their own. The fruit of the tree of the knowledge of good and evil would allow them to become self-actualized and fulfilled. They would be free to live a life on their terms. "God knows this is true," Satan said, "which is why He forbids you to eat the fruit."

When Eve saw that the tree was good for food and to be desired to make one wise, Satan knew he had won, for when he influences our thinking and emotions, our will blindly follows. She took the fruit, ate it, and gave it to Adam, who also ate.

Adam made his bid for supremacy, enthroned his reason in independence, and lost everything. For what Satan conveniently left out of the conversation was that man was created to be an image-bearer. A break with God's life would leave him empty and primed for another life to move in and fill him.

With a glittering lie, Satan put God out of His place in creation. He took the dominion God meant for man and used it to create a world system to actively oppose God as He worked to rectify what was lost. Satan filled man and creation with his own rebellious and corrupted life. He took Adam and all his children in hand to teach them what to think and then how to think about it. He gave man a corrupted worldview by thoroughly persuading him that the self-centered way he now viewed life was the correct and proper view.

The moment Adam and Eve ate the fruit, their soul eyes were opened and their spiritual eyes were blinded. They became confined to the limits of this earthly realm while the heavenly realm was closed to them. Death entered and became the great power that has continuously wrestled against God's eternal purpose. Separated from God, Adam was marked and destined to live his life not only with a darkened mind but under the thumb of a cruel taskmaster. All his descendants would suffer the same fate. Man and all his attempts to create a perfect utopia would be ultimately frustrated by death.

Adam did become all the things Satan promised him—independent, self-actualized, and self-governing. The lie Adam accepted entered into his very constitution. In himself, he now neither knew nor was capable of understanding the truth. That's the strength of the lie. Man doesn't even recognize that he is blind and living in a grave.

God's verdict upon the whole world is simple. In Adam, all die. The door is closed and the way is barred. God signified this truth by expelling Adam and Eve from the garden and placing cherubim and a flaming sword to guard the tree of life. His full thought is no longer with the first Adam. The door is closed and will only open one way: through God's provided way.

Cain and Abel

A conflict now raged upon the earth. Was the door really closed to Adam and his descendants? Or could man force the door open through his righteous works and worship? This conflict is the backdrop of the tragic story of Cain and Abel (Genesis 4).

It's important to note that Cain didn't exclude or ignore God. He recognized God and built an altar so he could worship Him. As an offering, he selected the best of what he grew—the product of his labor. Cain offered it, expecting it to be received. But he found a closed door when he laid it upon the altar. He grew sullen and angry that God had refused his offering and his motive in bringing it. But by sacrificing an offering from the earth and paying tribute to his strength, he proved worldly wisdom's influence over his worldview. He refused to accept God's verdict that the door was closed to fallen man.

The closed door had also passed to Abel. But when Abel brought his offering to the Lord, he found an open door. Why? Unlike Cain, Abel accepted God's verdict on fallen man. He understood that a sinful soul had to be poured out to death and not offered to God. Abel couldn't offer the life he had received from Adam. So he came to God through the life of another. That's why he sacrificed a spotless lamb.

Cain represents all those who seek to be accepted by God based on what they deem good. Abel represents those who seek to die to themselves so they can live by the life of another. For Cain, his worldview governed his perceptions about God and what God should accept. Abel accepted God's verdict and allowed the Spirit to rule his worldview. Even after God told

Cain how to be received, he refused to listen. Instead, the conflict reached its climax when he killed his brother.

Cain went out from God's presence unrepentant and resentful. He produced a civilization after his image and likeness, which had a fruitfulness apart from God. The flood was God's verdict on Cain's society.

The Road to Emmaus

When Jesus came in the flesh, He dealt with a whole universe of obstructions and limitations to God's eternal purpose. He tried to make the people understand but they dismissed His teachings as heresy, demonized His works, and ignored His claims that He was Messiah. No matter what He did—even raising Lazarus from the dead after he had been in the tomb for four days— He couldn't penetrate the spiritual blindness that held the people firmly in its grip.

To better understand the tragedy of the Fall and the limitations it placed on all men, let's examine the story of the two disciples on the road to Emmaus.

They had left Jerusalem to go to Emmaus, a village about seven miles away. Under the hot sun, they walked down the dusty road and discussed the events from the past several days. Jesus of Nazareth had been arrested at night and brought before the Sanhedrin, who, in an illegal trial, found him guilty of blasphemy and sentenced him to death.

Since the Romans made it unlawful for the Jews to kill anyone, the members of the Sanhedrin brought Him before Pontius Pilate so the Romans could execute Him on their behalf. Pilate questioned Jesus but quickly discovered He was innocent of the charges against Him. He ordered Jesus to be beaten with the scourge to appease the priests before he released Him. The priests were incensed. They threatened and pressured Pilate until he gave in to their demands and condemned Jesus to die by crucifixion. Six hours later Jesus died outside Jerusalem at a place known as The Skull. As the sun began to set, He was taken down from the cross and buried in a borrowed tomb.

The disciples' conversation progressed from the events of the past several days to those of the past three years. They had left everything to follow Jesus because they were sure He was the Messiah. They had studied the law and traditions in the synagogue since childhood. They and everyone in Israel eagerly awaited the Son of David to appear and release them from Roman tyranny.

There had been messiahs in the past, but they were all revealed as false in short order. But in the disciples' generation, a new prophet had arisen proclaiming the kingdom of God. Their hearts burned as they listened to His teachings. No one had the command of Scripture He possessed. Not even the Pharisees. But that didn't stop the priests from trying to trick Him into breaking the law so they could accuse Him before the people. He always confounded them with a wisdom that was not of this world.

The crowds and excitement around Him grew. Sometimes He couldn't even enter a village because of the crush of people begging Him to heal them from sicknesses and lifelong diseases. The two men had witnessed the impossible every day. The deaf could suddenly hear. The dumb spoke their first words. People who were blind had their sight restored. The lame walked home. The dead were raised to life. Oh, it was a great time to be alive. Then in one long night, it vanished.

At dawn, some of the women who had followed Jesus banged on the door of the house where the men were hiding from the religious leaders with the rest of the disciples. The women's weeping made it challenging to understand what they were saying. They had gone to the tomb to anoint Jesus' body, but an angel had rolled back the stone and showed them the empty grave clothes on the stone table. The angel asked them, "Why do you seek the living among the dead? He is not here but has risen" (Luke 24:5–6). John leaped to his feet and ran out the door. Peter hurried after him.

Those who were left stared at each other in stunned silence. Then all the disciples began to speak at once. Was it true? Was He alive? No, He couldn't be alive. If He was alive, why hadn't He come to them? They should wait until John and Peter return to hear what they found at the tomb. When they did return, they reported the tomb was empty but they didn't see any angels or Jesus. The faint specter of hope that had flickered in the two men's hearts all morning died out. The women were wrong. He wasn't alive. There would be no king on David's throne.

Suddenly, they found the small house suffocating. They needed to escape. They were still deep in conversation, walking along the road, when a stranger joined them and asked what they were discussing. Cleopas, one of the two, was flabbergasted. How could this man not know what had transpired in Jerusalem? They told him of Jesus' arrest and crucifixion. They explained how His death crushed their hopes for the future. They even told him that some women believed that Jesus had risen from the dead.

Instead of sympathizing with them, the stranger admonished them for being slow of heart to believe what the prophets had written in the Scriptures. Starting with Moses and working through all the prophets, he explained that Messiah had to suffer and die before He could enter His glory. As the men listened, their hearts burned within them. He was opening the Scriptures in a new way they had never heard before.

They reached the village and the two men asked the stranger to stay with them for the night. When they sat down to eat a small dinner, the man took the bread and blessed it. Suddenly, their eyes were opened and they recognized Him. It was true. Jesus was alive! Before they could speak, He vanished. They scrambled up from the table and retraced the seven miles to Jerusalem. They couldn't wait to share their news. Jesus was alive!

The two men running back to Jerusalem had spent years by Jesus' side and had performed mighty miracles in His name. They were known to friends and strangers alike as His disciples. More importantly, they knew His teachings and works. They had been right in the thick of it since the beginning, men who were incredibly full of teaching and experience when it came to the things of God. But they were none the better for it when the day of crisis came. They still lacked spiritual understanding of all they had heard and witnessed in the last three years. It was upon this deficiency they had foundered.

Their deficiency only pointed to the natural and earthly limits of their worldviews. They wanted to believe every word Jesus had ever uttered, but they couldn't. They were hindered by the same death Adam suffered in the garden. That death had been passed down to them. That's why they didn't believe the women's claims that Jesus had risen from the dead. There was no room in their worldviews for resurrection. Dead was dead. Their sight could only take them to the closed and sealed tomb and no further. Their Messiah's story had ended the same way all the other false messiahs' stories had ended. They died and left their disciples picking up the pieces of their shipwrecked faith.

15

God Has Not Changed His Mind

When we behold the Son, we see God's intention for our life. God never meant for us to live on the fringes of what He is doing on the earth but to interpret our life through the lens of His eternal purpose. We'll never see the need to change our worldviews until we, once and for all, reject what God has repudiated. Yet, the fallen nature has renounced God's verdict and seeks to carve out an independent life while also worshiping God. In our fallen states, we've nothing to bring that is acceptable to God. We must renounce the lie that has captured the very soul of all of Adam's descendants and corrupted our worldviews. In Adam, our destiny is futility and death. God has closed the door and barred the way into the fullness of His life to all of Adam's descendants.

And God has not changed His mind.

Chapter 3
THE LONG ROAD TO JABBOK
"What is your name?"

Genesis 32:27

JACOB'S STORY TEACHES that fallen flesh can never inherit the things of God. Since Jacob was born second after Esau, he was on the outside of God's redemptive plan. He chaffed at the poverty of his birth order and decided to obtain what he wanted through deceit. He didn't care about the tremendous damage his deceitful ways inflicted upon others. He lied to his father and stole the blessing from his brother because he believed his desire to be Abraham's heir justified his actions. Fallen man never goes wrong without having a very sound argument for doing so. Jacob's argument was simple: he wanted the blessing and knew how to get it.

In the aftermath of his deception, Jacob congratulated himself on his accomplishment not understanding that God would never allow man's independent ways to impinge on His eternal purpose. Jacob represented the fullness of independence. God's school of self-emptying was waiting for him in Haran for he could only inherit God's promises through faith, not the flesh.

God brought the cross into Jacob's life countless times to cause him to see that how he thought about the world and his place in it were contrary to God's ways. Jacob was a slow learner, but he learned, nevertheless. His years living in Haran finally produced in him a willingness to let go of his destructive worldview to grasp a new way—a way that didn't require him to live by his wits any longer.

At the fords of Jabbok, God was waiting for him to expose the pain and misery his worldview had caused him by asking a very simple question: "What is your name?"

Jacob and Esau

The twins were born almost at the same time. Esau was delivered first, and was covered in so much red hair that it looked like his little body was dressed in a hairy coat. His mother named him Esau, which means hairy. Jacob came into the world grasping Esau's heel. This action earned him the name Jacob, which has two meanings. The first one is to follow or to be behind—a name that fit him perfectly. He had followed his brother out of the womb, and due to the birth order, he would follow his brother for the rest of his life. The other meaning is to supplant, circumvent, assail, and overreach.

As firstborn, Esau was heir to the birthright. Upon Isaac's death, Esau would divide the estate into thirds. Each son would receive a third, while the last third would be reserved for the family. Esau would control these funds and use them to care for his mother and for any other financial interest that benefited the family. The only way the birthright could pass to the second son was for the heir to either die or to be proven unworthy.

The Scriptures don't tell us much about Esau and Jacob as they grew into adulthood. We have this one revealing story about their characters and worldviews (Genesis 25). Esau had been out hunting and returned with nothing to show for his efforts. He was hungry—so hungry he thought he was going to die. As Esau approached the family homestead, he spied Jacob sitting by a campfire, stirring a pot of lentil stew. Exhausted, he threw himself on the ground and asked his brother for some stew.

Jacob wasn't sitting in that particular spot by accident. He knew what he wanted, and he knew his brother well enough to know how to get it. As he scooped the stew into the bowl, he told Esau he would give him the stew in exchange for the birthright. His brother quickly agreed. A moment later, Esau was devouring the stew. Jacob watched him eat. He had the birthright—and now he had to find a way to secure the covenant.

The next time we see Jacob, it is at the pivotal moment in his life (Genesis 27). He was seventy years old and had reached maturity with a fully formed worldview. Isaac believed he was dying and wanted to lay hands on Esau and speak Abraham's blessing over him before Isaac was gathered to his fathers.

Rebekah told Jacob what Isaac was planning to do. Jacob hesitated. The thought of stealing the blessing from his brother didn't bother his conscience. He just needed to figure out some way to deceive his father so he would come away with the blessing and not a curse.

His mother came to his rescue. Her motivation for helping him was based on a prophecy she received before her sons were born. God had told her that Jacob would be the stronger of the two, and Esau would serve him. She dressed Jacob in his brother's robes, covered his arms and neck with goatskins so if Isaac touched him he would be hairy like his brother, and gave Jacob the stew that Esau was to bring as the covenant meal. The rest would be up to Jacob. He didn't disappoint her. He walked into his father's tent and announced he was Esau.

Isaac didn't believe him. His eyesight was failing, and he couldn't see the son standing before him, but he recognized Jacob's voice. So he asked him point-blank if he was Esau. Jacob lied with such conviction that Isaac believed him. All through the sharing of the covenant meal, Jacob sat next to his father and continued his deceit. If at any time his conscience did get the better of him, he could have stopped the charade, but he remained calm, cool, and collected. He allowed his father to continue to believe that he was blessing Esau. When Jacob left the tent, he had everything he wanted. He was Abraham's heir, and the land, the nation, and the blessing belonged to him.

Jacob had barely left the tent when Esau entered and greeted his father. This time the voice matched the son. Isaac began to shake at the magnitude of Jacob's deception. He told Esau what Jacob had done. At first, Esau was in disbelief. Surely Isaac could revoke the blessing if Jacob had gained it through deceit. But Isaac couldn't withdraw the blessing. What was done was done. Esau received a blessing, but Isaac warned his son that he would serve Jacob until his descendants finally grew restless and broke Jacob's yoke from their necks.

Jacob's lie shattered the family into pieces. Esau left his father's tent, determined that once his father was dead and the days of mourning were completed, he would murder Jacob and take back what he had stolen. He didn't care who knew. He told everyone what he planned to do, and someone told Rebekah.

She didn't tell Isaac what Esau was planning. Instead, she disguised her need to send Jacob far away by pleading with her husband to send him to her brother in Haran so he could marry a wife that would bring them both joy. Esau had married women from the surrounding tribes, and they were making her life miserable. She couldn't endure it if Jacob married outside the family. Isaac was only too glad to send him away. And just like that, Jacob was on his way to Haran.

That night, when he lay down on the ground, using a rock as a pillow, he slept so soundly that he could dream (Genesis 28). I don't know about you, but if I had deceived my father and betrayed my brother, the last thing I could do was sleep. Not Jacob. He dreamed of a ladder stretching from heaven to earth, with God's angels ascending and descending on it. Suddenly, the Lord stood above the ladder and promised not to leave Jacob until He brought him back to this land.

Jacob woke up, shaken to the core. He had chosen to make his camp on the very doorstep of the house of God and hadn't even known it. He poured oil over his stone pillow and knelt before it. His worldview poured forth in his prayer. He was all for the Lord mightily blessing him. That was why he wanted the covenant. To have bread to eat and clothing to wear.

But if the Lord was serious about bringing him back to the land, there was something the Lord would need to do first. He would have to clean up the mess Jacob had left behind in Beersheba. In other words, God would have to deal with Esau. To sweeten the pot, Jacob promised to tithe 10 percent of all the material goods the Lord blessed him with. How could the Lord resist such a deal? Satisfied with himself, he began the long walk to Haran.

Laban

Haran wasn't the haven Jacob believed it was (Genesis 29). Waiting for him was Laban, a man who shared Jacob's worldview and lied and deceived for the mere practice of it. Laban loved money, and when Jacob arrived on his doorstep, he realized his nephew was the heir of all that divine favor that had made Abraham wealthy beyond words. And it just got better, for Jacob was in love with his youngest daughter. Laban had caught Jacob in his web and schemed never to let him escape until he was more prosperous than Abraham.

Laban played up the family ties. He couldn't allow Jacob to work for free, so he told him to name his wage. Jacob said that he wanted Rachel's hand in marriage as his pay. Laban wavered. He was willing to betroth Rachel to him, but he couldn't give his daughter in marriage so cheaply. He had a reputation to uphold in the community, so he had no choice but to set a bridal price that would bring honor to the family's name. Hopefully, Jacob would think the price was reasonable. He could marry Rachel after seven years of labor. If Jacob agreed, the couple would marry at the contract's end.

The years passed quickly. Laban prepared a feast and invited his friends and family to help him celebrate the happy couple's marriage. As night fell, Jacob excused himself and asked his father-in-law to bring his new wife to his tent. The woman Laban presented to Jacob was heavily veiled, and Jacob could barely see her in the darkness. When the sun rose the following day, Jacob discovered Laban had deceived him. Lying next to him wasn't Rachel but her older sister, Leah.

Jacob found himself in a position he had never been in before. He was the victim of someone else's deceit, and he believed his outrage was justified. He had fulfilled the contract, and his uncle had flat-out betrayed him. He didn't want Leah. But now he was married to her, like it or not. He demanded to know why Laban had betrayed him. His father-in-law had an explanation ready. He couldn't allow Rachel to marry before Leah. The resulting scandal would ruin the family's reputation for years. Laban offered him Rachel's hand in marriage for another seven years of labor. This time, though, Jacob could marry Rachel once the week-long festivities celebrating his marriage to Leah had ended.

Leah and Rachel

What of the women who had been caught up in Laban's plot? Leah was complicit. Before they consummated the marriage, all she had to do was tell Jacob who she was. But she didn't. She kept quiet and pretended to be her sister. If Jacob had any self-awareness, he should have admired Leah's coolness. After all, her refusal to tell him the truth during their first night together was the same refusal he had mustered when Isaac asked if he was Esau. But this was too much to ask of Jacob's outrage. His feelings toward her grew into indifference.

If Laban presented Leah to Jacob as his bride, what had happened to Rachel? Where had Laban held her prisoner so she couldn't escape and ruin her father's plans? The news that she could marry Jacob once the wedding celebration ended brought little solace. By marrying Jacob first, Leah had solidified her place in the family and the community. She would be recognized everywhere as Jacob's wife, while the societal norms regulated Rachel to second place. Second to Leah in everything. Even her children would be second to Leah's children. The only place she wouldn't be second would be Jacob's love, but that wasn't enough. She could never be happy until she had gained back what her father had stolen from her—the place, position, and honor of being Jacob's wife.

The sisters immediately entered a lifelong battle for Jacob's affection. Each was resentful of the other's presence in the marriage and jealous of Jacob's time with her sister. They desperately wanted the position the other held. Rachel wanted to be the wife. Leah wanted to be loved. Leah did have one advantage over her sister. She could bear sons to Jacob while Rachel was barren.

Leah bore Jacob four sons in quick succession. She named her firstborn Reuben (behold a son) because she was firmly convinced that by presenting Jacob with his firstborn and heir, he would see her differently and finally love her. Simeon (to be heard) was born next. The little boy proved that God had heard how she was hated in the household. Levi (to be joined) arrived soon after. Leah believed Jacob would finally leave Rachel and be joined to her as a faithful husband. Finally, Judah (praise) was born. She praised the Lord, for how could Jacob ignore her and her sons?

As Leah gave birth to son after son, Rachel's fear that her sister would supplant her in Jacob's affections reached its breaking point. She was frantic to have a baby, so she turned to the day's custom and gave her handmaiden Bilhah to Jacob. She would adopt any children born of the union and raise them as her own. Rachel named Bilhah's firstborn son Dan (God is my judge). The baby was proof that God knew the injustice she had suffered at her sister's hands and had judged in her favor. Bilhah gave birth to one more son, whom Rachel name Naphtali (wrestling), for she had wrestled against her sister's presence in her marriage and finally prevailed.

Leah then realized she was having a hard time getting pregnant, so she presented her handmaiden to Jacob. When Zilpah gave birth to a son, Leah named him Gad (fortune), for good fortune had come to her. Zilpah bore another son, and Leah called him Asher (happy). She was happy that the women in the village would call her blessed and scorn Rachel for being barren. Leah would bear Jacob two more sons. She named her fifth son Issachar (wages). Her baby boy was her wage for giving Jacob Zilpah so he could have more sons. She called her final son Zebulon (dwelling of honor). Jacob would have no choice but to honor her as his wife, for she had borne him six sons. She also bore Jacob a daughter named Dinah (judged or vindicated).

In due season, God remembered Rachel and opened her womb. Nine months later, she held her newborn baby, Joseph (God will give). She wasn't satisfied to have just one son. How could she be? If she were going to compete with Leah and keep her hold on Jacob's love, she would need to bear many more sons.

Jacob Outwits Laban

When Jacob finally fulfilled the second contract for Rachel (Genesis 30), he wanted nothing more than to return home. He had very little to show for his years of service. His family was flourishing, but it was time for him to work for himself instead of being a hired hand. Laban resisted. He had grown wealthy in the years Jacob worked for him and was greedy for more. If Jacob wanted to be the master of his house, Laban wouldn't begrudge him that, just as long as he stayed. Laban told him to name his wage and he would gladly pay it.

Jacob wanted something other than a wage. He wanted something tangible, something he could look at and say, "That belongs to me." So he named all the speckled and spotted goats and black lambs in Laban's flocks as his price to stay in Haran. This way, ownership of each animal would be firmly established and there could be no misunderstanding. If his father-in-law came to inspect Jacob's flocks and found a white lamb or solid-colored goat among them, he could count the animal as stolen and take it.

Laban agreed, but as soon as Jacob left, he hurried to the pastures where his flocks were grazing. He ordered his sons to remove all the animals Jacob had listed and pasture them a three-day journey away from the main flocks. When Jacob arrived to claim what Laban promised, he discovered his father-in-law had cheated him again.

This time, though, Jacob came up with a scheme of his own. He took new limbs of poplar, almond, and plane trees and peeled back the bark to expose the white parts of the sticks. When the stronger of Laban's flocks came to the watering troughs to breed, he put the sticks in front of them. The ewes and does gave birth to black lambs and striped and spotted kids. Once the lambs and kids were weaned, he separated them and kept them far away from his father-in-law. As the years passed, his flocks increased while Laban's flocks grew sicker and weaker.

For Laban, it was an unexpected reversal of fortune. In all his scheming, he never considered that God's favor could turn against him. Yet it had. His sons angrily complained that Jacob was stealing their inheritance. If their father didn't do something about Jacob's continued prosperity, the family would be financially ruined. Tensions between the two men grew.

The Return to Canaan

The Lord appeared to Jacob and told him it was time to return home (Genesis 31). Because of the growing hostility between the two families, Jacob decided it would be best to leave as quickly and quietly as possible. He lived at the mercy of his father-in-law, who could easily claim ownership over his daughters, grandchildren, and flocks. Sheep-shearing season was near. Laban would be gone for at least three days overseeing the shearing and the price his wool would fetch in the local markets. Jacob would leave then. Hopefully, Laban would choose to let him go in peace.

Laban returned to find both Jacob and his household gods had vanished without warning. The theft of his gods enraged him. He would have gladly sent Jacob away with a feast and well wishes, but Jacob had revealed his true nature by stealing his gods. He was an ungrateful viper Laban had welcomed into his home as a son. For whoever possessed the gods would be considered his true heir and, upon his death, could claim his entire estate, impoverishing his sons for generations. He wanted revenge. He would strip

Jacob of everything he owned. Jacob had arrived in Haran as an impoverished man; he would return to Canaan as an impoverished man.

Laban gathered up his kinsmen to help him chase down Jacob. They caught up with his caravan in the hill country of Gilead. It was evening, so he was satisfied to wait until the morning to confront his son-in-law. But as he slept, the Lord appeared to him and warned him to be careful not to say anything to Jacob, whether good or bad.

A semi-chastened Laban stormed into Jacob's camp and demanded to know why he had snuck away like a thief in the night, depriving him of a chance to send the family off with a huge celebration. He could have easily overlooked such folly, but Jacob had stolen his household gods—a breach of trust he couldn't ignore.

Jacob denied the accusation. To prove his innocence, he permitted Laban to search his belongings. If Laban found the gods, he could put the guilty party to death. While Laban's brothers ransacked Jacob's tent and baggage, Laban searched Leah's tent. The gods weren't found.

Only Rachel's tent remained. He entered to find her seated on her camel's saddle. She didn't rise when he entered and explained that she was menstruating. He searched everywhere but the saddle. If he had demanded Rachel get up so he could dig under the saddle, he would have found his gods.

When Laban came back empty-handed, Jacob exploded. As any injured soul does, he had kept a list of all the wrongs he had suffered at Laban's hand and detailed them all, starting with the fourteen years he served for Rachel and ending with the fact that Laban had changed his wages ten times. He accused his uncle of only following him so he could rob him of his goods.

Laban brushed off Jacob's rage. He reminded his son-in-law that everything Jacob owned belonged to him and not to Jacob. But for the sake of his daughters and their sons, he was willing to allow Jacob to keep what he had obtained in Haran and make a covenant between them. Laban called the covenant place Mizpah, which would serve as a border between the two families. Neither man could pass over Mizpah to do the other harm. The next morning, Laban kissed his daughters and grandchildren goodbye and returned to Haran. Jacob watched him go. Then he headed south toward Canaan.

Esau

Jacob remembered all that had passed at Bethel twenty years before (Genesis 32). He remembered the Lord's promise to be with him and return him to the land. He also remembered the bargain he had struck. The Lord was to make it so Esau was no longer angry with him. Jacob had kept his end of the deal. He had given a tithe of all the Lord had blessed him with. Since the Lord had called him home, it was only natural for him to assume his brother was no longer angry and would receive him with open arms. So he sent messengers to Esau to announce his arrival, but when the messengers returned, they brought bad news. Esau was coming north with four hundred armed men.

Jacob panicked. He didn't understand why the Lord would have told him to return home if it wasn't safe. Suddenly, he found himself squeezed into a narrow place. His covenant with Laban made it impossible for him to retreat the way he had come. Esau's approach made it unfeasible for him to go forward. He was hemmed in, and, for the first time in his life, he didn't know what to do.

He turned to prayer and gave voice to his troubles. He begged God to save his wives and children from Esau. He wasn't above manipulating the Lord either by reminding Him that He had promised to make Abraham's descendants a great nation. How could that possibly happen if Esau's men killed all the children? Just in case his prayers weren't answered, he lay awake all night, plotting and scheming until he devised a surefire plan to mollify his brother. He would bribe him with an overwhelming display of wealth.

Jacob had his servants separate goats, sheep, camels, cows, and donkeys into groups. Each group would maintain a sizable distance from the other. He wanted his brother to be hit with wave after wave of his generosity. When Esau asked who the flocks and herds belonged to, his servants were to say that they were gifts from his brother, who was following behind.

There was nothing to do but wait for the plan to unfold. Earlier that day, he had sent his wives, his children, and all he possessed across the ford of the Jabbok River to make camp for the night. He was alone now with no one to stand guard over the chaos of his mind. One thought brought him peace, only to be quickly replaced by one that would freeze him in terror. He believed for one moment that his plan was brilliant. The next moment he was overwhelmed by the fear that if Esau hadn't forgiven him after twenty years, there was no way his pitiful attempts to bribe his brother would make Esau forget what he had done to him.

Jacob Wrestles with God

Jacob tried to quiet his mind by meditating on God's promise to give him the land, only to have his meditation disrupted by images of his wives' and children's dead bodies strewn over the ground. He groaned in exhaustion. Would this night never end? He was desperate for it to end but at the same time feared the coming sunrise. What if he was right and his brother embraced him? What if he was wrong and Esau killed him?

Jacob realized he wasn't alone as he paced back and forth along the river's bank. Someone was watching him. The man came near. Suddenly, Jacob was afraid. He took a few steps toward the river to escape, but the man reached out his hand and dragged him back. Who was this? What did he want?

Desperate to get to the other side, Jacob tried to pry the man's hands off him, but the man was strong. All night, he wrestled the man to defeat him and make his escape across the Jabbok to the safety of his camps. Hours passed, but the man refused to give up.

Jacob was panting with fatigue. Sweat poured down his face. In the east, the first glimmer of light appeared. If he could see the man, perhaps he could finally gain an advantage and be done with this torment.

The man reached out and touched Jacob's hip socket. Pain exploded through his body. His strength vanished. He fell face down into the dirt. He tried to get up, but waves of agony swept his body. He began to weep. He had to get up. Esau was coming. His family wasn't safe. His adversary started to walk away. Jacob reached out and grabbed the man's robe.

For the first time since he approached Jacob, the man spoke: "Let me go, for the day has broken." Jacob refused, saying, "I won't let you go until you bless me." He could see the man's face now. He hadn't even broken a sweat. *How can that be?* Jacob wondered. He was exhausted. "What is your name?" the man asked.

In the aftermath of this experience, Jacob grew to understand that the man he had wrestled with all night was the Lord. So when the Lord asked Jacob what his name was, He was seeking more than what people called him. His name was an indictment of what type of man he had become. Jacob was keen, astute, independent, cunning, clever, and always got what he wanted. He prided himself on his ability to be the smartest man in the room. He had gained the birthright and the covenant by his cleverness and finally bested Laban because of his cunning.

At Bethel, God promised He wouldn't leave him until He returned him to the land. But it was a land that couldn't be gained by cunning. It could only be given through faith. Jacob had zero faith in God. All his faith lay in his ability to outsmart others. But in the early morning light, the Lord had forced him to look at his worldview, which had always been the source of his pride. Jacob had never seen it as the root cause of everything that had gone wrong in his life.

God's exposure light flooded his heart. Finally, he could see that all his cunning had brought him heartache and misery. He had married a woman who had deceived him in the same manner he had duped his father—by pretending to be someone else. He had married his true love and saw nothing but hurt and betrayal in her eyes because, on his wedding night, he hadn't recognized that it was Leah lying beside him and not her. He had flocks and riches but no peace. He was terrified because twenty years ago, he had believed the end justified the means and had robbed his brother of what was rightly his. Esau had suffered ever since.

Just like Jacob had suffered at Laban's hands and Rachel had suffered at Leah's hands. With the covenant, Laban had washed his hands of him. Because of his betrayal, Esau was going to kill him. Jacob was the author of it all. No one had done this to him; he had done it to himself. He was to blame for all the suffering and pain he had inflicted upon those he loved. He could never make it right. What was done was done. Now he would have to live with it, but how?

"My name is Jacob," he finally confessed. It was a repudiation of his worldview. He no longer wanted to be that man. He wanted to be a different man but didn't know how. The man knelt next to him. "No longer will you be known as Jacob. For you are Israel, a prince with God. For you have

28

wrestled with God until He prevailed." Jacob asked the man for his name, but he refused. Instead, the man blessed him before he walked away.

The Villainy of a Worldview

In one encounter with the Lord, everything changed. Jacob had never been alone. There was never any need for him to take matters into his own hands. God was sovereign over his life, and God's sovereignty was good in its intentions toward him. Now he knew God had seen, heard, and cared for him more deeply than he realized. It mattered to God what kind of man he was. God was patient and waited until He could show him the sad truth of his life and Jacob would believe Him. The Lord no longer called him Jacob, a man forced to scheme his way through life to get what he wanted. He was now Israel, God's prince, a man who would represent God upon the earth.

Jacob had begun his journey at Bethel, a man who had stolen the covenant because he believed his desire for it was all that mattered. He was completing his journey here at Penuel, for he knew now that he had seen God face-to-face and had his life delivered. He didn't know what today would bring. He didn't even know how he would get up. But what he did know was that God was for him. For the first time in his life, he had enough.

Chapter 4
THE NECESSITY OF JOSEPH
His brothers also came and fell down before him.

Genesis 50:18

JOSEPH'S STORY IS told against the backdrop of his brothers' spiritual declension. *Declension* is defined as spiritual deterioration and decline. The brothers failed to live up to God's full thought for them. They were to be the genesis of a nation, but they were far from fulfilling their heavenly calling. So, God laid hold of Joseph, sent him to Egypt, and enrolled him in a school of intense suffering. For God must always have a person He can use to counter the contradiction between the position and condition of His people.

Forgotten and alone in an Egyptian prison, God brought Joseph to the cross where he had to learn to let go of the smallness of his worldview and become the link between his brothers' tragic condition and God's purpose for them.

Joseph learned to be emptied of his selfishness by the unjust things he suffered. He learned to serve without bitterness and complaint. His dreams were no longer about what they meant to him, but what they meant for God. When he looked down the long line of foreigners who had come to Egypt to buy grain, he recognized his brothers. Fortunately for them, he had more than grain for them. God had given him the heavenly bread needed to save them from their declension. He fulfilled God's calling on his life and saved his brothers alive.

Jacob's Family Difficulties Continue

After coming into the land, Jacob journeyed to Shechem, a city in northern Israel (Genesis 33–35). He purchased land and settled down in the shadow of the city's walls. One day, his daughter, Dinah left home to visit with the young ladies in the city. Shechem, the son of Hamor, the land's prince, caught sight of her as she walked through the fields. He was overcome with lust, so he seized and raped her. Here the story turns. He became utterly besotted with her and begged his father to go to Jacob and pay whatever Jacob demanded as the bridal price, for he had to have her as his wife.

Dinah's brothers were in the fields tending the flocks when news of her rape reached them. They rushed home and made a beeline for their father to find out how they could help him avenge Dinah's lost virtue. When they burst into his tent, they were shocked to find him sitting with Hamor and Shechem, calmly arranging a marriage between Dinah and her rapist.

When Hamor asked Jacob for the bridal price, Dinah's brothers answered. If the city's men wanted to marry within their family and become one people, circumcision was the only price they would accept. Hamor and Shechem convinced the city's elders that the bridal price would allow them to transfer Jacob's wealth to themselves through marriage. The elders agreed, and every male was circumcised. Three days later, when the men were sore and unable to defend themselves, Simeon and Levi entered the city and slew every man, beginning with Hamor and Shechem. They plundered the city, taking its wealth, flocks, herds, women, and children captive.

Jacob railed against Simeon and Levi for lying to Hamor and Shechem. What if the land's inhabitants found out what they had done? What if they mustered their forces and attacked them? They were strangers in the land and lacked the strength to defend themselves. The brothers' lust for revenge had put the whole family in danger. Simeon and Levi shrugged their shoulders at his rebuke. It was apparent Jacob cared nothing about Dinah's honor or dignity, nor did he care that she would have to spend the rest of her life married to her rapist. He had turned their sister into a prostitute by selling her into marriage. Since Jacob refused to act, they had no choice but to take matters into their own hands and avenge the crime perpetrated against her.

Jacob took his family and fled south. Rachel was heavily pregnant, and outside the small village of Bethlehem, she went into labor. As she delivered Jacob his twelfth son, she used her last breath to name him Ben-oni, the son of my sorrow. Jacob changed the baby's name. He wouldn't be the son of sorrow. He would be Benjamin, the son of my right hand. He had two sons by Rachel now. Joseph would be the son of his power, his heir who would reflect his will to the world. Benjamin would be the son set on his right hand, a place of honor and status.

Jacob disinherited Simeon and Levi for their actions at Shechem. He also disinherited his firstborn because Reuben had slept with Bilhah, Rachel's handmaiden, the mother of Dan and Naphtali. By sleeping with Bilhah, Reuben sent two messages to his father. First, he was the rightful heir and not Joseph, so when Jacob died, Reuben would lead the family by right of birth. Second, he wouldn't allow his father to marry Bilhah so she could take Rachel's place in the family.

The jealousy and resentment that had poisoned the relationship between Leah and Rachel hadn't remain confined to the women. How could it? As Leah's sons grew into adulthood, they grew indignant at Jacob's treatment of their mother and, by extension, of them. Were they loved? If they were, they felt they only received the scraps from their father's table. Was he proud of them? If he was, he was prouder of Joseph. When Joseph came of age, his father presented him with a coat of many colors to indicate that Joseph would be his heir and leader of the family. His elevation reduced Leah's sons to second place in the family when they should have been first. This was the most egregious of the slights and insults they felt they had received from their father.

Joseph and His Brothers

It was during this time that Joseph began to dream (Genesis 37). He was in awe of what the Lord showed him about his future. God had destined him to reign over his brothers and even his father. He was young and unwise, so he told his brothers all the Lord had shown him. Perhaps by revealing his dreams to his brothers, he was defending himself against their constant antagonism. His revelations had the opposite effect. His brothers grew more jealous and bitter about his place in the family.

Then one day, Jacob sent Joseph to check on the welfare of his brothers, who were with the flocks in a distant pasture, and bring back a report. The brothers habitually ignored Jacob's orders and did whatever they wanted. As heir, Joseph was responsible for ensuring his brothers carried out his father's will since the family's future prosperity rested on it. When Joseph brought back bad reports of their failures, he gave them more cause to hate him.

It took some time, but Joseph finally found his brothers near Dothan. They saw him coming since he was hard to miss in that multicolor coat. They put their heads together and devised a plan to rid themselves of him once and for all. There were many empty wells and cisterns nearby. They would kill him and throw his body in the nearest one, and no one would ever find him. Then they would tell their father that a wild animal had devoured him. They would be free of Joseph, and none of his dreams about reigning over them would come to pass.

Reuben talked them out of it. "Why should we have blood on our hands?" he argued. All they had to do was throw him into a pit. No one would hear his cries for help. Eventually, nature would take its course and he'd die. That way, they wouldn't be murderers. Reuben had no intention of letting Joseph die. Once his brothers had led the flocks to greener pastures, he would return to the pit and rescue him. The brothers seized Joseph, ripped his coat from him, and threw him into a deep pit. He begged them to release him, but they ignored his pleas. Instead, they sat down and ate their lunch.

The Bible doesn't explain why Reuben left the group, but he did. In his absence, the brothers devised another scheme to eliminate Joseph. A caravan of Ishmaelites approached on its way to Egypt. Trailing behind was a long line of slaves. Judah suggested they sell Joseph to the Ishmaelites for pocket money. That way, they wouldn't be guilty of killing their brother directly or indirectly. The rest agreed. They hailed the caravan and struck a bargain. Twenty shekels of silver for Joseph. The last they heard from him was his appeals for help as the Ishmaelites chained him to the line of slaves. Then the caravan moved off and his cries faded away.

Reuben returned to find the pit empty. He had a choice to make when he found out what his brothers had done. He could have ridden off after the caravan and repurchased his brother, but that presented difficulties he couldn't overcome, for Joseph would tell of his role in the plot. No one knew what Reuben had planned to do. His father certainly wouldn't believe him. His father barely tolerated him. Then there was the selling of Joseph. If Jacob found out, he would disinherit the rest of his brothers. He decided to protect his brothers and leave Joseph to his fate.

They took Joseph's coat and made it appear like he had met a gruesome end by a bear or lion attack. They showed tremendous grief when they presented the coat to Jacob and asked if he recognized it. Of course Jacob did. A wild animal had devoured his son. The brothers sighed in relief. Their plan had worked. Let Jacob be inconsolable. He didn't matter to them. They had rid themselves of Joseph, and no one was the wiser.

Well, it might be true that no one was the wiser, but the brothers knew what they had done. Even though they resented how their father treated them, he was still their father. They lived with his suffocating grief every day. They couldn't escape from it. Even if they wanted to rescue Joseph from the life they had consigned him to, it was impossible. They didn't get the make and model of the caravan that had dragged Joseph off. And if they did find the caravan, it was doubtful the Ishmaelites could tell them the fate of one slave. They had to live with what they had done. But it ate at them and corrupted any spiritual life they had. To God, they were the genesis of a nation. But as men, they were altogether inconsistent with the position they were to inherit.

Joseph in Egypt

What of Joseph? He had been sent to Egypt by God's providence. If the brothers were ever going to fulfill the destiny God had spoken over them, they would need someone to stand in the gap for them. Joseph became the link between his brothers' tragic condition and God's whole purpose for them. But before he could stand in the gap, God had a great work to perform in him first.

Joseph's dreams foretold of a reigning life. This had always been his understanding of them anyway. While dragged behind the caravan, he wondered why his life had taken this unexpected turn. He was about to be sold as a common slave. How does one reign from the lowest place in society? He was sold to Potiphar and rose quickly in the household ranks until Potiphar recognized the favor upon his life and entrusted him with administrating his estate.

Then Potiphar's wife entered the story as the temptress (Genesis 39). She begged Joseph to come and lie with her. He deflected her advances by stating that he couldn't betray Potiphar, nor would he sin against God. She wouldn't be refused. When they were alone in the house, she reached for him, but he fled, leaving his robe in her hands. Stung by his rejection, she lied to Potiphar and accused Joseph of rape. Potiphar gave Joseph no chance to defend himself. He was guilty as charged and dragged off again to a fate he didn't deserve.

Joseph had done everything right, yet it had gained him nothing. He wore an iron collar around his neck and fetters around his feet. An Egyptian prison wasn't Club Med. It was dark, dank, and smelled of urine and unwashed bodies. Night after night, he lay on his pallet and thought about the dreams of long ago. Those dreams now tested him by putting his inner life on trial. A long time had passed since his brothers had sold him into slavery, and the conditions he now endured only made the time go slower and seem longer. God always uses time to discipline His chosen vessels.

Joseph's imprisonment was slowly eroding his dreams. If he couldn't figure out how those dreams could come true as a slave, how could he possibly make them come to pass when he was a forgotten prisoner? Why did God give him dreams if they wouldn't come true? He didn't understand why he had to suffer. He didn't understand God's ways. It is easy to want to serve God when everyone kneels before you and you are the master of the situation. Now, he was the one doing the bowing and scraping.

He realized he had been foolish to tell his brothers about the dreams. It had only added fuel to the fire of their jealousy and resentment. Had he done it because of pride? Zeal? No, his true motive was that he had been selfish and self-serving. He wanted his brothers to know that God had chosen him over them. His brothers had mistreated him, and he wanted them to come and bow before him so he could lord over them.

But what Joseph wanted wasn't what God wanted. His plans for Joseph weren't tied to this earth. He had chosen him as part of the heavenly purpose, which was still at work to rectify the closed door suffered in the garden of Eden. Joseph would have to let loose his vanity and selfish interpretation of his dreams. He would have to come to learn why God had separated him and laid hold of him. To see God's hand in all the setbacks and sufferings he endured and realize that what he considered evil and unfair, God was using to make a vessel fit for the Master's hand. In Joseph's brothers' darkest hour, would he stand in the gap for God? Or would he demand justice for all they had done to him? In the scope of eternity, the slights he endured didn't matter. God had a greater purpose for him than revenge. He could enter a far nobler destiny if he could learn to forgive. He could see his brothers set free to live in the fullness of life God had intended for them.

Joseph had to learn service (Genesis 39). To teach him how to serve, the Lord put Joseph in a challenging school—in Egypt, where he had no name or voice. He could only learn to reign when he learned to serve without complaint and bitterness. He had to learn to have fullness without pride. He had to be emptied to be filled. He had to be humiliated to be exalted. The time would come when the dreams would come true. His brothers would appear before him. How would he handle the situation?

Most of us are probably familiar with the rest of Joseph's story. Pharaoh dreamed a dream that no one in his court could interpret. His cupbearer remembered Joseph from the time when Pharaoh had been angry with him and threw him into prison until the great king could determine his fate. The cupbearer had dreamed a dream but couldn't interpret its meaning, so he told the dream to Joseph, who said that Pharaoh was no longer angry with him and would soon restore him to his position. The cupbearer told Pharaoh about Joseph.

Joseph interpreted Pharaoh's dream (Genesis 40). Then with great insight and wisdom, he devised a plan to save Egypt from the famine Pharaoh had dreamed about. The king recognized that God was with Joseph, so he elevated Joseph to second in command in Egypt and ordered all his servants to obey him.

Joseph and His Brothers Reunited

The famine wasn't confined to Egypt (Genesis 42). It swept through the entire Levant. Crops failed, and the rivers and wadis dried up. Every family struggled to survive. Joseph's ability to ready Egypt for the famine meant that there was grain to buy in Egypt if one had enough money. Jacob had enough. He sent his sons to Egypt with gold to purchase grain for his growing family. The brothers were standing in line when Joseph recognized them and instructed his guards to bring them to him. The brothers bowed before him but didn't recognize him. Joseph realized it was the fulfillment of his dreams. He was reigning, and his brothers were bowing.

He accused them of being spies. They protested their innocence and explained who they were. They were ten of twelve brothers. One brother was dead. The youngest of them remained in Canaan with their father. Joseph told them he didn't believe them but would allow them to prove themselves. He would release one of them to return to Canaan and bring the other brother to him. Do this, and the rest of them would live. Then he put them in prison for three days to think about it.

After he released them, Joseph changed the conditions. He would give them grain and release all but one brother. That man he would hold in prison until the others returned with their younger brother. If they failed, Joseph would sentence them all to death. The brothers began to speak in Hebrew, thinking the Egyptian standing before them couldn't understand. But Joseph understood every word. They discussed what they had done to him those many years ago and how God's justice was now being served. Joseph couldn't control his emotions any longer. He left the room and wept.

When he returned, Joseph chose Simeon and bound him before the rest. He released the other nine and told them to make haste. The brothers hurried from the room. Later that night, as they fed their donkeys, they found their money bags in the grain sacks. Not only did the governor think them spies, but now he would also believe they were thieves. Why had God done this to them?

They returned home and told Jacob everything that had happened. He refused to allow Benjamin to go to Egypt with them. If it cost Simeon his life, so be it. At this moment, the brothers were reaping what they had sown. Jacob's refusal to let go of Benjamin was the natural consequence of their lies and deceit. Their youngest brother was all Jacob had left of Rachel and Joseph. Only Benjamin could ease his grief. But Jacob's refusal put the whole family at risk. Their wives and children would die if their father didn't relent and allow him to return to Egypt with them.

Reuben stepped forward and told Jacob he could kill his two sons if he failed to bring Benjamin home from Egypt. Jacob flatly refused. If

Benjamin died during the journey, it would send him to his grave. He had suffered enough. He wasn't going to risk his heart. There was nothing more the brothers could say.

The famine increased, and the food they had bought ran out (Genesis 43). Jacob called his sons and told them to return to Egypt and buy more grain. They couldn't. The governor had been clear. Unless Benjamin came with them, he would kill Simeon and send his guards to hunt them down and kill them. Once more, Jacob refused to allow Benjamin to go to Egypt.

Judah became the voice of reason. He asked his father to trust him with Benjamin. If Jacob couldn't, the entire family would die of starvation, including Judah's sons and daughters. He couldn't allow that to happen. Not when Jacob could prevent it. If Benjamin somehow was lost, Jacob could take his grief out on Judah, who would be willing to bear the blame forever. But time was of the essence. They should have returned twice by now, and the Egyptians might already be looking for them.

Jacob relented. The brothers prepared for the trip, took double the price for the grain since their money had been returned, and headed back to Egypt. Joseph was waiting for them. He had his steward invite them to his home and share in a feast prepared especially for them. When the dinner was ready, the men sat down to eat. Joseph ate, elevated above them.

After dinner, he released the brothers, Simeon too, to return to Canaan, but he had one more test for them (Genesis 44). He had his steward hide his silver divination cup in Benjamin's bag. Then he sent guards to arrest the brothers for thievery. His brothers trembled before him. They pleaded their innocence and told Joseph that if one of them had stolen the cup, then that man would pay for his crimes with his life, while the rest of them would become the governor's slaves. Joseph partially agreed. Only the man who had stolen the cup would pay with his life. The rest would be free to return to Canaan.

A Son of Leah Pleads for the Life of a Son of Rachel

One by one, the bags were spilled out, beginning with Reuben and working chronologically from eldest to youngest. The brothers were too agitated to realize that the governor knew in what order they had been born. Finally, the guards began to search the last sack. The brothers breathed in relief.

Benjamin was no thief. Yet, when the guards spilled the grain, they found the silver cup.

Judah pleaded for his brother's life. If Benjamin were to die, it would also be their father's death. "I promised my father I would return the boy to him," he told Joseph. "You can punish me if you wish, but let Benjamin go so my father will live happy and content."

It was too much for Joseph. A son of Leah pleading for the life of a son of Rachel. He ordered everyone but the brothers from the room (Genesis 45). He burst into tears and spoke to them in Hebrew. "I am Joseph. Is my father still alive?" The brothers didn't know what to make of this weeping Egyptian confessing to be the brother they had sold into slavery. They just stared at him. So Joseph told them once more who he was. He begged them not to be dismayed because of what they had done to him. God had sent him to Egypt to preserve their lives.

If Joseph thought it was for this moment that God had brought him to Egypt, he would be wrong. The Lord had commanded Isaac to remain in the land during a famine, and He would provide a hundredfold return. Isaac obeyed, and the harvest was abundant. The Lord could have done the same for Jacob. If food wasn't the issue, what was? Why had God sent Joseph ahead to preserve a family alive? God's answer would be fully revealed seventeen years later.

Joseph Forgives His Brother

The brothers believed the only reason Joseph hadn't retaliated against them for selling him into slavery was because Jacob wouldn't allow him to. But after Jacob died, they realized nothing prevented Joseph from taking his revenge. So they lied and told him that their father had commanded him to forgive them for what they had done (Genesis 50).

When Joseph saw their terror of him and heard their lies, he began to weep. His brothers were still haunted by their actions. Their betrayal of him had been a drag upon their hearts. They couldn't stand before him without feeling guilt and shame. He knew now that this was the fulfillment of his dreams. How perfectly had God prepared him for this moment. With just one sentence, he could free his brothers from the burden of sin they had carried since that long ago afternoon.

At the sight of Joseph's tears, his brothers fell before him, proclaiming, "We are your servants." Joseph knelt and reached his hands out to them. "I forgive you," he told them. "I forgave you all long ago. You meant it for evil. God meant it for good. God sent me here to save your lives." Not with grain, for grain could always be had, but for the one thing they needed above all else. More than they needed to eat. Possibly, more than they needed to breathe. They needed Joseph to forgive and release them from the guilt that had consumed their lives. They couldn't forgive themselves. Only Joseph could do that. God hadn't failed any of them.

One Father, Two Worldviews

Leah's resentment and jealousy toward Rachel had shaped her sons' worldviews. She felt she had never received the honor or love she deserved. As the boys grew older, they witnessed the disrespect with which Jacob treated her. They held their father in utter contempt and struck back at him whenever they could. The situation became intolerable after Rachel died. Jacob didn't attempt to disguise his love for Joseph. He disinherited Leah's sons and made Joseph his heir. Their hatred toward their father and, by representation, Joseph, caused them to sell their brother into slavery.

His brothers viewed everything through the lens of their guilt. Their consciences constantly accused them, and their worldviews reinforced their guilt. There was no escape. When the "Egyptian" spoke severely to them and accused them of being spies, it forced their worldviews into the open. They were the ones who brought up Joseph and their beliefs that God was using the "Egyptian" to finally punish them for selling their brother and ignoring his pleas for help. When Jacob died, they lied once more to forestall the justice they always believed would be served upon them.

Like a chip off the old block, they lied to cover up what they had done. Except they weren't like Jacob. The lie wore at them and led them into declension—a moral or spiritual decay. Things weren't as God had meant for them to be. The brothers no longer answered to His thought for them. God couldn't leave them like that, for their destiny was to grow into a nation that He would one day set among the surrounding nations to be a light, an ensign, so the gentiles could come and know His goodness. God had to call them back to their divine purpose. His means were the object of their hatred.

His brothers viewed everything through the lens of their guilt. Their consciences constantly accused them, and their worldviews reinforced their guilt. There was no escape. When the "Egyptian" spoke severely to them and accused them of being spies, it forced their worldviews into the open. They were the ones who brought up Joseph and their beliefs that God was using the "Egyptian" to finally punish them for selling their brother and ignoring his pleas for help. When Jacob died, they lied once more to forestall the justice they always believed would be served upon them.

Joseph's dreams shaped his worldview by allowing him to view himself as his brothers' master, with them bowing in submission to his great authority. He could have held on to his worldview and would have probably died forgotten and alone in an Egyptian prison. But God didn't abandon His man. Through Joseph's suffering, the Lord taught Joseph to release the smallness of his thinking and his interpretation of his dreams in order to serve a heavenly purpose—to restore his brothers. To that calling, Joseph said yes, and God raised him up and set him as the second power in Egypt.

God Has Not Changed His Mind

Joseph was necessary. In every generation where there is declension, Joseph is necessary. His ability to forgive his brothers was wrought in the iron collar and fetters that rubbed his ankles raw. God put His vessel upon the potter's wheel and produced a man who stopped seeing his dreams in terms of himself.

The dreams were never about him. They were about what God needed to accomplish in a dysfunctional family tearing itself apart. God's purpose for Jacob's sons could only be fulfilled once they knew Joseph had forgiven them, so Joseph forgave them freely, without reluctance. Then he proved his forgiveness by providing for his brothers and their families until the day he died.

Chapter 5
FAILURE IN THE WILDERNESS

*But they did not listen to Moses, because of their broken
spirit and harsh slavery.*

Exodus 6:9

THE STORY OF the generation that came out of Egypt has become a
cautionary tale for all believers. That generation's lives can be divided into
two very distinct parts: the lives they lived before God came down to deliver
them, and the lives God called them to as His treasured possession among
all peoples (Exodus 19:5). But the Israelites didn't see any difference in the
lives they had lived in Egypt and the lives they were living since being
brought out of Egypt.

That was the problem. They were being forced, against their will, to
live in a wilderness that could not provide for them. As far as they were
concerned, the wilderness was more precarious than Egypt ever was. This
God they were following required faith for even the most basic of needs.
They didn't want to fight the good fight of faith. They were tired of fighting.
They wanted their every need met without having to do anything for it. God
had proven no different than Egypt, despite His promises and His mighty
work.

They set a romantic version of Egypt before them and talked about their
former home's goodness incessantly. They hardened their hearts toward
God and chose to believe their fears, appetites, and, especially, their desire
to know what tomorrow brings.

This is why this generation's story is a cautionary tale. When we don't
know what to do, we do what we know. When we don't believe, we disobey
and seek our own way, understanding, and outcome. The people wanted to

be in control of their lives. So, they chose to return to Egypt because they knew how to navigate Egypt, and there was familiarity and comfort in knowing that.

Moses and the Israelites

The nation God sent Moses to deliver from Egypt consisted of people with broken spirits and severely damaged worldviews. The harsh slavery they endured in Egypt for generations had entirely conquered them. They lived under the constant fear of death, which produced little hope, no expectations, and few dreams. Then Moses appeared and, for a day, they allowed themselves to have hope.

Their hope didn't last, for Pharaoh laughed at Moses' demand that the children of Israel be allowed to go three days into the wilderness to worship God (Exodus 5). In Pharaoh's worldview, this God couldn't be much of one because Egypt had exercised its dominion and power over Israel and enslaved them. So Pharaoh refused to listen to the Lord's voice and refused and refused until Egypt lay in ruins.

Then deliverance came. The people were free. They went out of Egypt rejoicing, praising the Lord who had come down to deliver them. Waiting for them was a Promised Land where their children would know peace. But this new worldview born on Passover didn't survive the first sign of trouble. The people continually accused Moses and the Lord of wanting to kill them. If there was no food, God was starving them. If there was no water, God was allowing them to die of thirst. God drew the Egyptians out after them, and now the only thing they could do was finally die at the Egyptians' hands. Like they always knew they would.

The people set up camp at Mount Sinai and awaited the next blow to come. Three days later, they awoke to the peals of thunder and flashes of lightning. They rushed out of their tents to see the mountain enveloped in a thick cloud. Loud trumpet blasts echoed over the land. Only Moses could approach the mountain. The people had been forbidden to come near under the penalty of death. They didn't want to anyway. As the trumpet blasts continued, the elders informed Moses that the people had elected him to speak to God on their behalf. Whatever God told Moses to do, they would do. They didn't want God to talk to them anymore.

This God wasn't like the Egyptian gods, who might have been demanding and capricious but they could also be placated and appeased. Most of the time, they ignored your requests, but now and again they answered your prayers. The gods' avatars were nature's most benign and familiar things. They rarely spoke except through the cycles of nature or through their priests. Their voices never sounded like loud trumpet blasts that shattered the peace and eardrums. They had never been terrified of a God before, and never had a God made such demands on them. To believe the impossible every day! How long were they expected to live like this?

The Golden Calf

Moses disappeared into the cloud at the top of the mountain forty days ago, and that was the last the people had heard from him (Exodus 32). What if he were dead? What if this God of fire and smoke had killed him? What would become of them? They needed to appoint a new leader and a new god. A god they could understand and who understood them. They chose Aaron to be their leader, and Hap, the god of courage, strength, and kingship, to be their god. He possessed all the qualities the people needed to continue their journey, for they lacked courage, strength, and a true leader. And if in the end, they died as they expected, Hap could even raise them from the dead.

Aaron commanded the people to give him all the gold they had, and he would fashion for them a god. When he finished his work, he presented a golden calf to the people, who shouted joyfully and credited Hap for bringing them out of Egypt. Finally, they had thrown off the terror of the God on the mountain. Hap was a familiar friend they would gladly follow.

As their revelry reached its frantic climax, Moses appeared carrying two stone tablets. He raised them high over his head, dashed them into the ground, and then plowed through the dancing crowd, for not everyone had stopped at the sight of him. He dragged Hap from his altar and had the idol broken up and ground into fine gold dust. He took the dust, put it in the water the Lord had provided, and made Israel drink it.

Next, he turned his wrath upon Aaron, who he had left in charge of the camp. "What were you thinking about allowing the people to sin so greatly?" he demanded. Aaron's response could have been better. He blamed the people for insisting. He blamed Moses for disappearing. But he saved the best for last. He explained that all he did was throw the gold into the fire. The calf appeared all by itself.

Moses went into the tent of meeting to ask the Lord to forgive the people of this terrible sin and to go up with them into the land. The Lord replied that since Israel was a compromised and sinful people, He couldn't go up with them. He would send His angel instead. The people heard the news, and suddenly they were sorry. They had brought this calamity upon themselves. There was nothing they could do to atone for what they had done.

Their fate rested in Moses' hands. Would he be able to convince God not to abandon them? Every morning, they stood outside their tents and watched as the pillar of cloud descended upon the tent of meeting (Exodus 33). When it did, they fell on their faces and worshiped. Moses prevailed. He returned from the mountain with new stone tablets God had written upon—a framework for daily living to keep the people from sin. The covenant was renewed.

The people gave offerings for a tabernacle, for this God was coming to dwell among them. The people were grateful to the Lord for sparing their lives. They expressed their gratitude by overwhelming those building the tabernacle with gold, silver, spices, and expensive cloth. Once the artisans completed the tabernacle and Moses consecrated Aaron and his sons as priests, God's presence filled the Holy Place.

Giants in the Land

A year after arriving at Sinai, the cloud lifted from the tabernacle (Numbers 10). Before the people left for the Promised Land, the Lord explained to Moses how He would empty the land of the Amorites, the Hittites, the Canaanites, and all the other "ites" who made their homes there. He would send a terror before the people to confuse the enemy and release swarms of wasps to drive out the inhabitants. He wouldn't empty the land all at once, but bit by bit, as the people could occupy the towns and cities. He didn't want the land to become desolate and have the wild beasts multiplied against them.

Moses sent twelve spies to search out the land and bring back a report for the people. They beheld a land as bountiful as the Lord had promised—a land to be desired and possessed. When they saw the giants in their walled cities, the land suddenly lost its appeal. The giants were a game-changer. Up until that moment, the land had been something to be valued and desired. Now, to possess the land, they would have to go to war against (in their minds) an invincible enemy. They were bricklayers, not warriors. In their terror of the giants, the Lord had been rendered powerless. Once provoked, the giants would wreak havoc until all Israel became their prey. When the spies told the people about the giants, they used this revealing phrase: "We seemed to ourselves like grasshoppers, and so we seemed to them" (Numbers 13:33).

The people refused to go up to a land that devoured its inhabitants (Numbers 14). Their worldviews wouldn't permit them to go forward. It would only allow them to retreat into their past lives in hopes of finding a safe haven. Miraculously, Egypt was no longer a place of hard labor and easy death. Now it was a place of plenty where they knew nothing but security. In their fear, they created a romantic, idealized version of Egypt that lost all sense of reality. "At least in Egypt, we had an abundance of food," they told each other, "an abundance of choice. We feasted in Egypt. We always knew from where our next meal was coming. Not like the wilderness where we have to eat this worthless bread (manna) that makes us want to vomit."

They knew what Egypt demanded. Yes, it was true they had spent their lives in hard toil. Yes, it was also true that some of them would die at the Egyptians' hands, but they also knew how to keep their heads down and avoid their masters' wrath. They knew how to navigate Egypt, and there was security in that knowledge. They didn't know the Lord and collectively decided they would no longer live in terror that today was the day He would finally kill them.

Caleb and Joshua tried to talk to the people, but they would not listen to this faith talk any longer. They took up stones to silence the two men. The glory of the Lord suddenly appeared at the tent of meeting. Moses entered to plead on the people's behalf. When he came out, he told the people that the Lord wouldn't allow them to return to Egypt. Instead, they would go into the wilderness where everyone twenty years of age and over would die. The children they feared would become the giants' prey would inherit the land.

When the people heard that they wouldn't be allowed to return to Egypt, they suddenly changed their minds. They would atone for their sin by taking the land. Except it was too late. God had disqualified them, and He was no longer with them. The people armed themselves anyway and went up to do battle. The Canaanites soundly defeated them.

The Israelites' Faulty Worldview

Israel's unbelief and lack of trust in the God who had delivered them from Egypt contributed to their failure in the wilderness. But there was another factor in that failure: the land itself. Throughout their sojourn in Egypt, they heard stories of a land flowing with milk and honey that the Lord had promised to their ancestors Abraham, Isaac, and Jacob. A land of inheritance. In the cool of the evenings, they spoke of how wonderful it would be to live in their own land. To have a little piece of real estate where they could settle down and raise their children in peace and security. The land's only worth was what it meant to them. The giants caused the land's value to skyrocket beyond what Israel was willing to pay.

Never once did the people look at the land from the divine perspective. Never once did they ask why the Lord had promised Abraham a land. Nor did they ask why God had come down to deliver them from Egypt. They weren't even curious about why He systematically destroyed Egypt's gods or reduced Egypt to a wasteland.

God intended the land to be where He would continue His work to rectify what Adam had lost in the Fall. What He began in Abraham would continue through Abraham's descendants. The Lord would put His name in the land and dwell among a chosen people. He would be their Father, and they would be His sons, reflecting His will and ways to the surrounding pagan nations who lived under the reality of a closed door—hundreds of thousands of people who served many gods because their worldviews were as fear-based as Israel's had proven to be.

The nations would see a people at peace, secure in their borders. God would bless Israel beyond words. He would permit no disease or sickness to be found among the people. They would be prosperous and their harvests

47

would be bountiful. The nations would put away their false gods and worship the living God. It would be a generational revival where darkness would lose ground and light would shine throughout the earth.

The Villainy of a Worldview

The *self* was at the center of Israel's worldview, which never allowed the people to change how they viewed themselves, even after God had delivered them by His mighty hand. They lived under the threat of death before the Exodus, and they lived under the threat of death in the wilderness. This wasn't true, of course, but since the people expected to die, every setback, test, and trial wasn't about His love and care for them—it was about death finally catching up with them.

The generation that came out of Egypt feasted on the wrong things and filled their hearts with wrong thoughts. They viewed God and themselves through distorted lenses. Everything in their lives prior to Moses coming to Egypt had led to death. They saw every day as a pending catastrophe. That's why every crisis produced a meltdown of faith. They were convinced that they would die in the wilderness, either by the hands of their enemies or by the hands of this God they were ignorant of. The tragedy was they never linked their disobedience to their difficulties.

Wrong thinking will always give you the wrong context. The wrong context will always produce bad fruit. In the wilderness the context was survival, and the fruit of that context was unbelief, hardness of heart, and, finally, rebellion along the borders of Canaan. And the consequences of their worldviews were eternal.

Chapter 6
THE INSECURITY OF SAUL

"Though you are little in your own eyes."

1 Samuel 15:17

WHAT WOULD YOU say if you had to describe King Saul in a sentence? Was he a people-pleaser? Mad? Perhaps insecure? All those descriptions are accurate, but they give only a one-dimensional understanding of Saul's worldview. The insecurity that held him captive didn't belong exclusively to him. He shared it with his family, his relatives, and all those who were born into the tribe of Benjamin. It was a shared tribal trauma that scarred Saul's *self* and produced his insecure worldview.

The Levite and His Concubine

In the final chapters of Judges, we have the story of the Levite and his concubine (Judges 19 through 21). The concubine was unfaithful and ran away to her father's house. The Levite followed her to convince her to come home. Her father was in no hurry to lose his daughter again, so he stalled the Levite's departure for four days by occupying him with conversation, good food, and wine. When the fifth day arrived, the father tried the same tactics. They worked for the better part of a day, but as evening approached, the Levite suddenly announced he was leaving with the concubine. No amount of persuasion could convince him to spend another night in that house.

When the Levite's small party reached Jerusalem, his servants begged him to go into the city and find lodging. The Levite refused. Jerusalem belonged to the Jebusites, and he wouldn't spend the night in a foreign city. They would continue to Gibeah, a town in the territory given to Benjamin. As was the custom, he went to the town square to wait for someone to offer him hospitality for the night. No one did. Then an agitated old man agreed to take him in, but he had to hurry. It was unsafe to spend the night in the square.

The old man was an enjoyable host. There was plenty of food and wine to make their hearts merry, but a loud banging on the door shattered the evening. Worthless fellows had surrounded the house and ordered the old man to bring the Levite out so they could have intercourse with him.

The old man opened the door and begged his fellow citizens not to behave wickedly toward a guest under his roof. He forced his virgin daughter and the Levite's concubine out the door and into the streets to satisfy the mob's lust. He permitted them to do to the women anything they wanted, but they were to leave the Levite alone.

It was a terrible thing to do, and terrible things happened. The men abused the concubine all night. She crawled back toward the house at dawn and died with her hands on the threshold. The Levite exited the house and saw her lying there. He ordered her to get up, for they had to go. When she didn't answer, he realized she was dead.

He threw her body over one of the donkeys, returned to his home, and cut her into twelve pieces. He sent a piece to the elders of every tribe to announce the suffering he had endured at the hands of the men from Gibeah. He demanded justice for his concubine.

Israel Fights the Benjaminites

All the people of Israel gathered at Mizpah to listen to the Levite recount his story and take counsel on how they should avenge this great sin done within their midst (Judges 20). They decided to attack Gibeah and slaughter the guilty parties. Every tribe would participate. No tribe would be left out. First, though, they would ask the elders of Benjamin to surrender the men of the city so they could put them to the sword. The elders replied that they wouldn't allow the rest of the tribes to slaughter their brothers. They mustered twenty-six thousand men to defend Gibeah against Israel's four hundred thousand armed soldiers.

The men of Benjamin were scrappy fighters and won the victory. Israel reformed their battle lines to attack the next day. Behind the lines, a stunned people wept and cried out to the Lord. Should they continue the fight or return to their homes? The Lord commanded them to fight. The next day, the lines attacked, and once more the Benjaminites prevailed, killing eighteen thousand men. The people retreated to Bethel to fast and weep before the Lord. They inquired if they should go up against Benjamin or return to their homes. This time, the Lord promised them victory.

They set an ambush around Gibeah. The battle unfolded as before. Israel's lines broke, and the soldiers fled from the battlefield. The Benjaminites, confident in victory, gave chase. The trap was sprung. Those waiting in ambush seized the city and set it on fire. The soldiers fleeing before the Benjaminites saw the smoke and knew they had won the victory. They stopped running, turned, and fought.

The Benjaminites tried to retreat, but the battle had turned against them. Only six hundred men escaped to the natural fortress at the rock of Rimmon. Israel's soldiers swept through Benjamin's territory, killing everything that breathed and burning down every city. Nothing remained. Benjamin's inheritance in the land had become a desolate wilderness.

While the men of Israel were still at Mizpah, they had made a covenant that not one family would give their daughters in marriage to any man of Benjamin under the penalty of death. Now, they thought better of their pact. If the men of Benjamin couldn't marry, they would be wiped out. How could they allow this to happen? They couldn't break the covenant, but there had to be a way around it. They searched the records to see if any city wasn't at Mizpah to sign the covenant.

They discovered Jabesh-gilead hadn't answered the original summons. They sent soldiers to kill everyone in the town but the young virgins. They brought them back to give to the men holed up at the rock of Rimmon. They were two hundred virgins short. What should they do? They permitted the remaining Benjaminites to kidnap the young women of Shiloh when they came to the fields to worship.

Israel returned to their homes, leaving the tribe of Benjamin to rebuild their cities and towns. Their reputation suffered greatly. Gibeah's sin had branded their tribal conscience. It also branded the nation's conscience. The people still remembered what happened by the time Saul was born, approximately eighty-two years later.

Saul, Israel's First King

Israel's last judge reigned in the land as Saul grew to adulthood (1 Samuel 8). Samuel spoke to the people on the Lord's behalf. As he grew old, he appointed his sons to be judges in his place, but they were corrupt. Anyone could buy an innocent or guilty verdict if they had enough money. If the people couldn't trust Samuel's sons to judge fairly and without prejudice, to whom could they turn? They came to Samuel to ask him for a king to judge them just as the kings in the surrounding nations did.

Was kingship ideal? No, but it was to be preferred over Samuel's dishonest sons. Samuel considered their request a repudiation of his life service. He took his complaint to the Lord, who told him that the people hadn't rejected him but had rejected the Lord's kingship over them. He commanded Samuel to tell them what living under a monarch would be like.

Samuel painted a bleak picture of Israel's future under a king. A king would be the ultimate corruption because he would have the power to carry out his every law or whim. He would heavily tax the people and take whatever he wanted, and everyone would be helpless to stop him. He would even take their children and put them in his service. They would become his slaves. The picture ended with a warning. If the people decided to go through with their request, there would come a day when they'd cry out because of the king's injustice. On that day, the Lord wouldn't answer their prayers. The people refused to listen. They stubbornly insisted on a king. So, God gave them one—Saul from the tribe of Benjamin (1 Samuel 9).

When Samuel told Saul he would be king, Saul's first reaction revealed his worldview. "Why me? I am from Benjamin." He described Benjamin as the lowliest of the tribes in the land—one who wore Gibeah's great sin like a cloak of shame and sorrow. The people would be better off with another man.

Samuel gathered the people together to present to them their king. When he called for Saul to come forward and be crowned, he was nowhere to be found. It wasn't an auspicious beginning. The crowd began to murmur. Perhaps they had the wrong man. They inquired of the Lord, who told them

Saul was hiding among the baggage. They rousted him out of his hiding place and were thoroughly impressed by what they saw. Saul was a handsome man who stood head and shoulders over everyone else in Israel. What a physical specimen! He looked every inch the king on the outside.

Saul hid because he couldn't bear to hear the crowd's reaction when they discovered God had chosen their new king from Benjamin. He was correct. Not everyone was impressed. Talk began to circulate throughout the land. How can this man save us? They despised him and brought him no gift to honor him. Saul heard the rumors but held his peace. He returned to Gibeah to wait for something kingly to do. A test of leadership came two years later.

Saul had finished the day's work, and as he was leading his oxen to the barn, he became acutely aware that those gathered near his home were weeping with loud cries and pleas to heaven (1 Samuel 11). He asked for a report, and the people told him that the Ammonites had besieged Jabesh-gilead. The city's elders had tried to lift the siege by promising to serve the Ammonites, but Nahash, their leader, had rejected the offer. He would only lift the siege if the people surrendered and had their right eye gouged out. If they agreed, Nahash would win the city and bring great disgrace upon all of Israel. The city's elders asked for seven days to consider the offer. Nahash agreed. The elders slipped messengers through the enemy's lines to ask Saul for help.

Saul grew angry. The Spirit of the Lord rushed upon him. He slew his oxen, cut them into pieces, and sent them along with a message throughout the land. Whoever doesn't come out to fight with Saul and Samuel, the same thing would happen to their oxen. The dread of the Lord fell upon the people. They left their homes and gathered at Bezek. Saul led them to a mighty victory over the Ammonites the next day.

During the next two years, Israel skirmished with the Philistines, but after Saul's son, Jonathan, defeated the Philistine garrison at Geba, war came to Israel. Saul blew a long trumpet blast and mustered the men of Israel at Gilgal (1 Samuel 13). The Philistines marched through the land with little to no opposition. The people were forced to flee and hide in empty cisterns, pits, and caves, and among the rocks. Any place where they would be safe from the enemy, who killed everyone in their path. As the stories of the Philistines' atrocities grew, the men surrounding Saul grew afraid.

The Insecurity of Saul

Insecurity and Fear

Before Saul went to Gilgal, Samuel had sent word that he would come and offer a sacrifice before the army went into battle. Seven long, tension-filled days passed. Rumors multiplied, as did the fear. The army questioned why Saul didn't attack. Saul wondered why Samuel delayed. Then it happened—men began to leave. They had families to protect, and if Saul was too afraid to fight, they needed to go and defend their homes from the Philistines. The enemy was already at Michmash, and it would be only a matter of days before they attacked Gilgal. Still, Saul did nothing. Was he afraid? What kind of king was he? He was a king from Benjamin.

Saul heard the murmuring and complaining. He knew what the men were saying. It was an attack on his character. He had to do something, or no army would be left when the Philistines arrived. He could only go in to battle after the sacrifice was offered and prayers made to the Lord. So, he made the sacrifice. As soon as the flames consumed the offering, Samuel came into camp. The prophet wasn't pleased and demanded an explanation.

Saul explained he couldn't go in to battle without the Lord's blessing, so he forced himself to sacrifice the burnt offering. He was telling the truth. He did force himself. One of the traits of an insecure worldview is that it views the world through fear. And that worldview doesn't just fear one thing. It fears everything. Saul was afraid of the Philistines. He was afraid he couldn't be king enough to inspire his men to stay. He was afraid that the men would desert him. He was afraid of the Lord. He was afraid of Samuel's disapproval. He was afraid that no matter what he did, it would be the wrong choice. So, he took stock of the situation and decided that if Samuel wasn't coming, he would offer the sacrifice, unite his army, and go to battle.

Samuel rebuked him. The only thing Saul should have been afraid of was disobeying the Lord's commandment, which Samuel had made clear to him. He was to wait at Gilgal until the prophet came to offer the sacrifice and entreat the Lord's favor. If Saul had done that instead of giving in to the many voices of his fear, the Lord would have established his kingdom forever. For his disobedience, his kingdom couldn't be allowed to continue. The Lord would raise up a new king to reign in Saul's place.

The Bible doesn't tell us Saul's reaction to Samuel's decree. All we know is that he gathered the army and marched to Geba. Neither army attacked. Instead, they settled down to watch each other. The Philistines sent raiding parties from Michmash to occupy the surrounding territory. In response, Saul moved his headquarters to the outskirts of Gibeah.

Jonathan broke the stalemate (1 Samuel 14). He and his armor bearer went to pick a fight with the Philistine garrison encamped at Michmash. The two men would show themselves to the Philistines. If the Philistines invited them to come up to them, they would know the Lord had given them into their hands. But they would retreat if the Philistines responded that the two should wait until they came down to them. The Lord was faithful. The Philistines invited them to come up.

Jonathan scrambled up the rocky crag. When he reached the top, he slew the Philistines, causing the remaining garrison to panic. The Lord caused an earthquake, which increased the Philistines' terror. The watchman at Gibeah saw and heard the tumult. Someone was fighting the Philistines and winning. Saul commanded a headcount to see who was missing from his ranks. One of his men told him it was Jonathan and his armor bearer skirmishing with the enemy.

Before he sent his men into battle, Saul's worldview caused him an additional problem. Rebuked by Samuel, he decided to prove that he was a mighty king. The insecure aren't only constantly afraid, but that fearful worldview causes them to assert themselves, sometimes very foolishly, to show everyone they are brave, courageous, and more than capable of handling the responsibility they have been burdened with even when they're not.

The men had always been ready to fight. He had their loyalty. Now Saul felt he had to establish his authority. He didn't do this for the men. He did it for himself. To prove to himself that he wasn't insecure and afraid. He ordered his men not to eat until he was avenged of his enemies. The army chased the Philistines into a surrounding forest, where the weary soldiers found a beehive on the ground oozing with honey. Even though they were starving, they refused to eat. Jonathan stuck his spear into the hive, drew out the honey, and ate. The moment he did, those who had witnessed his actions told him of his father's orders.

Saul asked the Lord if he should continue his pursuit of the Philistines, but the Lord was silent. Saul interpreted the silence as proof that someone had sinned during the battle and earned the Lord's displeasure. As king, it was his responsibility to root out the guilty party and not spare him, even if that man was Jonathan. The men cast lots, and the lots revealed that Jonathan was the man who had sinned. Saul held firm. For his sin, Jonathan would die.

The men vehemently protested. Why should Jonathan die for this sin? They were only victorious because of Jonathan's courage and strength. They stood against their king and ransomed Jonathan's life. Saul gave in to the people. His fear-induced bravado had almost cost him the life of his son. He dismissed the army to their homes and returned to Gibeah.

God Rejects Saul

In 1 Samuel 15, the Lord instructed Samuel to have Saul attack the Amalekites as punishment for their attack on Israel when they came out of Egypt (Exodus 17:14). Saul wasn't to spare the people or their livestock; they were devoted to destruction. After the battle, Samuel entered the camp. Saul bragged about keeping the Lord's commandment and winning a great victory. Samuel stared at him in disbelief. If Saul had obeyed the Lord, why did the sounds of bleating sheep and lowing cattle fill the camp? Saul had a ready answer. The people spared the livestock to sacrifice them to the Lord in thanksgiving. What could be wrong with that?

Everything was wrong with that answer. Samuel held up his hand and ordered Saul to stop talking. He already discerned the problem. The root of this great sin Saul had committed was that he saw himself as too weak to exercise authority and control over the people. His worldview had led to his destruction.

Saul protested. He had done what the Lord commanded. The people were responsible for sparing the flocks and herds, not him. They wanted to sacrifice them to the Lord, and he couldn't muster a reason to tell them no. Samuel's anger grew. Because Saul had rejected the word of the Lord, He had rejected Saul from being king. One who isn't wholly and utterly committed to God to do God's will is wholly repudiated. This was now Saul's fate.

Saul quickly repented and confessed his sin. Samuel was right. He now understood that he hadn't done what the Lord had commanded because he feared the people would reject him as king and raise up another in his place.

But he was very sorry. He begged Samuel to pardon his sin, go with him to the Lord, and make intercession on his behalf. It was too late. The Lord had disqualified him.

First Samuel 16 is the introduction of David. Since this is Saul's story, I will spend little time on Saul's jealousy and hatred of David. Suffice it to say, Saul wasted the rest of his life trying to destroy this usurper of his throne. Saul oscillated between playing the victim and ruthlessly holding himself responsible. Like anyone with an insecure worldview, he blamed himself for all his failures until his *self* could no longer stand the torment he was inflicting upon it. The torment drove him mad. He became unpredictable in his moods and actions. He was still king, but the Spirit of the Lord had abandoned him. He raged at the unfairness of it all.

At the end of his life, Saul was desperate for someone to tell him what to do (1 Samuel 28). Samuel had died, and the Lord had turned from him. No prophet visited him, and his dreams were fruitless. The Philistines had invaded, and he didn't know if the Lord would give him victory. He visited a medium and asked her to summon Samuel's spirit from the grave. Samuel had always been honest if severe with him, and hopefully Samuel would tell him what he should do. When Samuel appeared wrapped in a robe, Saul bowed himself low to the ground. Samuel spoke with the severity and honesty Saul expected and told him that his anguish would end tomorrow. The Philistines would win the battle. He and his sons would be killed on Mount Gilboa. The kingdom would pass to David.

The Villainy of a Worldview

History wouldn't be kind to Saul. It wouldn't remember that Saul united the tribes into a nation and fought valiantly to drive out the enemies that occupied the land and oppressed the people during the time of the judges. He should have been a hero. Instead, he was the mad king who persecuted David before dying an ignoble death. Saul had great potential but never fulfilled the calling on his life.

Samuel had gotten to the root of the matter when he said that Saul was little in his own eyes. No matter how many people followed him, how many victories he won, and the good he accomplished in giving the people a national identity, he couldn't overcome the worldview instilled in him by the misfortune of his birth. The events of the past, which had occurred long before he was born, had written the story of his life. He had changed the people's opinion of him through his bravery and wisdom, but he didn't see it and wouldn't allow himself to believe it. The most powerful man in the kingdom lived every moment, fearing that he would be revealed as a fraud, and the people would take his throne from him and give it to another. Ultimately, it wouldn't be the people who did this to him but his entrenched worldview. The last image of Saul is him seeking a medium because he was desperate for anyone to tell him what he should do. His insecurity had devoured him, leaving it as the defining characteristic of his life.

So, when you hear the name of Saul, do you think of a people-pleaser? A mad king? A failure? Or do you see the tragedy of a life destroyed by his worldview?

Chapter 7
NEHEMIAH TAKES A STAND

"Why should the work stop while I leave it and come down to you?"

Nehemiah 6:3

WHEN THE REMNANT returned to Judea after spending seventy years in exile, they returned with a royal decree from Cyrus to rebuild the temple and reestablish the nation. Cyrus' decrees were the law of the land. A person disobeyed one under the penalty of death. There was nothing to prevent the remnant from rebuilding the temple—except their worldview.

The surrounding nations pushed back against the remnant because they were afraid Israel would reign over the region as it once had under David and Solomon. The remnant heard the nations' threats and stopped building. Their worldview convinced them they were too weak and helpless to withstand the nations' constant ultimatums. They decided it would be better for them just to settle for what little the nations would allow them to have.

A worldview never stays hidden no matter how much we think we hide our true selves. It's revealed in a thousand different ways, and nefarious people take advantage of our weaknesses to manipulate us to live how they want us to live. The remnant had shown themselves to be afraid, and the nations capitalized on their fear and submissiveness to enrich themselves at Judah's expense.

How long the remnant would have lived under those conditions is not known. What is known is that God raised up Nehemiah to remind the people who they were in God and who God was for them. The nations believed Nehemiah was just another Jew who shared the same worldview as the remnant and, therefore, could be bullied just as easily. The nations were wrong. Nehemiah's worldview had been shaped in the fire of intercession.

He came to call God's people out of their spiritual declension by reminding them it was time they lived as if God was for them and not against them.

Exile

As Israel was preparing to possess the Promised Land, the Lord told them that the land was vomiting out the current inhabitants because their worship of false gods had made the land unclean. He warned the people that if they did the same, the land would one day vomit them out. The northern kingdom of Israel refused to heed the Lord's warning, and the ten tribes worshiped Baal and Ashteroth and passed their children through the fire of Moloch. The prophets proclaimed judgment, but Israel refused to repent and return to the Lord. In 740 BC, the Assyrians attacked and captured Samaria, Israel's capital.

History tells us that Assyria's king instituted a policy throughout the territories he conquered To prevent rebellion among the people, he uprooted whole civilizations and transported them to lands that weren't theirs. Before these people arrived, the Assyrians stripped the lands of their assets. This way, the new arrivals would be occupied with survival and not with patriotic zeal to restore the land to its former glory and freedom. The Assyrians chose people from the conquered territories of Babylon, Cut-hah, Ayya, Hamath, and Sef-ar-vaeem, and sent them to Israel. They brought with them their false gods and quickly set up altars and groves for worship. The Lord judged their sin of idolatry by loosing lions among the population.

The people requested the Assyrians send priests to teach them how to please this God so they could live safely within their new borders. The Assyrians sent one priest who returned to Bethel and instructed the people in the law of Moses. In response to this teaching, the people added the God of Israel to their pantheon of gods. They continued their pagan worship, including burning their children in the fire to Adram-melech and Anammelech. But to appease the Lord, they appointed men to be His priests. These nations eventually became the Samaritans.

Unfortunately, the kingdom of Judah didn't learn from the northern kingdom's experience. Despite the prophets' many warnings, they refused to repent of their sins. Nebuchadnezzar, king of Babylon, attacked Judah in 605 BC to secure his trade routes throughout the region. Nineteen years later, he captured Jerusalem, burned the city, and destroyed the temple. He adopted the Assyrian policy of relocation and emptied the land of most of its inhabitants, sending them east to Babylon. There the Jews would stay for seventy years until God brought them back to the land.

Cyrus the Great

The seventy years passed. Belteshazzar ruled over a declining Babylon. Cyrus and the Persians had successfully invaded the land and stood before the city's gates. Belteshazzar felt safe behind Babylon's thick walls and massive gates, but the people were anxious and nervous. The king called for a grand celebration to occupy the people's attention. As the festivities dissolved into drunkenness, he commanded his servants to bring out the consecrated gold and silver vessels his grandfather had captured from the temple and disburse them among his guests.

As they drank from them and praised the gods of Babylon, a disembodied hand appeared and wrote on the wall: *Mene Mene Tekel Parsin* (Daniel 5:24–25). Terrified, Belteshazzar called for Daniel to interpret the writing. Daniel studied the words, turned to the king, and pronounced God's judgment. The Lord had weighed Belteshazzar in the balances and found him wanting. His kingdom would be divided and given to the Medes and the Persians.

Outside the city, Cyrus had found a way to exploit the city's design. Babylon was situated next to the Euphrates River. A moat had been dug around the city, making the city an island in the middle of the river. Cyrus diverted the river from its course. As the moat emptied, the Persians ducked under one of Babylon's many bronze gates and entered the city. That night, Babylon fell, Belteshazzar died, and Cyrus ruled the Middle East.

The prophet Isaiah had written about Cyrus one hundred twenty years before he ducked under the gate (Isaiah 45). According to the historian Josephus, Daniel showed Cyrus what the Lord had declared long before he was born. In those verses, Isaiah prophesied how the Persians would capture the city.

The Lord stirred up Cyrus's spirit. He declared that the Jews could return to Judah and rebuild Jerusalem and the temple. He returned the temple vessels to the first wave of exiles and ordered the governors of the nations in the province Beyond the River to assist the Jews by giving them silver and gold, goods, and animals to serve as free will offerings on his behalf.

Rebuilding the Temple

By now, the Samaritans had been in the land for 187 years. They were still semi-pagan, but a subtle deception had taken hold of their national worldview. They believed their worship of the Lord made them equal to the Jews in the Lord's eyes. When the Samaritans found out that the Jews were planning to rebuild the temple, they sent an envoy to Zerubbabel, the newly appointed governor of Judah. They asked that they be permitted to aid in the temple's construction, but Zerubbabel said no (Ezra 4).

The remnant quickly laid the foundation and appointed counselors to help them with the reconstruction. The Samaritans, still smarting from the Jews' refusal to allow them to participate, bribed the counselors to sabotage the project. They also sent messengers to Darius, who ruled in Babylon. The Samaritans, along with the governors of the province, informed the king of Jerusalem's former fame and power and warned him that if the remnant rebuilt Jerusalem, they would rebel against the Persians by not paying tribute, custom, or toll, and the royal revenue will be impaired (vs 13).

Darius had the archives searched and learned that the governors hadn't exaggerated the threat a revitalized Jerusalem could pose for his kingdom. He sent a royal decree ordering all work on the temple and Jerusalem to cease until he sent another command permitting the Jews to build. The people stopped building and focused on making a living in the land. They were perfectly willing to settle for what the enemy would allow them to have instead of pursuing God's destiny for them.

When Israel failed to go up into the land because of the giants, their worldview was exposed, but only to themselves. The giants had no idea the spies were even in the land. The remnant revealed their worldview by capitulating to the nations and abandoning the temple. They had shown themselves to be afraid, and the nations capitalized on their fear and submissiveness to enrich themselves at Judah's expense.

The Lord raised up the prophet Haggai to warn the people to consider their ways (Haggai 1:7–11). They had looked to their own houses while leaving the temple in ruins. It was time for them to do as the Lord commanded and rebuild the temple so the Lord might be glorified. If they didn't, the judgment of famine that now held the nation firmly in its grips would continue. Zerubbabel and Joshua, the high priest, added their voices to Haggai's and implored the people to obey God and rebuild the temple.

Bolstered by the word of the Lord, the remnant earnestly started to rebuild the temple. The governors in the surrounding nations sent an envoy to remind the Jews that Darius had forbidden all construction in Jerusalem. This time the people didn't care. They refused to back down. When the envoy demanded who had permitted the Jews to rebuild, they said, "Cyrus" and kept right on working.

The governors sent another letter to Darius to report that the remnant had defied his decree and were rebuilding the temple. Not only that, the Jews brazenly justified their rebellion against him by stating Cyrus had ordered the temple to be rebuilt. They politely asked the king if he would search the royal archives to see if Cyrus had made such a decree. Darius acquiesced to the governor's request and ordered a search. Cyrus' decree was found and upheld.

God was on the move. Darius allowed a third wave of Jews led by Ezra, the priest and scribe, to return to Jerusalem. The king decreed that Ezra should teach the Law of Moses throughout the region and appoint judges and magistrates to administer justice by upholding the law. Darius' decree warned the nations that they would suffer banishment, confiscation of goods, imprisonment, or death if they didn't obey the Law of Moses. This decree would have made Jerusalem the center of justice, culture, and worship in the province.

The remnant should have seized upon the opportunity the Lord had given them to rule and reign over their enemies. They had been brave and obeyed the Lord for a brief few years before their worldviews convinced them they were far too weak to impose their will on the surrounding nations. They didn't send priests from Jerusalem to teach the law. Neither did they appoint judges and magistrates. Darius' decree giving them favored-nation status slipped through their fingers. They had a temple but very little else.

Judgment for Disobedience

The people abandoned the law, which allowed corruption to creep into every aspect of their lives. The governors who served after Zerubbabel were no longer righteous or God-fearing. They quickly forsook their responsibility to rule justly. Instead, they exploited the people and the land to sustain their lavish lifestyles. Jerusalem's nobles and leaders entered into business alliances with the enemy and cemented those alliances through marriages. Society restructured itself on the principle of the few getting wealthy at the expense of the rest.

Foreigners took over large segments of Judah's economy, making it harder and harder for the poor to pay both the Persian tribute and the governor's exorbitant taxes. With all their money going to taxes, the people had nothing left to feed their families. They had no choice but to go to the nobles to borrow money. The nobles offered loans at usurious rates in direct contradiction to the law. The people took out loans even though they knew they could never repay them. When the loans came due, the nobles demanded payment and foreclosed on lands, vineyards, flocks, herds, and houses. When the poor had nothing left to foreclose on, they sold what remained—first their daughters and then their sons into slavery. Judah's wealth flowed into their enemies' purses.

The people grew poorer. They were oppressed, and the oppression grew. They were suffering, but their sufferings worsened. All this only intensified the truth of their worldview. They lived at the mercy of others. They thought they were returning to a land of peace and security. Instead, the elders robbed them of everything they owned. They didn't have time to worry about walls, gates, and the Lord's commands. They were too busy trying to survive. After they were through selling their children, they would have nothing left for the taxes and interest they owed. They were living, balanced, on the edge of a knife.

That was the way their enemies preferred it. To make God's people too busy and overburdened for anything else but survival. The nations feared that if the people ever stepped into their identity as God's covenant people, the Jews would turn the region's balance of power on its head. So the nations were constantly reinforcing what the people believed about themselves. They were too weak and helpless to do anything about their lives.

Nehemiah Stands in the Gap

In 445 BC, Nehemiah's brother, Hanani, accompanied by a group of men, came to Susa, the Persian capital. Scripture doesn't reveal the purpose of Hanani's journey, but he used it as an opportunity to visit his brother in the palace. Nehemiah was the king's cupbearer, a position of significant influence within the court. Nehemiah asked his brother how the remnant was faring in Jerusalem, and his brother's response grieved him. The people were in great trouble and shame. Jerusalem's walls were still broken, and her gates burned with fire. The remnant was living unsecured, taunted by their enemies, and unable to govern themselves.

When Nehemiah heard the news, he recognized Jerusalem's sad state as a spiritual problem, not a political one. Edicts and decrees couldn't solve it. The glory of God had been lost. Glory is always lost when we become occupied with ourselves, and the remnant was occupied with themselves. Jerusalem needed someone to stand in the gap and remind them of who God was for them and who they were in God.

He also realized he couldn't pack up tomorrow and depart for Jerusalem. He was the king's servant and would need Artaxerxes' permission to go. He would also need Artaxerxes' authority and treasury to help him rebuild the walls and gates. Five or six months later, while Nehemiah was serving wine, Artaxerxes noticed his cupbearer was sad even though he wasn't sick. He demanded to know the reason. Nehemiah explained that his sadness was because Jerusalem still lay in ruins. Artaxerxes agreed to let him go to Jerusalem as a temporary governor and oversee the city's rebuilding.

When Nehemiah arrived in Jerusalem, Sanballat, the governor of Samaria; Tobiah, an official of Ammon; and Geshem the Arab, their sidekick; challenged his authority. They were displeased that Artaxerxes would send a governor empowered to seek the welfare of the people. However, they could do nothing to stop Nehemiah from accomplishing his goals. To do so would mean to go against Artaxerxes' decree, a losing proposition if there ever was one.

But they believed they still held all the cards. Sanballat and Tobiah married their sons and daughters into Jerusalem's nobility. These marriages allowed them considerable influence in Jerusalem's affairs. They would have to pressure their familial alliances to force the nobles to revolt against Nehemiah and refuse to do the work.

What Sanballat and Tobiah were counting on was that Nehemiah was just another Jew with a fearful and timid worldview. They were wrong. Nehemiah had never shared the remnant's worldview. God forged his kingdom view in the many days and nights he spent interceding on the remnant's behalf. He had come to do more than build the city's walls. He came to vindicate the holiness of the Lord's great name, which had been profaned and diminished throughout the territory. The remnant dared to claim they were God's chosen people yet lived as if they had no God.

Nehemiah gathered the elders together. He was frank. The city was in great trouble because they had disobeyed the Lord and left the city in ruins. The nations held them in derision because the people allowed them to steal their goods while they wrung their hands in fear. The time to go to work had arrived. Artaxerxes had blessed their endeavors. If they worked together, they would be able to rebuild the walls.

Word filtered back to Sanballat, Tobiah, and Geshem. They jeered at the Jews' foolish attempts to rebuild the city. But they had severely underestimated Nehemiah. He recognized their insults and scorn as spiritual warfare. It was the greater enemy that motivated these men. He didn't argue or enter into a debate with them. He spoke the truth: "God is the One prospering us. We are His servants. You are not. Even though you think you have a portion in Jerusalem, you don't. We'll take what belongs to us." His words strengthened the people. They rose as one and began to build. Every household in the city took part in building the wall because Nehemiah had the entire wall under construction simultaneously.

To intimidate the workers, Sanballat mustered his army. He laughed before his men and mocked the Jews' attempt to build a strong wall from ruined and burnt stones. He used his connections within Jerusalem to spread rumors that the army would attack the workers.

Fear overtook the remnant. They couldn't build the wall fast enough to keep the enemy out. There was too much rubble in the way. They needed help. Men from the surrounding villages poured into the city and begged the people to give in to the Samaritans and stop building. The nations resorted to their old playbook and tested Jerusalem's resolve. They hoped to make the people afraid by convincing them they would die if they continued to build the wall.

When word reached Nehemiah, he didn't fret, wring his hands, or ask a dozen people what he should do. He sprang into action. He stationed warriors in all the areas through which the enemy could attack. He placed people by their clans behind the wall and in all the open places and gave them swords, spears, and bows. He told the nobles to stop listening to the voices threatening them with death. "Who is greater, the enemy or the Lord? Who is more to be feared? So, if the Samaritans attack, fight—not just for your lives, but for your children's futures."

Sanballat, Tobiah, and Geshem now realized they had misjudged Nehemiah. All their previous ploys of manipulating the remnant's worldview failed with him. They couldn't make him afraid. They needed a more violent solution. They sent messengers to Nehemiah, asking him to come down to Hakkephirim in the plain of Ono to discuss the situation. Nehemiah recognized the three men only wanted to do him harm. He returned a message informing them that he was doing a great work. Why should he stop it to come down to them? There was nothing for him to gain from a conversation with them. He had a job to do.

The enemy couldn't go up to Nehemiah. Artaxerxes protected him. Their only course of action was to get him to stop the work on his own. To leave it to come down and hear all the reasons that it would be to his benefit to stop building. When Nehemiah refused, they sent the same invitation three more times, imploring him to come down to them so they could talk. He declined each time. He had nothing to say to them, and they had nothing he wanted to hear.

The fifth time the messengers approached, they carried a handwritten letter from Sanballat. He warned Nehemiah that he had heard rumors and that Artaxerxes might hear them also. It was being said that Nehemiah wasn't building the wall for the Lord but because he would proclaim himself king and rebel against the Persians. These reports were catastrophic toward him, and it would be best if Nehemiah would come down and talk to them so they could protect him from Artaxerxes' anger. Nehemiah knew better than to accept the premise of the enemy's accusations. If he did, he would have to defend himself against lies and baseless allegations for the rest of his time in Jerusalem. He wrote back that Sanballat was making up rumors out of whole cloth, and Artaxerxes would never believe them.

Finally, Sanballat and Tobiah hired a prophet to warn Nehemiah that someone had put a contract out on his life and he needed to seek refuge in the temple. The two men wanted to force Nehemiah into an open display of hypocrisy. The remnant would be left to build the wall, armed for war, while their governor fled the battlefield to save his life. Nehemiah's reputation would be in ruins, the people would no longer follow such a coward, and the work would cease.

Nehemiah refused to attribute the prophet's words to God. It was the Lord who had sent him to build the wall. Why would He change His mind and now tell him to flee for his life and hide in the temple? He asked the prophet if such a man as he should run away and hide. Of course not. He was the governor, appointed by the king, and anointed by God to restore the city. He wouldn't give the people a reason to abandon the work and slip back into a life of fear and passivity.

Fifty-two days after the work commenced, the remnant had built the wall and set the gates. All the enemies' threats had come to nothing.

The Villainy of a Worldview

Every time the people tried to break free from the fear that bound them, the enemy would apply pressure, and they would submit to their worldviews' counsel that they were too weak to resist. The best thing they could do for themselves would be to remain small and passive. The enemy exploited their worldview repeatedly until the remnant became impoverished and powerless.

The enemy's worldview was just as fearful as the Jews, except the remnant didn't know it. The nations' shared histories involved Jewish conquest and subjugation of their lands. Instead, they used their worldview to fuel them into action. They were determined not to see Jerusalem rise to her former glory. The spiritual wickedness in the nations worked incessantly to keep the people occupied with the necessities of life so they wouldn't have time to remember their prophets and kings who served a God who fought for them. If Israel remembered, they would subjugate the nations as their former kings had.

Things might have remained unchanged, but Nehemiah's arrival challenged the status quo. He had a kingdom view that answered to the Lord. The tactics that had worked so successfully on the remnant failed miserably on him. He refused to be intimidated by their empty threats. He knew they would never go against Artaxerxes's decree. He knew it, and they knew it. So he didn't care what they said about him. All their threats, bluffs of war, and intimidation were nothing more than kabuki theater for the remnant. He knew the only way to stop them was to stand in God's truth and not waver. His stance was enough to bolster the remnant's resolve. Once they realized they could stand up to the enemy, they were able to finish the wall.

Chapter 8
WHAT ABOUT ME?
"What about you?"

Jacob to Ben Linus

FOR THIS CHAPTER, I'm going to leave the Bible (only temporarily) and choose two scenes from the television series *Lost* to illustrate just how our worldviews hinder our walks with the Lord. Our worldviews will always triumph over God's work in us if they can get us to ask one simple question in every situation we find ourselves in: *What about me?*

The question is a trap. If we ask it, our worldviews will continue to exercise their complete mastery over us. How? By convincing our *selves* we have the right to ask the question. One of the foundational tenants of Christianity is His command that we die to *self* so we can live to God. If we find ourselves asking, "What about me?", there will be no growth or maturity into image and likeness.

What About You?

In case you haven't seen *Lost*, let me set the stage. The series opens with a plane crash on a mysterious island. The island serves as a metaphor for the battle between good and evil. Evil is swirling about, always present, trying to break free and infect the world. The island is like a cork on a bottle. It's the only thing keeping evil at bay. Jacob is in charge of protecting the island and making sure the wickedness remains bottled up. Jacob's brother, known as The Man in Black, is the personification of that evil. He wants nothing more than to escape from his prison. The island has two rules by which the brothers must live. One is that The Man in Black can only leave the island if Jacob is dead. The other is that The Man in Black can't kill Jacob; he must have someone else do that for him.

One of the main characters from the plane crash, John Locke, has died, and The Man in Black is using his body (you have to go with it) to communicate with the other survivors to convince someone to kill Jacob. He finds his murderer in Benjamin Linus, the right-hand man of Jacob's right-hand man. There is nothing Ben won't do for the island. In one of the more dramatic scenes of the show, he had to make a heartbreaking choice— save his daughter or the island. He doesn't believe Jacob would ask him to sacrifice his daughter, so he chooses the island. He watches as a group of mercenaries murder his daughter.

Ben is the focus of the scene. As a character, he is an enigma. Is he a good man? Is he a villain? The audience is never quite sure. What we do know is that he is an amoral sociopath consumed with his duty to protect the island. Even though he has killed on Jacob's orders, he has never actually talked to Jacob face-to-face. If Jacob has a task for Ben to complete, he always sends the aforementioned right-hand man to pass along instructions.

The scene opens with Locke and Ben entering Jacob's sanctuary. It's Ben's first time there, for you can only enter upon invitation. A tapestry hanging on the wall catches his attention, and he examines it. Suddenly, he hears a man ask him if he likes what he sees. He turns to see Jacob sitting in a chair. Locke orders Ben to do what he asked him to do. When Ben hesitates, Jacob intervenes. He tells Ben that no matter what Locke has asked him to do, he has a choice. He can leave the sanctuary and allow the men to discuss their issues.

Ben replies with hurt, anger, and bitterness. He reminds Jacob he has lived on the island for thirty-five years, and all he ever heard was Jacob's name. His intermediary would bring instructions, and Ben would complete them without question. But whenever he asked to see Jacob, he was told he would have to wait and be patient. Locke asked just once and received an immediate audience.

Ben continues his lament. "What makes Locke so special? What was so wrong with me?" Then he asks the question he has been waiting for years to ask. "What about me?" Jacob looks at him long and hard and responds, "What about you?" For Ben, it was as if Jacob just spit in his face. He takes a deep breath while the truth breaks over him. He was nothing more than a rube, a pawn to this man. "Well." That is all he says before he raises the knife and kills Jacob.

When watching the scene, one feels Ben's resentment of Jacob's treatment of him. His worldview convinced him that the island chose him to protect it because he was special. So he gave everything in pursuit of duty. He was loyal to Jacob and the island. Even though he wanted to dismiss the intermediary and have a face-to-face relationship with Jacob, he accepted the arrangement as just another aspect of his duty. One day his time would come, and Jacob would reward him for his loyalty.

But when Locke received an immediate audience, Ben realized Jacob didn't want to speak to him. He was good enough to do all the dirty work Jacob required but too dirty to be invited into the sanctuary. This revelation stunned him. How dare Jacob dismiss him as if he didn't count? As if he didn't matter? As if the sacrifice of his daughter didn't matter? He sides with Locke and kills Jacob.

What About Me?

You probably haven't survived a plane wreck on a mysterious island. Still, there may have been times when you felt as if the world has dismissed you in the same superficial and indifferent manner that Jacob dismissed Ben after years of loyal service. In the aftermath of such a momentous rejection, you may have demanded answers to some very reasonable questions: "What about what I want? What about how I feel? What about me?"

You were bewildered by the unfairness of life, cruelly dismissing you as if you didn't count, as if your dreams and aspirations didn't matter. Why would the world give you a talent only to treat you as if you weren't special? You're not special to the world because the world doesn't have special people. Satan hates equally, destroys equally, and kills equally. He has one purpose for your life: to devastate and scar your heart so that when you hear the gospel's good news, there is nothing good about it.

No matter how often you ask the questions, you have yet to receive the answer you desire or believe you deserve, giving birth to an unsettled soul. Tired of being ignored by the world, you insist on your way. It's not overt. It isn't you standing in the middle of a room shouting everyone down until they have no choice but to listen to you. No, it just appears like a summer storm. You explode over something small and insignificant because you feel small and insignificant. Looking back over your life, you'll see the same words and situations constantly triggered the same storms. No one is listening. Everyone is telling you what is good for you. And the anger builds. They don't know you at all.

You feel violated as people dismiss your rights. There is a feeling of inequity growing in your heart. A sense that you aren't receiving your due. You're constantly aggrieved. You're tired of other people demanding their rights at your expense. Your worldview rises and demands justice for all the slights—real or not—you have suffered at the hands of a system that coldly dismisses you.

So, you claim your rights. Your right to be angry. Your right to hold unforgiveness in your heart. Your right to mistreat someone because they have mistreated you. How often have you begun a sentence, "You don't know what they did to me"? This one sentence justifies all the anger, resentment, and unforgiveness. The root of bitterness takes hold, poisoning you and everyone around you. The cork is out of the bottle. Evil has escaped.

Years and perhaps decades of demanding your rights, whether vocally or not, has set a wildfire in your life. A fire that is on the verge of consuming you. You can't put it out. You are deficient in the necessary spiritual understanding needed to douse the flames. Upon this deficiency, you are foundering. Meanwhile, Satan sifts you like wheat for the sheer pleasure of doing so. The ground of his sifting is your constant offense. You're tired of other people demanding their rights at your expense. You recognize these people as the petty tyrants they are. The truth is, though, very few people will sacrifice themselves for another's needs. That is the consequence of the Fall. People want what they want. Their justification for doing so is that everyone else is out for themselves, so it's only reasonable they should be too.

You insist no one understands what you have gone through, what you've suffered. You're right. Probably no one does. But I do know the great harm you're doing to yourself. You're the author of a far greater tragedy than what they (whoever they are) did (whatever they've done) to you. You're a greater villain in your life than they ever could be. You're inflicting upon yourself significant spiritual damage. Your insistence that your rights receive their day in court has cost you spiritually. It's keeping you immature in the nature and character of the Son. God has promised you so much, and you have discounted it all because you need and demand justice. You're wasting years of your life. Years you can never get back.

Two Masters

In the Sermon on the Mount, Jesus tells His disciples that no one can serve two masters. For he will hate the one and love the other, or he will be devoted to the one and despise the other. One cannot serve God and mammon (Matthew 6:24). Over the years, teachers have reduced the word *mammon* to mean money, but that isn't the definition of mammon in Greek. *Mammon* means the one thing in which you put your trust. Whatever it may be, that one thing becomes a master in your life.

The conflict arises when you try to serve two competing masters. No one throughout human history can ultimately serve two different masters when both demand absolute fidelity. The outcome is predetermined. You will love one of the masters and hate the other. You can only serve one while giving lip service to the other. You also can't place absolute trust in two masters at one time. It's impossible.

You can't come onto God's ground to worship Him and bring your outraged and offended *self* with you. Your prayers can't be a constant demand for justice and a litany of your troubles. To serve God, you must be governed by God alone. If you hold on to whatever others did to you, your master is this world. You're living captive to its influence. There is no spiritual realm in your life. God isn't greater than all the things that have happened to you.

Where Will You Go?

Let's return to Ben Linus. After he murdered Jacob, he was taken captive by a woman named Ilana. She came to the island to protect Jacob from The Man in Black, only to discover that she has arrived too late. Jacob is already dead. When Ben falls into her hands, she will have her vengeance. She puts him to work digging his grave. Locke shows up and sees him slowly digging. He tells Ben that he has placed a rifle in a clearing near the half-completed grave. All Ben has to do is decide what to do. With that, Locke leaves. Ben makes his run to freedom with Ilana in hot pursuit. He reaches for the rifle and turns it on the woman but doesn't shoot. Instead, he wants to make her understand why he killed Jacob.

The turning point in Ben's character arc was his daughter's death. It was his fault she died. He had a chance to save her but chose the island over her. All in the name of Jacob. He tells Ilana that he sacrificed everything for Jacob, only to find out that Jacob didn't even care. He was angry, so he killed him. But then he realized that's not why he did it. He killed Jacob because he was terrified that he was about to lose the only thing that ever mattered to him, his power. But now he knows the only thing that mattered was his daughter. He apologizes for killing Jacob. He doesn't expect her to forgive him because he will never be able to forgive himself.

Ilana asks him what he wants. He wants to go. Go where? Back to Locke. His answer dumbfounds her. Why? "Because he's the only one who will have me," Ben replies, heartbroken over what he has allowed his life to become. She battles within herself for a brief moment. Ben is, after all, the man who killed Jacob, but the internal battle ends quickly. "I'll have you," she says before walking away.

If you continue to demand retribution for all the real and perceived injustices done to you throughout your life, sooner or later you will have to decide to whom you will go. To this world because it is the only one who will have you? The only one who truly understands why you nurse all your resentment, unforgiveness, and bitterness? Or will you hear the Lord say, "I'll have you, but your resentment, unforgiveness, and bitterness must be left behind"? You can tell Him, "But you don't know what they did to me," and He will still insist they be left behind, for He did not create you to be governed by your pain but by His love.

"What about what I want? What about me?"

The Worldview's Tyranny Must End

What about you? The answer doesn't seem as cruel as when Jacob said it to Ben. For now, you understand that the question is asking which life you will choose. You can choose a life and have the Son revealed in you. But for that to happen, for you to carry His image and likeness, you must stop living under the control of your outraged and offended *self*. You must deny your *self* so that you can finally live to God. Or you can go to the world for sympathy and understanding and find someone who will agree that you're justified in your demands for justice.

No matter which choice you make, there is only one way this is going to end. You will stand before the Lord, and He will judge your life based on one standard—the measure of His Son's nature present in you. You are closer to that day than you were yesterday. So choose wisely.

Chapter 9
YOU HAVE ONE TEACHER
"You have heard that it was said . . . but I say to you . . ."

Matthew 5:21–22

BEFORE GENESIS 1, the Father contemplated how He would communicate His purpose and destiny to the creation He was about to speak into existence. That is why He chose to create through His Son, so His Son would forever be His voice. Jesus was the Word (John 1:1) who brought light out of darkness and declared man to be made in His image and after His likeness.

He was the Word who sought Adam after the Fall and promised Eve her offspring would crush the serpent's head. He was there when Sarah gave birth to Isaac, when Israel came out of Egypt, when Solomon dedicated the temple, and when the remnant returned from Babylon. In the exact moment He formed Adam from the dust of the earth, He beheld an innumerable multitude standing before the throne and the Lamb (Revelation 7:9). He is at the beginning and the end and every point in between and knows the Father has never changed His mind about His desire that you be made in His image and after His likeness.

Jesus—The Word

When the fullness of time came, the Father took His Word, the utter expression of who He is, wrapped Him in flesh, and sent Him into this fallen world. In the incarnation, the Father expressed Himself in a language men could understand.

Jesus was a carpenter who knew the value of hard work and the challenges of daily life. When He taught, He used earthly examples to convey spiritual meanings: a sower, a sheepfold, a prodigal, and a wedding feast. He was approachable. People could ask Him questions and He would answer. He always went to where the need was. He was tireless, healing whole villages of sickness and disease. No devil could stand before Him. He exposed worldly wisdom as the foolishness of men. He revealed what God hid due to the Fall.

The Father was no longer shrouded in shadows and confined to the priests' and scribes' misunderstanding. He stood in a light so bright that darkness couldn't overwhelm it. He spoke through His Son the good news that what He purposed for your life is still valid.

This means your life is no longer about where you've been and what's happened to you. Your life is about a Father, sonship, and love. Jesus knows the truth about you because He was there when the Father chose you in Him before He created the world (Ephesians 1:4). Even after Adam ate of the tree, the Father looked down and still saw who He made man to be. In the Father's heart, nothing changed. Man still has the same purpose, the same destiny, and the same value.

But that's not what the disciples grew up hearing. The rabbis taught that instead of love, there was duty. Instead of grace, there was legalism. Instead of forgiveness, there was punishment. Instead of a loving Father, there was a taskmaster they could never satisfy and please no matter how hard they tried.

Jesus told the Pharisees and the crowds that the Father kept nothing secret from the Son but revealed everything to Him. In turn, He revealed all these things to the disciples (John 15:15). This revelation forever changed the disciples' relationship with God. Before Jesus came, they were the equivalent of servants who didn't understand why the master did what he did. It wasn't their business to know. It was their business to hear the master's command and obey without question. They were now His friends, and their friendship allowed them to understand the immensity of His purpose in making them sons worthy and satisfying to Him.

A False Teaching Exposed

I have sat through many teachings where preachers emphasize there will be times when you won't understand what God is doing in your life. When that happens, you must grit your teeth, steel your will, and blindly obey Him. That's what God expects of us in those times. But that teaching runs contrary to what Jesus taught the disciples. Only the servant doesn't understand and is expected to obey his master blindly. You're not a servant. You've become His friend. He has made known to you all He has purposed for your life. He didn't call you into something still undecided or open to change and speculation. The strength of His call is the one thing the Fall couldn't overcome.

The Lord doesn't hide your life's purpose in a mystery you aren't allowed to know. Your course through life isn't one of mindless obedience. God didn't create you to live ignorant of His will for your life. Neither did He create you to live in gross darkness. It's always a false teaching that states you can't know, so the only course open to you is to obey without comprehending why you're suffering.

This is why it's so important to change your thinking. Trials and tribulations are going to come. They come because of the Word. They come to challenge your commitment and see if hardship can put you out of the fight. If you don't know His purpose, you'll quickly become discouraged. Instead of trust, there will be prayers of bewilderment and demands that your suffering be alleviated immediately or explained to your satisfaction. Your lament over the situations and circumstances you find yourself in only exposes the limits of your thinking. You're stumbling over what He has said to you. If you allow your life to speak louder than His voice, it becomes easier to draw back due to offense.

Trials and tribulations, no matter how severe and unfair, don't have the power to change who God is for you and who you are to God. The truth of the unchangeable nature of God toward you is the firm foundation on which you are to build your life. Jesus told the disciples that in their lives, the rains will fall, the floods will come, and the winds will beat against their houses in an attempt to destroy what they had built. But He also told them that if they built their houses on His teachings alone, they would remain intact (Matthew 7:26).

You were His choice from the beginning. When you settle that in your spirit, you'll discern that testing times are your proving ground. A proving ground is an environment that demonstrates whether something is true. He loves you enough to expose the motives, thoughts, behaviors, and emotions that keep you from reaching maturity. All His teachings come together in times of trial. You are not your own. You have been bought with a price for a greater purpose than you could ever imagine—the Father's satisfaction revealed in His Son.

Who Are You?

His satisfaction was revealed when He declared that Jesus was His beloved Son in whom He is well pleased (Matthew 3:17). You get to be one with Him in that satisfaction. During life's difficulties, He teaches you what is valuable and worthy. He also teaches you what fullness is: a mature son living in his inheritance. No longer will you live as *just* a sinner saved by grace.

This false teaching that insists Christians are *just* sinners saved by grace is a carefully designed trap to keep you less than who Jesus says you are. When you refer to yourself as a sinner saved by grace, you argue against the power of His death and resurrection. He died to empower you to live in Him and be conformed to His image and likeness. Even though this is the message of the New Testament, the language that fills our churches is the opposite.

Some find it easy to believe that Christians are *just* sinners saved by grace because that teaching excuses their spiritual poverty (the state of not being able to meet their spiritual obligations) and explains why they constantly fail and sin. "Look around," they say. "Everyone sins. No one is perfect. What a relief I'm not alone." They remain captive to sin because their lives back up their theology. And because their lives back up their theology, they believe it all the more. That's why they push off image and likeness to the day they finally make it to heaven. Then things will be different, but for now, everything about living in this world for Christ is just hard.

No. He has made you the righteousness of God in Christ Jesus. He died to set you free from the power of sin. This is what He paid for on the cross.

This is why He tells you to reckon yourself dead to sin and not allow sin to reign in your mortal body (Romans 6:6). How? By living in the righteousness He gave you when you were born again. The false teaching that you're *just* a sinner saved by grace steals from you the power His righteousness has in your life to conform you to His image and likeness, and makes that power null and void.

If you believe you're *just* a sinner saved by grace, then you don't understand the harm that confession does in your life. Instead of a Father, sonship, and love, there is the overwhelming and discouraging belief that you can never measure up to the impossible standard of the Son of God.

Into this discouragement comes another false teaching: If you obey a list of man-made or even self-imposed rules, you'll be accepted and loved. How you keep or fail to keep those rules becomes the barometer you use to judge your relationship with the Lord. This forces your eyes inward, and your behavior determines how righteous you are at any given moment. When that happens, you find yourself living on shaky ground, for there will be days when you are pleased with your behavior and days when you want to run away and hide from God's presence just like Adam did in the garden.

You may not realize it, but you're building your house on a foundation of feelings, emotions, works righteousness, and false teachings. When life's storms come (because Jesus says they will) and beat against your house, it'll fly apart in the wind, leaving you demoralized and disappointed. You'll look around at the wreckage and not understand how you got here because you love the Lord and want nothing more than to please Him.

But everything will always remain the same if you constantly rebuild the house on the same foundation. The enemy will increase his pressure on you. The storms will become more and more frequent. Eventually, you'll stop rebuilding. No wonder Jesus says false teaching is a thief and a robber. This teaching that you are *just* a sinner saved by grace is the wretched hireling stealing your true identity and heritage.

You Are Who God Says You Are

You are your Father's son. Let me stop here for a moment and explain why I use *son* and not *sons* and *daughters* when describing Christians or, at times, describing myself. I'm well aware that women aren't sons, but daughters. But Paul utilized the word *son* in his epistles to describe all believers. He was writing to gentiles who knew the practice of a Roman nobleman adopting his own son so he could teach the churches that the same thing happened to them when the Father adopted them in Christ. Unlike the Romans, Paul didn't limit adoption to sons. Daughters were also included. Paul continued to use the word *son* to describe male and female because gender wasn't the issue—the position a Roman son assumed when he was adopted was.

A Roman adoption recognized that the son had passed from childhood and had reached adulthood. He was given the privileges and responsibilities that came with being an adult in Roman society. If he was the first-born, he was proclaimed the heir of his father's estate and political power. If he wasn't the first-born, he was proclaimed a joint-heir and enjoyed the same privileges and responsibilities the first-born received. The sons were free to conduct business in the marketplace, and their father's friends and enemies understood that the sons were to be received as if they were their father.

You walk in the newness of life under an open heaven. Jesus came to give you life and life more abundantly (John 10:10), so how can a situation or a circumstance triumph over His truth unless you allow false teaching to warp your perspective and diminish who you are to Him? What He says is the only thing that matters. If He says you are holy, blameless, qualified, and beyond reproach, that's who you are. You can build your house upon His words or continue to build them on how you feel about yourself at any moment.

Please believe me. I know what I'm talking about. I squandered my life because I couldn't believe I was a son worthy of His love. That truth was for someone else. Not for me. And throughout my life, the winds blew, the rains fell, the floods came, and the fall of my house was great. Then He showed me in one incredible moment that I was made in His image and after His likeness. I repented of my wrong thinking.

My life became more than my feelings and failings. I had one teacher, and He was saying some incredible things about me. I summoned the courage to believe Him. All the other teachings that made it their life's work to steal from me, kill me, and destroy me were vanquished. He did that for me. He will do the same for you. That's why I wrote this book.

Jesus' appearance changed the language by which you're to live. Instead of a multitude of voices, there is only one voice that speaks. Only one voice that teaches. Only one voice to be believed and obeyed. Now that Christ has come, all other teachers and teachings must be abandoned. You have one teacher. One glorious teacher who knows you better than you know yourself. It's time to hear His voice and believe the gospel's good news.

Part 2
IMAGE
AND
LIKENESS

Chapter 10
THE HEAVENLY PATTERN

Our fathers had the tent of witness in the wilderness, just as he
who spoke to Moses directed him to make it, according
to the pattern that he had seen.

Acts 7:44

THE FUNDAMENTAL TRUTH of your faith is that the Lord Jesus has become the Father's standard for your life. The strength of His call is to conform you to the Son's image so you may reach the age of majority and inherit the responsibility of manifesting the Son to the world. Your life is the proving ground of His resurrection, for it's His life that destroys the works of the devil. God is conforming you to His nature, character, and authority.

Image and Likeness

Image and likeness are the physical representations of the invisible—a precise reproduction in every aspect. The incarnation is the heavenly pattern—the union between the divine and humanity. The incarnation was the Father present in the Son, and the Son possessing the Father's glory and occupying the Father's throne. The Father and the Son were two persons but one in purpose, will, and mind. The people couldn't tell them apart, nor could they force them apart.

Since the garden, a war has raged over the governance of the universe. The first casualties were creation and man. Death's corruption defiled every inch of creation. Man's nature underwent a fundamental transformation. He was reconstituted in Satan's image and after his likeness. Darkness filled his mind, and sin lorded over him, making him a captive to his appetites and emotions. When God closed the door to fallen man, it appeared Satan had won the war, for in the earth's current condition, how could the door ever be opened again?

To ensure the door remained closed to man and the earth continued in its corrupted and lawless state, Satan worked tirelessly to extinguish any revelation from heaven. As God worked through His chosen vessels, He deposited something of His life in them. These deposits were a menace to Satan's kingdom. He would bring death's great might against God's rectifying work. He couldn't attack life directly, for what power does death have over eternal life? So he diluted God's truth with men's opinions and ideas, which proved a most effective tactic. Truth became almost unrecognizable as men dragged the heavenly revelation from its exalted position to the dust of the earth. It was the garden played out over and over again. Man's independence and selfishness became the lens through which he defined truth. He became the final court of appeals on whether following the Lord's commandments was good or evil.

Jesus came into this world as the living revelation of the Father's goodness to all men. His baptism changed the status quo. He stood as the federal head of a new race, just as Adam was the federal head of the old. Even though both races shared their beginnings in God's eternal purpose, they could never dwell together peacefully due to the Fall. Nor would they share in God's inheritance. For in the new man, judgment day had arrived for the old. If man didn't repent, he would die in his sins.

Jesus' appearance along the banks of the Jordan meant the war had entered its endgame. Both God and Satan would try this new man. Would Jesus depend solely on the Father and allow God's glory to govern Him? Would He deny Himself and be obedient, even if that obedience meant death? Satan knew if he were to win, he would need to tempt Jesus into acting of His own volition by elevating His opinions over what God had made known. No matter how the war ended, there would be a victor and a vanquished.

What made Jesus different from all the other men who came before Him was His intimate knowledge of the Father's nature, which is love. A love without limits. He demonstrated God's love for man by overthrowing the poverty of their condition. This is why He healed the sick, cast out demons, fed the multitudes, raised the dead, calmed the storms, and exercised an authority no one in Israel had ever witnessed. His compassion toward the crowds that thronged Him gave the people hope that the God of Abraham, Isaac, and Jacob was a Father who would genuinely welcome the prodigal home.

The compassion He displayed to all people was also why the religious leaders feared and hated Him. A loving God wasn't good for business. The religious leaders had carefully cultivated a God who was never pleased as a way to keep the people in line and submitted to their authority. Take that away, and there would be spiritual anarchy. So when they questioned His teachings or motives, they were argumentative and defensive. He responded with a wisdom that baffled them. When they tried to trick Him or trip Him up with a small detail of the law, He turned the tables on them to expose their hearts. He never let a lie stand. He was the only one who knew God and had come to manifest the Father's heart to the people.

During the Last Supper, Jesus commanded the disciples to love one another as He loved them (John 13:34). He was calling them back to their purpose—image and likeness. When man fell, he fell from love into selfishness, which can never produce true love. Even though he believes he loves purely, it isn't selfless. Therefore, it isn't love. There are always conditions attached to his love, whether he recognizes it or not. If those conditions aren't met, then his love dries up and dies. God's love never fails. When your love toward others truly equals the love Christ has shown you throughout your life, the world will see the Lord in His fullness. That's how powerful His love is.

Love Is Everything

Paul makes this clear in 1 Corinthians 13. He asked what good are tongues, prophetic powers, the ability to understand all mysteries, and faith to move mountains if there isn't love. Love is the more excellent way. It doesn't seek its own and takes no recognition of the wrongs done to it. Love is kind and patient without envy or arrogance. Love bears all things, believes all things, hopes all things, and endures all things (1 Corinthians 13:7). Love is the heavenly pattern in fullness.

God has revealed this heavenly pattern to you so you can know His love and be transformed. He has persevered with you, has held you when you cried, rebuked you when you were wrong, and shined a light in the darkness that was suffocating you. He forgave everything you've done. He also raises you from the death that operates in you so you can live in the fullness of His life. This is true freedom. Finally, to be free of the petty tyrant of *self* and its worldview that demands you live for yourself.

At the same time, Jesus gave the disciples His commandment and told them that He was going away and they couldn't follow (John 13:36). Peter asked Jesus where He was going. Jesus answered that Peter couldn't follow for now, but the time would come when he could. Peter insisted he would follow Jesus to prison and death. His insistence perfectly demonstrated why he was unable to follow. There is only so far the flesh, will, and intellect can carry you. None of these things can bring you into image and likeness. Peter believed his love for Jesus equaled Jesus' love for him. So if Jesus were going somewhere, Peter would also go. Even if it meant he would have to die alongside Jesus.

Peter's love carried him as far as the enemy's campfire in the high priest's courtyard (John 18:15-27). But when the young woman asked him if he was Jesus' disciple, he denied knowing Jesus because he feared the soldiers warming themselves around the fire would kill him. When he denied Jesus the third time, the blast of a Roman sentry's trumpet sounding the watch pierced the night's quiet. At that moment, Jesus turned and looked at him. Peter's love couldn't overcome the Fall. Self-preservation in the face of death overwhelmed him, and he couldn't make himself go where Jesus was going.

The cost of discipleship is high. Jesus says the first thing you must do to follow Him is to deny your *self* and the *self's* fallen instinct to preserve its authority to govern your life as it sees fit. To the *self,* Jesus' call to denial is the same as death. Don't define death as your final breath on earth, for the *self* defines death as being denied what it thinks it needs most to survive—whatever the "it" is. Because the *self* doesn't want to die, it works unceasingly to prevent the heavenly pattern from forming in you.

God's love is the only power that can overcome a *self* bent on preservation. No matter how much Peter believed his love was powerful enough to follow Jesus to the cross, his *self* and worldview yanked him back from the threat of death. It was a devastating moment. Peter fled the courtyard, but the enormity of his failure followed him, crushing his heart. He found a secluded place and wept bitterly (Luke 22:62).

There will be times in your Christian life when you arrive at the point where your love and sincerity can take you no further. You'll need Jesus to show you how powerless you are in your strivings and desires so He can be life to you. When you come to that place, rejoice. The heavenly pattern is at work in you. You are about to witness a dead thing raised to life. Even though your *self is* exposed, more than leaves will cover you this time. His life will flood in and produce fruit that remains.

The war that has raged throughout the ages will come to you, for Satan is still warring against the kingdom. In these times of difficulty, he will try to convince you that you must have sinned mightily to have God abandon you in your sufferings. It's not true. The difficult time comes for the same reason Peter was allowed to go to the enemy's campfire. Because you believe something about yourself that isn't true. This is a monumental thing. Peter believed he loved Jesus enough to die for Him. His love gave way to his need to save his life when he was in peril. Peter didn't emerge from his dark hour the same man. Your life is undergoing the same transformation in your dark hour. The fruit of the Spirit, which is love, is increasing in your thinking and life. It is proof His life triumphs in you.

Living Under the Holy Spirit's Government

To see His heavenly pattern manifested in your life, the Father gave His Son. If this is how the Father started His relationship with you, how will He not provide you with everything necessary to bring you into the full measure of image and likeness? The Holy Spirit is developing in you a life that satisfies God's heart. But the only way you'll see and understand God is at work in you is if you genuinely live under the Holy Spirit's government. His government isn't a negotiation where you get to weigh the cost of obedience and decide whether or not it's to your benefit to deny your *self* and be faithful to His call.

The more you possess the living knowledge of the Lord, the more God's fullness and glory will be manifested in you. You must consciously decide to live for God's satisfaction and not in your dissatisfaction any longer. This means recognizing the work He is doing in you and committing yourself to its fulfillment.

His glory is a tremendous influence in your life. When you live for His glory, the possibilities are eternal. Nothing will remain that doesn't have significance and importance. If you allow God to have His way, no matter the cost, at the end of your life you'll be a mature son made in His image and after His likeness—the full expression of His love.

Chapter 11
THE SON OF GOD
"This is my beloved Son, with whom I am well pleased."
Matthew 3:17

IN THE FALL'S aftermath, Adam's descendants had no choice but to live imprisoned in the *self's* discontentment, which is never satisfied no matter how much it gathers to itself. Man's independent ways produced a fruitfulness separate from God, and this fruitfulness ended the same way for every man in every generation—in futility and death. But in one act of love that defies description, the Father sent His Son into the world to be a beacon—a shining light to reveal that God has not changed His mind about image and likeness.

John the Baptist

The news swept into Jerusalem on the hot desert wind. A prophet had come out of the wilderness proclaiming a baptism of repentance for the forgiveness of sins (John 1). His name was John, but the people called him the Baptist. The priests thought him a ridiculous figure in his garment of camel skins with a leather belt tied around his waist. They believed he was trying too hard to associate himself with Elijah, the great prophet God promised to send before the great and awesome day of the Lord (Malachi 4:5).

The priests took counsel and decided the best course of action was to ignore him. He wasn't the first prophet or messiah to come out of the wilderness. He would streak into the national consciousness like a shooting star streaks across the night sky. He would dazzle and amaze, and the crowds would hang on his every word, and he would baptize them. But just like a shooting star, he would soon burn out. The people would turn their attention to the next new thing and quickly forget the Baptist.

As time passed, it grew harder for the priests to ignore John. His growing stature presented a threat to their authority. Most people who went to be baptized believed John was Elijah come back to life. So the priests sent spies to Bethabara, where John was baptizing, to report all that he said and did. The spies' reports only confirmed the priests' suspicions. John was baptizing the people with water as a sign of repentance but taught them that he could only make them conscious of their spiritual poverty. He lacked the power to change their condition. Even as he admitted his limitations, he proclaimed that another one, mightier than he, was coming. When He appeared, He would baptize the people with the Holy Spirit and fire.

The priests were troubled by this man who would come after. John described Him as coming with a winnowing fork in His hand to clear His threshing floor. He would gather the wheat in barns but burn the chaff in an unquenchable fire. John was proclaiming that a prophet was coming with the authority to judge, purge, and purify the people. Who in Israel would dare take such a mantle upon himself?

The priests agreed to send an envoy to ask John questions about who had authorized him to baptize. The envoy's members arrived at the Jordan and found John standing in the river, speaking to a large crowd. One of the members dispatched a Levite to ask John to join them in the shade of some trees at the river's edge.

John spotted them before the Levite could make his way through the crowd. He pointed his finger and shouted, "You brood of vipers! Who warned you to flee from the wrath to come? If it was God, bring forth fruit in keeping with repentance."

The priests scoffed at the notion. No one had to warn them to flee, for they weren't under wrath. They were Abraham's descendants and priests ordained by Moses. Unlike the rabble surrounding John begging him to baptize them, they didn't need to repent.

John reached down and plucked a rock from the river. He thrust it toward them. "Don't think you're safe because you have Abraham as a father. Being Abraham's son means nothing. For God can raise up children for Abraham from these very rocks."

John dropped the rock, and it splashed water everywhere before disappearing. "Even now, the axe is laid to the tree's root. Creation is under God's wrath, for sin and death have corrupted it. None shall escape unless they repent."

The priests stiffened in outrage. How dare John disparage them in front of the crowds. They dropped any attempt to be conciliatory toward the Baptist. They would ask the questions they had been sent to ask and leave as quickly as they had arrived.

"Are you the Messiah?" they asked.

John shook his head. "No."

"Are you the prophet Moses spoke about?" (Deuteronomy 18:15).

Again, John shook his head and replied, "No."

His answer surprised them, for they were sure he would have been only too eager to claim that prophet's mantle. "Then who are you? The Sanhedrin needs to know."

"I am the voice crying in the wilderness. Prepare the way of the Lord and make His path straight."

In a moment, the atmosphere along the river bank became electric. The people were aware of Isaiah's writings. All they had believed about John was true. God had sent him to prepare the way, for God was coming to them. The people surged into the waters, calling his name. He turned his attention from the priests to the people.

The priests left the Jordan. John's ministry was more dangerous than the Sanhedrin had suspected. If the people truly believed John was the forerunner prophesied by Isaiah, then any man could say he was the one of whom John spoke. If the people believed that man, he could deceive them and lead the nation to sin. The priests needed to discredit John before his message spread throughout the land.

The Lamb of God

Days went by, and the crowds doubled and then tripled in size. John lifted a sobbing tax collector from the water. The man wiped his tears and asked what fruit he should produce to prove he was sincere in his repentance. "Be content with your wages," John replied. The man waded out of the river.

The next in line stepped up. John froze, too stunned to move. Standing before him was the One for whom he had been waiting. The Lamb of God who would take away the sin of the world. But why was He in line to be baptized for the repentance of sin? He didn't need to be baptized. "No," John said in a strangled voice. "I need to be baptized by You. Why have You come to me?"

"Because we must do all God requires of us," Jesus answered.

As Jesus came out of the river, John watched the heavens open and the Spirit of God rapidly descend and fill Him without measure. Then a voice spoke from heaven. "This is My beloved Son in whom I am well pleased" (Matthew 3:17). The voice belonged to the Father. He was presenting His Son to Israel and declaring Jesus as the focal point of creation. Here was the image and likeness to which the Father would conform humanity.

In the Old Testament, the Jordan River represented death and resurrection. Jesus' baptism represented the moment Jesus died to all He had been on the earth until that moment, though none of it was wrong or sinful. He was still God's Son in the carpenter shop. But now He had come to the place where all consideration for reputation, honor, and any such realm of the natural man had to be set aside. He was to be governed by God's glory alone. He publicly declared that He was dead to the *self's* demands and would voluntarily live a life dependent on the Father for everything.

God fully committed Himself to a man, and the man committed Himself to fulfill God's eternal purpose. The Son's commitment wouldn't just be outward but also in His inner life, the life only the Father would know, where He would never negotiate or compromise the glory bestowed upon Him. Men would behold His miracles and listen with burning hearts to His teaching, but His inward life belonged to the Father, and the Father was satisfied.

Tempted in the Wilderness

From the Jordan, Jesus went into the wilderness to be tempted by the devil (Matthew 4). In the garden, Satan tempted Adam with the physical first. He presented the fruit of the tree of the knowledge of good and evil as something desirable to the palate. He also combined the physical temptation with a plea to the soul. The fruit would also make him wise. Finally, he attacked the spirit by deceiving Adam into believing he could fulfill his destiny by overthrowing the Son's government and establishing a new one based on his image and likeness. When Satan approached Jesus in the wilderness, he didn't feel the need to change his methods. If he could tempt Jesus to act independently of God's expressed will, he would secure his kingdom forever. The good news was that Jesus had been fasting for forty days, which weakened Him and left Him susceptible to temptation.

Satan's first attack was on Jesus' apparent need for food. He told Jesus that since He had been anointed by the Holy Spirit and invested with divine power, He should use His anointing for His benefit. He could turn the stones littering the wilderness into bread and satiate His hunger. Satan was disguising the temptation by making it appear a reasonable course of action to turn stones into bread to break His fast.

If Jesus had accepted the premise of Satan's temptation, it would mean that His *self* had gained ascendancy over His Father's will. You must fulfill God's will God's way. Jesus reminded Satan that God had already made His mind known in the matter (Deuteronomy 8:3). His life wouldn't be about His convenience and comfort. His life would be about the glory He carried.

Satan didn't give up. He transported Jesus to Jerusalem and set Him on the pinnacle of the temple. He told Jesus to prove to the priests that He was the Son of God by throwing Himself down. The Father's angels would catch Him before He hit the ground. Satan perverted the Scripture to make it appear that this action was necessary for fulfilling His ministry. He could gain the Sanhedrin's acceptance and avoid all the trouble, misunderstanding, and offense that would come if He challenged their authority.

The battle is always more significant in the soul than the flesh. The whole matter of reputation, standing, favor, and advancement is a powerful temptation. Jesus rejected Satan's offer. God had also made His mind known about the sin of tempting God (Deuteronomy 6:16).

Satan took Jesus from the temple's pinnacle to a high mountain and showed Him all the world's kingdoms and their glories from that moment forward. Satan offered him a trade. He would give Jesus the kingdoms so He could rule and reign over them, for he had the authority to give them to whomever he wanted. If Jesus accepted his offer, He would avoid the difficult and lonely life of denying Himself and going to the cross. The price for the kingdoms and the avoidance of the cross? Jesus would have to bow down and worship him.

Satan understood the incarnation was the final campaign in the war that began in the garden. If Jesus were allowed to redeem creation, it would be the annihilation of all Satan had fashioned and formed in his image. It would also be the end of him, and he didn't want to vanish. He wanted to remain the god of this world. To do so, he was willing to give up the kingdoms and their glories but not their images and likenesses. He would allow Jesus to rule over the nations and enforce any laws He desired, but humanity would remain constituted after his nature. They would still be liars, murderers, and eternally separated from God. But most importantly, he wouldn't have to go into the ash heap of history where all his glory and achievements would be forgotten.

"Be gone," Jesus told Satan, refusing and repudiating any attempt to subvert the price of redeeming His inheritance from death (where it lay) to life (what it was always supposed to have).

Satan left Him, but only temporarily. He would watch and observe, awaiting an opportune moment to tempt Him again.

Adam's Failure/Jesus' Victory

Adam and Eve ate of the fruit of the tree of the knowledge of good and evil because they wanted to build something in their images and after their likenesses that would be lasting and permanent. God had made His mind known about the tree and the fruit, but they disregarded His commandment and made the conscious decision to exalt their opinion over His revealed will. They opted for independence and not dependency. They ate, failed, and the rest is history (so to speak).

When Satan employed the same lies in the wilderness against the Son, he failed. Jesus brought everything back to what God had already said about the issue. No matter how hard Satan tried to entice Jesus into acting in His own self-interest, self-comfort, or self-promotion, He refused. He would have nothing but the Father.

At the heart of all Satan's temptations is a demonic pressure that is applied against the *self's* fear of death. He coerces the *self* to break from God's revealed will in order to seek its own will so it can live in control of its destiny. Jesus chose differently than Adam. He refused to be independent and self-actualized because He knew there was death in self-centered living. He chose to do only what He saw the Father doing (John 5:19).

The law of life in Christ is a life that is always away from *self* and toward God. It no longer relies on reason, emotions, or appetites to inform its decisions. It relies strictly on what God has said about the situation. This is the image and likeness we were created to bear. And God will not change His mind.

Chapter 12
"IF I TELL YOU EARTHLY THINGS"

*He who is of the earth belongs to the earth and speaks in an earthly way.
He who comes from heaven is above all. He bears witness to what
he has seen and heard.*

John 3:31

WHEN NICODEMUS SECRETLY came to Jesus, he was hoping to engage the young rabbi in a theological discussion, much like the debates he participated in with his peers in the temple. This give and take of ideas about the mystery of God's ways had been foundational in his advancement within the ranks of the Sanhedrin. He was *the* teacher of Israel, and people looked to him for answers because of his great wisdom and understanding of the Scriptures.

He believed he knew everything a priest could possibly know about God. There was nothing left for him to learn. The first thing he wanted to convey to Jesus was that he was different than the priests who had confronted Him after He cleansed the temple. He knew Jesus had come from God, for only a man sent from God could perform the miracles Jesus did (John 3:2).

Jesus responded to Nicodemus' declaration by informing this teacher of Israel that all his learning had produced a learnedness without light. His study and teaching had brought him to the closed door. A man would need to be born again before the door would open. Only then would he be able to see the kingdom of God.

Jesus in the Temple

During His first trip to Jerusalem, Jesus went into the temple and was angered by what He saw (John 2). The Sanhedrin had allowed the Court of the Gentiles to become a marketplace. The money changers at the court's entrance charged the people a penalty to change Roman coins into temple ones so they could buy sacrifices to offer to the Lord. Those who sold animals did so at an excessive amount. The worshipers were at the money changers' and merchants' mercies, for the two groups coordinated their efforts. The merchants would accept only temple coins, and the priests would sacrifice only animals bought in the market. It was quite a racket and diminished the temple, for the priests operated it like any other pagan temple in the Roman Empire.

Jesus made a whip of cords and drove the merchants from the temple. He poured out the money changers' boxes and overturned their tables. Pandemonium reigned. People scrambled for the scattered coins. Animals bleated in fear and panic, and some rushed from the court. When Jesus finally spoke, He rebuked the merchants selling pigeons, the only offering the poor could afford. "Take these things away; do not make My Father's house a house of trade" (v. 16).

The priests were not pleased. According to John's Gospel, this was the first time they had met Jesus, and His cleansing of the temple challenged their authority. They confronted Him in the now demolished court and asked Him what authenticating sign He would perform to prove God had sent Him. When God called Moses to return to Egypt, He gave Moses three signs to prove his commission to the children of Israel. Moses then became the standard for any prophet or teacher who came to the nation in the name of the Lord. They would need to perform a sign to prove that God had sent them.

Even though the priests were insincere in asking for a sign, Jesus gave them one. He told them to destroy this temple and in three days He would raise it up. The raising up of the temple would be the only sign He would ever give them. The priests were astounded by the audacity of what He was declaring. They reminded Jesus and the curious crowd that it had taken Herod the Great forty-six years to build the temple. There was no way Jesus could rebuild it in three days. They dismissed Him.

The priests labored under a misconception. They believed God's presence dwelled behind the veil in the Holy of Holies, but it didn't. During the Babylonian conquest, God's glory had departed the temple due to Israel's idol worship. Now His glory had returned in His Son. The priests' ancestors hadn't noticed when the glory left, and their descendants didn't notice when it returned. The priests didn't even ask whether there was some spiritual significance in what Jesus had said.

Since they didn't ask, Jesus didn't explain. Only after His resurrection would His disciples understand that the temple He spoke about that day was His body, not the second temple. The priests didn't give His rebuke of the marketplace another thought. They allowed the money changers and the merchants to return to the Court of the Gentiles. It was business as usual.

All this happened at Passover. The people flocked to this new rabbi, bringing the sick and demon-possessed for Him to heal and deliver. They believed in Him, but it was a belief based on expediency. There was a shallowness to their faith. They were willing to believe a series of smaller signs (the healings) while ignoring the larger sign (His death and resurrection). They settled for so little when He would have shown them incredible things. He wouldn't entrust Himself to them, for He knew their hearts (v. 25).

Nicodemus Comes to Jesus

Then Nicodemus came to Him at night, in secret, and here was a man Jesus did entrust Himself to (John 3). Nicodemus represented the best Judaism could offer. From the time he was a boy, he had studied the Scriptures and learned at the feet of great teachers. He absorbed it all. His studies shaped his worldview. His dedication to the Torah and the traditions didn't go unnoticed by the other priests, who offered him a seat on the Sanhedrin. Once there, he put his knowledge to use in judging the people.

But he wasn't like the other priests in the Court of the Gentiles that day. He hadn't closed his mind to what God might be doing in Israel. He watched Jesus leave the temple and minister to the people and recognized Jesus could only perform such miracles if God were with Him. He was willing to engage this new teacher and learn more about His doctrine. He didn't want the other priests to know what he was doing. That's why he came to where Jesus was staying that night and asked to see Him.

We'll never know what Nicodemus planned to discuss with Jesus. He only got as far as telling Jesus all he knew about Him before Jesus cut him off (v. 3). The issue was one of seeing. Nicodemus may have known many things, but the kingdom wasn't about what a person knows but about what they see.

When Adam fell, man's spiritual eyes were closed. A man must be born again so God can open his spiritual eyes. Nicodemus was the perfect specimen of the limitations of the old man. He can only know what others taught him. But the born-again man, the new man, lives by the Spirit of revelation. There is a vast difference between learning about the Lord and seeing Him in glory.

"How can a man be born when he is already old?" Nicodemus asked, perplexed by the absurdity of Jesus' statement. "Can he enter a second time into his mother's womb and be born?" If being born again was the prerequisite to seeing the kingdom, he was hopeless because a second birth is impossible in the natural world.

Jesus responded that one cannot enter the kingdom of God unless one is born of water and the Spirit. For that which is born of the flesh is flesh. It is unsuitable for the kingdom because it carries the curse of the Fall—death and corruption. The door is closed, and the way is barred to the flesh. The cherubim still stand watch over the tree of life. Only the Spirit can open the door. To enter, one must be born of the Spirit.

The look on Nicodemus face must have been one of amazement, for Jesus told him not to marvel when He told him that he must be born again. The kingdom doesn't originate in classrooms in the temple nor through the many debates the priests participated in over the minutiae of Scripture. The kingdom of God is not earthly, for the earth could never contain it. If the kingdom did originate through man's studies, then it would be limited by man's blindness to the things of God.

The kingdom is spiritual, birthed in the Spirit. The Spirit moves like the wind, free from all earthly boundaries. When the wind blows, men don't understand where it originated or where it is going. They can only hear the wind's sound and feel its effects. The wind blows over them and then is gone. But its fruits remain as proof that it had been there. The same is true of the Son of Man. He came from heaven, will return to heaven, and His incarnation's fruits will remain as proof He had come to earth.

"Are you *the* teacher of Israel, and yet you do not understand these things?" Jesus asked Nicodemus (v. 10).

No, Nicodemus didn't understand. He had come to see Jesus because he thought he had discernment his fellow priests lacked. But now he had come to the end of himself. All his learning and studying hadn't produced any insight or understanding into what Jesus was speaking about. He may have been *the* teacher of Israel, but listening to Jesus made him realize he didn't know anything.

If Nicodemus didn't understand earthly things, how would he ever understand heavenly ones? No man had ever ascended into heaven, for the door is closed. There is no teaching that can open it. If Nicodemus had any hope of entering the kingdom, someone had to come down from heaven to open the door. That someone needed to be a person who knew the Spirit's origin and where the Spirit was going, so He could identify the fruits of the Spirit's presence to the people.

Nicodemus' problem wasn't that he was old and couldn't re-enter his mother's womb. His problem was more desperate and tragic. Without someone opening the way to the tree of life, he had no hope of ever living for God. When he came to speak to Jesus, he never suspected Jesus would shine a light on his spiritual poverty. Before Jesus spoke, he had been rich in the things that mattered. His teachers taught him that he was acceptable to God based on his bloodline and good works. He was one of the chosen ones. Jesus had torn that belief asunder, leaving him hopeless because he didn't understand how to be born again to see and enter a kingdom that he already believed he ruled and reigned in. Jesus' teaching left him on the outside of the kingdom looking in.

Nicodemus needed to know how to see, how to enter, and how to be part of it. If all his learning had brought him to naught, then how was he to be born again?

To answer how, Jesus brought up an incident that happened to the children of Israel during their sojourn in the wilderness (Numbers 21:4-9). The people had complained because there was no food or water. All they had to eat was loathsome manna, which they considered worthless. As judgment for their contempt for the manna (a type of the Bread of Life), the

101

Lord sent fiery serpents throughout the camp. If a serpent bit a person, death was inevitable. The people repented of their sins and asked Moses to intercede on their behalf. The Lord instructed Moses to make a bronze serpent, place it on a pole, and put it in the middle of the camp. If a serpent bit anyone, all the person would have to do was look at the bronze serpent. If they looked with faith, they would live. The answer to Nicodemus' question was faith.

Just like Moses lifted up the serpent because of sin and judgment, so would Jesus be lifted up because of sin and judgment. The human race had been snake bit, and death was the only outcome. But God intervened on man's behalf by sending His Son from heaven to be lifted up so men could look and believe that He had saved their lives by this one act.

Nicodemus stumbled over being born again because he couldn't figure out how to do it in the natural. The impossibility of such an act revealed the closed door at work in him. The gospel's good news is that the Son became the door through which the Spirit passed from heaven to earth and could inhabit men. Being born again was the heavenly answer to Nicodemus' earthly problem.

God's Answer to Man's Separation

You too were perishing, and God rescued you. Even Nicodemus, in all his wisdom, was perishing. Your association with Adam caused your permanent separation from God. The meaning of condemnation is separation. God's answer to man's separation is the Son. In the most famous verse in the Bible, Jesus told Nicodemus that God so loved the world that He gave His only Son that whosoever believes in Him should not perish but have eternal life (John 3:16). The Son came down from heaven to stand between you and death.

Whosoever believes in the Son is not condemned, for the very elements that separated you from the Father have been defeated by the Son. The only way out of your predicament is to believe in the Son the Father sent. What stops people from coming to faith? From coming to Him? It's where He dwells—in the light.

In Jesus there is light, but in His light there is also the exposure of all the things you never want anyone to know. The most challenging thing you'll do in your life is stand before Him in the light and have all your wrong motives, judgments, imperfections, weaknesses, sins, and selfishness exposed. There is no defense or justification you can offer to the Lord for the condition of your life. You're just naked and exposed.

But you're not abandoned. In coming to grips with your actual condition, you can see your need for something to look to so you can live. Israel had the serpent on the pole, but God has given the world His Son on the cross. Faith in Him is the putting away of your wrong motives, judgments, imperfections, weaknesses, sins, and selfishness. It is the burying of the old man in a tomb and the raising up of a new man clothed in God's righteousness who is alive to God. It is image and likeness. It is glorious and wonderful.

The light is shining, but men draw back into the shadows. They can't face the exposure because they know their deeds are evil. In the darkness, all their illusions can remain because darkness gives them the perfect cover for the acts they do, the choices they make, and the morality they champion. There is no light in the darkness, and men prefer it that way. They don't want to stop living for themselves, so they live in darkness, condemned and separated.

Learnedness Without Light

Nicodemus secretly came to Jesus to interrogate the young teacher on His doctrine. He never suspected that Jesus would tell him that all his learning and study hadn't given him eyes to see the kingdom of God. In that simple statement, "You must be born again to see," Jesus brought all of Nicodemus's study to its inevitable conclusion and end. His position in the Sanhedrin, the robes he wore that gave him status in society, and his judgments and pronouncements to the people were meaningless because he was blind to his actual state.

Learnedness without light is futility. Nicodemus needed to be born again to see and learn in the light. For that to happen, he didn't need more teaching and study. He needed the Son of God.

So do we.

Chapter 13
OLD THINGS PASS AWAY

For the law was given through Moses; grace and truth came through Jesus Christ.

John 1:17

"THAT'S NOT WHAT I heard." With that simple statement, I have cut off discussions about a topic that could alter the way I think about life. Why am I so quick to shut down a conversation that challenges my worldview? It's purely a defense mechanism. For if my worldview could be wrong about something that rudimentary, what else could it be wrong about? Foundational truths were being shaken and rather than follow the evidence, I closed my mind to such "foolishness."

The people Jesus ministered to had built their society on the teachings, customs, and traditions their ancestors had passed down through the generations. These things provided a solid foundation for life. Plus, there was the added bonus that if they kept hold of their faith until the end, they would be rewarded with an eternal paradise.

They didn't want to be challenged to think differently about God and themselves. They wanted to be fed, healed, and delivered. That's all. Jesus' teachings struck at the very bedrock of their worldviews. They listened politely to Him until He told them truths that forced them to make a choice between clinging to the old ways or stepping into the new age that was dawning. It was too big of an ask. They closed their minds to such "foolishness" and perished.

Jesus and the Five Thousand

At the beginning of John 6, Jesus fed five thousand men (not including women and children) with five loaves of bread and two fish. It wasn't the miraculous bread that registered with the crowd as much as it was that they had eaten until they couldn't eat anymore. But the next day they woke up hungry. So they sought Jesus, and when they couldn't find Him, they sailed across the Sea of Galilee and found Him in Capernaum.

Jesus was fully aware of why the people sought Him. He recognized their hunger as a temporary earthly need He could quickly remedy. But tomorrow the people would wake up hungry. He took up their expectation that He would feed them to teach them there was a bread that could eternally satisfy and cause them never to know hunger again. He counseled the crowd not to labor for the food that would spoil, perish, and eventually cease to exist. If they were going to give their labor, or the strength of their lives for something, let it be for food that endured to eternal life.

The people had come to Capernaum seeking another miracle. If they were willing to believe Him for bread that would leave them hungry, they could believe Him to give them bread that would satisfy them forever. The people asked, "What must we do to do the works of God?" They kept the law, read the prophets, and strictly adhered to the traditions, so what did they still lack? If He told them what was missing, they would perform those works also to partake of the bread of life.

Jesus told them that the work of God wasn't something they needed to do. It was something they needed to believe. They needed to believe the Father had sent and sealed Him and had become the surety for all Jesus said and did.

The crowd rejected the Father's seal and demanded one of their own. So they asked Him to produce manna, which Scripture told them was bread from heaven (Exodus 16:4). Manna fed their forefathers for over forty years, not just a day. They demanded He surpass or at least equal Moses' miracle, for Moses had produced food from nothing. Jesus used five loaves of bread and two fish to feed the people. They would neither believe nor follow Him if He couldn't perform their chosen miracle.

Jesus reminded the people that their fathers ate manna in the wilderness but they died outside the Promised Land. Manna might have been a spectacular miracle, but it couldn't produce faith or obedience. Israel's failure in the wilderness was an indictment against manna's failure to produce life in those who ate it. The Father had chosen to give this generation something far superior. He was giving them the true bread from heaven. The difference between the manna they demanded He produce and the bread of life wasn't from whence they came but in what they produced.

The crowd asked Jesus to give them this bread continually. He replied that He was the Bread of Life. All other bread was imperfect, defective, frail, and uncertain. He appealed to them to stop working and eating worthless bread that left them hungry. They would find satisfaction, fullness, and life if they came to Him.

A New and Living Way

The crowds had sought Him in hopes of getting a free meal. Now He was making them choose between the old ways they knew and were foundational and a new and living way that was foreign and unknown. There was security in knowing who they were, keeping the law, and following the traditions. Judaism gave them their identity and governed their lives. Standing before them was a man declaring His flesh was the true food and His blood was the true drink. Whoever consumed both His body and blood would have eternal life. They would abide in Him, and He would abide in them. And just as the Father was His source of life, He would become theirs.

Jesus expressed Himself in words and imagery that evoked the Passover because the crowds gathered that day were on their way to Jerusalem to celebrate the sacred feast. After Passover would come the Days of Unleavened Bread, and both feasts represented putting away the old life and putting on the new. They would eat the Passover lamb. The priests would pour the lamb's blood on the brazen altar in the temple as a reminder that the nation had been purchased from slavery in Egypt when the angel of death passed over them.

By telling the people that their fathers ate manna in the wilderness and died disqualified outside the Promised Land because of unbelief, Jesus gathered up everything their forefathers had received from Moses, including the Passover lamb. When their fathers ate the lamb that night and put its blood on the doorposts, they were only temporarily delivered from death.

But God had sent His Lamb into the world, and if they believed in Him, their deliverance from death would be permanent and eternal.

His teaching scandalized them, and they weren't sure they wanted any part of Him or the food He was offering. They weren't sure they wanted to set aside their identity to take up the new one He proclaimed. Centuries had passed since their forefathers had come out of Egypt. Their history was rich in God's exploits. Their kings were mighty warriors who, if here, would have defeated the Romans and returned the land to its rightful owners. Their prophets had spoken God's will and their destiny into being. They believed those prophecies and looked forward to the day God would deliver them as He did in the past.

Jesus said He was the bread come down from heaven and promised a deliverance on a far grander scale than they could ever imagine. They began to grumble, which exposed the limits of their worldviews. They stumbled over whether He could be from heaven. For if He was, they knew they would be responsible for responding to all He was saying about Himself and the Father. They would have no choice but to forsake the old, no matter how comfortable they were in their traditions and culture.

It was too much to ask. The people didn't want to set aside their identity and the teachings that brought them hope, even if these teachings didn't deliver them from Rome's brutal occupation and burdensome taxes. They wanted a warrior king like David and not a Lamb. They would have been satisfied with receiving manna and not this bread come from heaven. Their needs were earthly, just as their forefathers' needs had been temporal— deliverance from their enemy and a land flowing with milk and honey.

Jesus told His disciples that if they were scandalized by His teaching that He had come from heaven, how offended would they be when they saw the Son of Man ascending to His rightful place at the Father's right hand? They needed to stop judging His words through their narrow and rigid worldviews. They needed to stop thinking that the knowledge they possessed was the only knowledge they needed. Their thinking caused them to misinterpret His words and dismiss them. And because they believed they were correct in discerning His teachings as revolutionary and counter-productive to their current circumstances, they ignored the very life those teachings bestowed upon the hearers.

It was another generation refusing to go up into the Promised Land.

The crowd had searched Jesus out so they could receive a free meal. Their interest was personal and selfish. They would only accept His teachings if they gained some advantage by adhering to His words. They refused to believe the God they knew would give His authority over life into this Man's hands. They couldn't conceive it, and in the end, they rejected Him for the same reason Israel refused to go into the Promised Land. They didn't believe Him.

Jesus and the Twelve

Jesus turned to the Twelve and asked if they were also leaving. I don't believe the Twelve understood His teaching more than those leaving the beaches. But when Peter answered for the rest of the disciples, he answered from what he did know: Lord, to whom shall we go? You have the words of eternal life, and we have believed, and have come to know, that you are the Holy One of God" (John 6:68–69).

As the Twelve followed Jesus, they knew He was different from them. They lived with Him, ate with Him, followed Him down dusty roads, and knew His life embodied a quality they had never witnessed before. He was a man devoid of all self-interest. He wasn't looking to receive anything from this earth. He refused to play the games that would have guaranteed His acceptance into the religious hierarchy of Jerusalem.

Jesus lived for one thing—the glory of the Father. His life had impacted their worldview. They might not have understood the tremendous spiritual truths He espoused. Still, they did understand that if they had any hope of appropriating the life He spoke about, they must follow Him, for there was no other teacher who could reveal truths that originated in heaven. They wanted to learn, so they stayed, hoping light would come one day and they would fully know what they couldn't currently comprehend. They didn't care about the cost. They would pay that price even if it meant that the old ways and teachings had to give way to the new. It wouldn't be easy for them, but it was necessary.

Choosing Time

The crowds stumbled over His words because He was forcing them to choose, and they didn't want to. They wanted to keep the law, the traditions, and their identity as God's chosen people. They had only come for food and not to be challenged to rethink all they believed and held dear. They were Abraham's children and didn't want to be anything else. They certainly didn't want to be the generation that abandoned the old ways instead of passing them down for their children to inherit. They recoiled at the thought. Their society had always been this way, and their society would always remain this way. They abandoned Him and continued their journey to celebrate Passover. That familiar truth was all they wanted to know.

The disciples made a different choice. They wouldn't let their lack of comprehension deter them, for they believed He was the Son of the Living God. They would follow Him until the fullness He promised shone in their hearts.

Chapter 14
WHICH IS EASIER TO SAY. . .

*If you can't find it in the life or words of Jesus,
then why is it in your theology?*

Dan Mohler

I THOUGHT LONG and hard about whether I should add this chapter to the book. I'm not sure I'm qualified to write on the topic of healing, and, I knew if I included it, I could possibly be limiting the book's audience. But this book is about image and likeness, and Jesus healed everyone who came to Him. He didn't turn anyone away because healing was proof His life always triumphs over death. I knew if I took the safe route and ignored Jesus' healing ministry, I wouldn't be true to the Lord or the reader. So here goes.

Jesus Heals the Leper

After Jesus finished preaching the Sermon on the Mount, the crowds besieged Him, making it difficult for Him to navigate His way down the mountain (Matthew 8). Suddenly, the mass of humanity parted like the Red Sea, leaving Jesus face-to-face with a leper, who fell on his knees. "Lord," he said, "if You will, You can make me clean."

Jesus didn't hesitate. He stretched out His hand and touched him. "I will. Be clean." Such a simple act of healing and compassion that it is often overlooked, but it shouldn't be. The leper's healing shows us the very heart of image and likeness.

Sometimes we can read the Scriptures and miss the impact the writer wanted to press upon us. This man had leprosy, and the disease was laying waste to his life. Because leprosy was highly contagious, a leper lived isolated from society, usually in a colony with others who suffered from the same disease. Lepers were forbidden to come into a city or town or live in a house with another person. They had to stand six feet away from people on a calm day and 150 feet away on a windy one. If a leper recovered from their affliction, they could show themselves to the priest and receive a clean bill of health. Those were the fortunate ones. Most didn't recover, and the progression of the disease was terrifying. It eventually attacked the flesh, disfiguring the person as their fingers, toes, and nose rotted away.

If a leper did venture out, they had to dress in special clothes that identified them as a leper, wear bells so people could hear them coming, and shout with every step they took that they were unclean to warn someone from coming too close. It was a lonely life and a lonelier death. They received no sympathy from anyone. Just like the man born blind in John 9, the leper faced the same harsh judgment from the priests. Their illnesses were proof of God's judgment. They were sinners. Case closed.

No wonder the crowds that pressed in around Jesus that day so quickly dispersed when the leper approached with his clanging bell and shouts of unclean. No one wanted the disease because no one wanted to live as a lonely outcast. News of Jesus' miraculous healing power had reached the leper colony, and this one leper believed if he asked Jesus to heal him, Jesus would. It was a gamble, but the leper was desperate.

When the man asked Jesus to heal him, he was seeking more than physical healing. He was asking Jesus to restore his life. To cure the disease and remove the stigma, remove his forced isolation, and allow him to return to the land of the living. Jesus didn't hesitate. He touched the leper and healed the man. Jesus instructed him to go to the priests to obtain a clean health bill that would legally allow him to live among people once again.

Jesus' reaction to the leper was the same reaction He demonstrated to anyone who came to Him for healing. He recognized sickness and disease as the work of Satan. None of it came from God. Sickness served no purpose but to steal, kill, and destroy. As the Father's representative on earth, Jesus was anointed by the Father to do good and heal all those oppressed by the devil. He never told anyone that they had to continue in their sickness.

The Pharisees and Sadducees had linked illness to sin and declared all sickness as the judgment of God. They were the shepherds and teachers of

Israel, so they shaped the Jewish people's worldview until they, too, saw the correlation between sin and illness. People who were born blind or struck with leprosy, for example, were only getting God's just punishment.

Jesus Heals the Paralytic Man

One day Jesus was teaching in Capernaum (Mark 2:1-12). The house, courtyard, and surrounding areas were jam-packed with people pressing in to hear Him and to be at the front of the line when He began to heal the sick. Four men brought a paralyzed man to the house so Jesus could heal him, but they couldn't get near because of the crowd. The men were resourceful and decided to climb up on the roof, rip it open, and lower the paralytic down to Jesus. He saw their faith and told the man lying on the bed that his sins were forgiven.

The scribes, witnessing the unfolding events, were offended by His words. They didn't express their thoughts out loud, but if they had, they would have told the crowd that Jesus had committed blasphemy by giving Himself, a mere man, the authority to forgive sins. Jesus knew their thoughts because He, too, had sat under their teachings and had listened to them oppress Abraham's children with false teaching.

He challenged the scribes' understanding of sickness. "Which is easier to say?" He asked them. "Your sins are forgiven, or rise and walk?" If sin and illness were the same to the scribes, what did it matter what He said? If He healed the man, it was proof God had forgiven his sins. It also proved the same if He told the man his sins were forgiven and he was healed.

"But that you may know that the Son of Man has authority on earth to forgive sins," Jesus said, His attention now fixed on the man lying at His feet. "Rise, pick up your bed, and go home."

Why were the priests so eager to equate sin and illness as coming from God? Because they couldn't fully comprehend that the Fall meant all men, including themselves, lived under the law of sin and death. In the kingdom of darkness, the wages of sin is death. They never considered that Satan exercised power over their lives because Adam had seceded that authority to him the moment he ate the fruit of the tree of the knowledge of good and evil. Satan slandered God by convincing men God was responsible for all the evil on the earth because He had the power to stop it. This slander became the priests' theology.

For it is slander to equate sickness with God. Jesus said, "I came that they may have life and have it abundantly" (John 10:10). He didn't come to steal, kill, and destroy. If this is true, why do we accept sickness as something God allows or initiates? Jesus never said to anyone in the Gospels, "I desire to heal you, but My Father has given you this sickness to work His greater purpose in you." Never once.

Two thousand years ago, believers recognized sickness as the work of the evil one, and as they preached the gospel of reconciliation, they healed the sick, raised the dead, cleansed lepers, and cast out demons. It was God's evidence to those listening that His life had thoroughly triumphed over the death at work in them.

The Thorn in the Flesh

I know that when you write or teach something that strong, it raises the inevitable questions. One counterargument to the ministry of healing is Paul's thorn (2 Corinthians 12:7-10). Why didn't God heal Paul if it was His will to heal everyone? Poor Paul's thorn. It gets blamed for so much and made to uphold a theology contrary to Jesus' life. As soon as you make God the culprit, it's a sure sign you're deceived.

There is great danger in ripping a verse out of context and basing a whole theology on it. Paul sought God to remove the thorn, and God said no because His grace was sufficient. But if you read all the verses before and after 2 Corinthians 12:7, Paul identifies his thorn as the messenger of Satan sent to harass him. The messenger came from Satan and not from God.

God says He exalts His Word above His name. Isaiah 53:5 prophesies that by His stripes, we are healed. Peter emphasized this truth when he wrote that by His wounds, we have been healed (1 Peter 2:24). Peter uses the present perfect tense of the word heal to show an action that started in the past and is still happening today. The Father has shown you in Jesus His absolute willingness to heal to the extent that Jesus left no one who came to Him unhealed.

By making Paul's thorn an illness God refused to heal, you're saying that from time to time, God sovereignly nullifies what He accomplished in Christ and allows His children to suffer illness for many reasons, but mostly to work His purpose in them. This teaching devalues God's Word and makes Him untrustworthy. If God can sovereignly change His mind about what He has promised His children, then His promises become meaningless. He tells you He will until He won't, and when He goes back on His word, it's always for your good, so you're to submit to your suffering. This false teaching robs you of your inheritance. Christ suffered greatly at the hands of ruthless men to obtain healing for you in His atonement.

When God called Paul to the ministry, He did so with the promise that He would show Paul how much he would suffer for His name (Acts 9:16). This was not a new teaching, for Jesus had warned His disciples that they would be persecuted for righteousness' sake.

Paul preached Christ crucified. He didn't preach a gospel of works righteousness that was prevalent in Jewish and pagan cultures. For his understanding that we are made righteous by the finished work of Christ alone, he suffered tremendous spiritual and physical persecution.

Paul also suffered mental anguish over the state of the churches. The Judaizers were going behind his back and overturning his work by instructing new converts that righteousness didn't come from faith alone but must be augmented by circumcision and keeping the Law of Moses. Not only did Paul have to deal with the Judaizers, he also had to contend with false apostles who defamed him in the churches he founded, turning the people against him. He spent plenty of time and energy defending his work. Three times He prayed for the Lord to remove the thorn (or stop the persecution) and allow him to work without the obstacles that constantly arose.

To this request, the Lord said His grace was sufficient, for Paul's trials and tribulations would establish His church. God didn't send the persecution. It was the natural result of preaching righteousness. Jesus had defeated Satan, but the devil was still contesting every piece of ground on which the church was advancing.

If you talk about God's desire to heal everyone as proof that the kingdom of God has drawn near, you'll receive stout opposition from Christians who base their theology on their experiences and not on the truth of Jesus' life. When their prayers go unanswered, they don't hesitate to drag God's Word down from its exalted position and make it subservient to their opinions. After all, God doesn't heal everybody.

These Christians insist they are right because... and then they will tell you of the time they prayed for God to heal someone and that person didn't recover or, worse, died. God didn't answer their prayers, so they absorbed their disappointment and loss into their theology and now believe the doctrine of laying hands on the sick and commanding sickness to depart isn't true. They have reasoned themselves into an entirely different understanding of how Jesus deals with illness today. He no longer heals all those who come to Him. For if He did, God would have answered their prayers. And, just like the priests in Jesus' day, their opinions and history become more significant than God's truth.

Jesus Heals the Epileptic Boy

Jesus came off another mountain to find another man needing healing (Matthew 17:14-20). This time it was a father seeking healing for his epileptic son. He had brought his son to Jesus' disciples, who had healed countless people and cast out many demons in the past. When they commanded the demon to leave, the demon refused. After their failure, the scribes began to argue with them. Jesus asked the scribes why they were arguing with His disciples.

It was the father who answered. He explained that he had brought his son so the disciples could heal him, and they failed. Jesus responded to the disciples' failure by calling all those gathered about the boy a faithless and twisted generation, or a generation with a twisted and distorted way of thinking. All the participants in the argument were wrong. The disciples were wrong because they didn't believe it was God's will to heal the boy and gave up. The scribes were wrong to be arguing with the disciples over their failure. The father was wrong because he doubted Jesus' will and power to deliver his son from the demon that possessed him. Jesus rebuked the demon and healed the boy.

The disciples came to Jesus afterward and asked why they couldn't cast out the demon. He said it was because of their unbelief. Even after all they had seen and done, they still had unbelief. He told them this kind of unbelief comes out only through prayer and fasting. Many preachers have said Jesus was talking about the demon, but He wasn't. He was talking about the unbelief that had caused the disciples to doubt God's will to deliver the boy from his oppressor.

If Jesus was talking about the demon, everything He said to the disciples about their twisted and distorted thinking and unbelief was meaningless. When the disciples asked why they hadn't been able to cast out the demon, He would have said that you can only cast out these types of demons through prayer and fasting. That would have made the disciples feel better. "Oh, now we see. We just haven't fasted and prayed enough." But when Jesus learned of the situation, He said their worldview caused their unbelief. They failed to understand that when the demon didn't come out the first time they commanded it, it was still God's will for them to cast out the demon. Instead of drawing back in unbelief and questioning God on why it didn't happen, they should have stood in their understanding of God's will and commanded the demon until it obeyed.

Two Types of Faith

This story reveals the difference between sentimental, fear-based faith, and biblical faith. Jesus explained biblical faith is displayed when a person speaks to a mountain to be moved from here to there, and it moves. Nothing will be impossible for those who believe. Sentimental and fear-based faith believes faith is revealed in the act of speaking or praying. You pray, and the rest is up to God. Biblical faith is only satisfied once the mountain is moved. Jesus assures you it only takes faith the size of a mustard seed to move a mountain.

Suppose you aren't entirely convinced it's God's will to heal a person, and you lay hands on them anyway—what is operating in you? Faith or unbelief? If you aren't sure God didn't give the person the sickness in the first place, what is working in you? Faith or unbelief? What is operating in you if you believe that healing the sick, casting out demons, raising the dead, and cleansing the lepers is not for today? Of course, it's unbelief. You may be praying, but you're unsure of God's will.

In most cases, you hope God will have pity on you and move the mountain anyway. Your unbelief and uncertainty prove you don't know

Him, for you have failed to clearly see the price He paid so you can demonstrate the power of resurrection and heal the sick. Your worldview and unbelief has devoured your mustard seed of faith.

Sentimental or fear-based faith is unbelief, no matter how sincere your heart is when you pray. If you pray and someone doesn't get healed, you need to look at the condition of your heart. I don't say that to offend. I say that because it's true. Jesus told His disciples the mountain would move if they spoke to it. Period. There is no Plan B. His will is for the mountain to move. If it doesn't move, it's because you never expected or believed it would. The only remedy for your unbelief is to seek God until you know His will for every mountain you encounter (it's for the mountain to move).

The Revealed Will of God

John writes in his Gospel that no one has ever seen God at any time, but the Son came into the world and declared the Father to us (John 1:18). Jesus manifested image and likeness every time He prayed for the sick and they recovered. If you pray for the sick and they don't recover, the fault doesn't lie with the person you prayed for, nor is it a sure sign God must not want that person healed. You must return to the Lord and ask, "Lord, what aren't I seeing?" He is faithful and will reveal His Son in you. Only when you see the Son in all His glory and majesty will you see the Father, for the Father is revealed in the Son.

Jesus is the revealed will of God for your life. No matter where it comes from, you shouldn't permit any other voice to rob you of this truth. So, if you're saying and doing things you know Jesus never said or did, you must ask yourself why you keep saying and doing them. And if you're not saying and doing things that Jesus said or did, then you must also ask yourself why you're not saying and doing them.

Chapter 15
THE CLOSED DOOR
Jesus wept.

John 11:35

JESUS STOOD IN a graveyard in front of Lazarus' tomb. People were weeping in sadness and grief. Those who weren't weeping were murmuring against Him. As far as they were concerned, He had arrived too late. Death had claimed another prize.

Jesus groaned deep inside, troubled by what He felt in His spirit. He began to weep, not from grief, but because He had come up against the closed door once more. Martha, Mary, and even His disciples were rooted in death, for they had been born in death, and death was all they knew.

That day, everyone gathered to mourn Lazarus would learn the greater eternal truth: Death must bow its knee to Resurrection Life. "Take away the stone," He said.

Lazarus is Dying

The servant rode into the large camp at Bethabara (John 11). He threw himself off his lathered horse and, with a slap on its flank, sent it toward the river to drink. The servant asked the nearest person where he could find Jesus. The man pointed toward a large gathering at the Jordan's bank. The servant nodded before heading off in the direction of the man's point. He pushed and shoved His way through the crowd until he saw Jesus sitting in the shade under a clump of trees. John and James were with Him.

The servant ran the last couple of steps and threw himself down before Jesus. He drew in a big breath, then sharply exhaled. "A message, Master," he said, thrusting a small rolled-up piece of parchment toward Jesus. "Lazarus is dying. Martha and Mary beseech You to return to Bethany and lay hands on him so he will live." He kept pushing the parchment forward to emphasize the urgency of the situation. Finally, John took the parchment from his hand.

Unbeknownst to the servant, by the time he reached Jesus, Lazarus had already died, and if not buried, preparations for his burial were taking place. We know this is true because by the time Jesus arrived in Bethany, Lazarus had been in the grave for four days. After hearing the news, Jesus remained at Bethabara, ministering to the crowds for an additional two days. It would take almost a full day for Him to walk to Bethany. That adds up to three days. The fourth day or the first day Lazarus was in the tomb would have been when the servant departed Bethany.

Jesus knew Lazarus was dead but instructed the servant to tell Martha and Mary that Lazarus' sickness was not unto death. Instead, God would use the illness (not cause the sickness) to reveal the Son's glory. The servant arrived home to find a house in mourning. He dutifully reported Jesus' words to the sisters, but it was too late.

Jesus' words fell to the ground. They meant nothing now. If Lazarus had been alive when the servant returned with Jesus' promise that this sickness was not unto death, the sisters could have held on to their faith and hope. Now, they had to live with the knowledge that if only they had sent the servant before Lazarus' condition became critical, it would have given Jesus enough time to make the trip from Bethabara and heal their brother. But now, the grave had swallowed the promise of healing and glory. Death had triumphed once more.

Three days later, Jesus told the disciples they needed to return to Bethany, for Lazarus had fallen asleep. The disciples misinterpreted what He said. They thought if Lazarus could finally sleep, he was recovering. There was no reason for Jesus to return to Judea. The priests' hostility toward Him was out in the open. If they went back, the priests would arrest Him.

Jesus told them Lazarus was dead, and, for their sakes, He was glad He wasn't there so they might believe. *Believe what?* the disciples probably wondered. Did they think they were traveling to Bethany to witness another resurrection? No, they didn't. They thought they were traveling to Bethany to die. They gallantly resolved themselves to their possible fate.

Did I Not Tell You

When the news of Jesus' arrival reached the sisters, Martha left a house full of mourners and met Jesus at the edge of the village. She assured Him that she knew her brother wouldn't have died if He had been there. Despite what happened, she still believed in Him.

Then Martha said a remarkable thing. She knew even now that whatever Jesus asked of God, God would give Him. Was she saying that she believed Jesus could raise Lazarus from the dead? No, because the rest of their conversation proved she didn't. Her brother had been dead for four days and had already begun to decay. In her worldview, life was no longer possible.

So what was she saying? She was telling Him that she still believed He was the Messiah, and God still answered His prayers. She had witnessed too much of His power to be convinced otherwise. Even though His word had failed her in her moment of need, it didn't alter her belief in Him. She would have still sent Him word that Lazarus was sick and dying. She would have still believed that Jesus could heal her brother. Death just proved too powerful an enemy in this case.

Jesus told her Lazarus would rise again. As a devout Jew, Martha knew God would raise Lazarus on the last day. It was the one thing that brought her comfort. Her brother was gone, but it was only temporary. In God's paradise, they'd see each other again.

"I am the resurrection and the life," Jesus said. There could only be a resurrection on the last day because He had power over death. Whoever believed in Him, though he died, yet shall he live. If a man believed in Him, that man would never taste death. "Do you believe this?" He asked her.

He was challenging the limits of her faith. It was one thing to believe in an event in the future, but would she bring that future into her present? Would she believe that God would still give Jesus whatever He prayed for even now? Amid her grief and loss, would she believe that life triumphs over death even after four days? Would she believe that His glory was bound up in defeating death wherever He found it? To God, nothing is impossible. Did she believe this?

She didn't answer His question. Her unbelief limited Him. She didn't have faith for the "even now." She had been taught and firmly believed that the only remedy for death came on the last day when God intervened and raised the dead to life. Today was not that day. She told Him that she believed He was the Son of God who was coming into the world. She left Him outside the village, returned home, and told Mary that Jesus was asking to see her.

Mary followed Martha from the house, and the mourners followed Mary because they believed she was going to Lazarus's tomb to weep and lament, and they wanted to comfort her. When she saw Jesus, she fell weeping at His feet and repeated what Martha had said: If Jesus had been here, Lazarus wouldn't have died.

Jesus looked around. Everyone was weeping in genuine grief. Death had won the day. His appearance had made no impact on their worldviews. He groaned deep inside, troubled by what He felt in His Spirit. The closed door was evident. He began to weep, not out of grief for Lazarus, but because He had come up against the limits of man's darkened mind once more.

Those gathered around Him and accusing Him of not caring enough for Lazarus to heal him before He died lacked the spiritual discernment necessary to see past the great calamity of death. No man had power over death. Not even the king in his palace. They believed even God's power over death was constrained until that last day when He would call the righteous to life. Even if they wanted to believe that Jesus could raise Lazarus as He said, it was too late. Lazarus had been dead for four days, and his spirit was no longer on earth.

Take Away the Stone

Some strong men were standing in the crowd. Jesus ordered them to remove the stone. Martha vigorously protested. Her reasoning was sound. If they opened the grave, all that would come out would be the odor of a decaying corpse. She didn't want this to be her last memory of her brother. She wanted him to be left in peace.

"Did I not tell . . ." He said. When did He tell her? The day Lazarus died. Everyone standing there believed Jesus had given the servant the message not knowing Lazarus was dead, but He had known. He didn't say this sickness wasn't unto death to be cruel or to fail them. He gave the servant that specific word to evoke faith in them. If they had truly believed He was the Son of God, and God heard and answered His every prayer, the moment the sisters heard He was approaching the village, they would have sent men to remove the stone from the grave because this sickness was not unto death.

But dead four days later was more potent and impossible to defeat than a sickness that brought a loved one to his inevitable fate. Why subject themselves to further heartache? Why not just leave well enough alone and let them finish mourning their brother so they could learn to live without him? What did Jesus want from them? Was He still expecting them to believe even now?

"Did I not tell you that if you believe, you would see the glory of God?" He asked. They had a choice to make, for there is always a choice to make. By now, they knew this would end with either Lazarus coming out of the tomb alive or Jesus failing and being exposed as the fraud the priests believed He was. Martha could have remained in unbelief, suffered the loss of her brother, and protected Jesus and herself. If she refused to open the tomb, no one would have ever known whether He could have raised Lazarus from the dead. Or she could stop making what was happening about her and obey the Lord. One must genuinely deny one's *self* to step out of the way to allow God to work.

Martha relented, and the men removed the stone. Jesus prayed that He knew the Father heard His prayer. He used the past tense verb *knew*. What Jesus was about to do had already been settled in heaven four days ago when He told the servant that this sickness was not unto death. God's word doesn't return to Him empty but accomplishes what He purposes (Isaiah 55:11). This time, His word would accomplish the Son's glory.

"Lazarus! Come forth."

The crowd waited breathlessly. Would Lazarus come forth? There was movement in the cave. Then Lazarus appeared bound in grave clothes, which restricted his movement. Jesus ordered the men to loose Lazarus from the things that bound him and let him go.

It was a glorious moment. It revealed the Son's power given to Him before the world's creation. In Him was life, and the life in Him was the revelation of man (John 1:4). Now, He had shown all those present that this is what it meant to have His life. It was the calling forth of the dead and the loosening of grave clothes that darkened their minds and restricted their faith.

The Endgame

Death had been struck a fatal blow. Satan knew that as long as Jesus walked the earth, death would have to bow the knee to God's Son. But he wasn't about to lose his power to enslave men through the fear of death so easily. He influenced some who had witnessed the miracle to hurry to Jerusalem and tell the priests.

The members of the Sanhedrin met with Caiaphas, the high priest, to discuss how they should react in the light of Lazarus' resurrection. They had to do something to discredit Jesus before the people forcibly took Him and made Him king. If that happened, the Romans would take away their religious autonomy and subjugate them as they had other conquered provinces.

Caiaphas rebuked the priests for their lack of discernment. Discrediting Jesus was no longer an option. The time had come to settle their "Jesus" problem once and for all. He would have to die, for it was better if one man died than the whole nation perish. No one disagreed. Starting that night, they changed their strategy. They would no longer seek to discredit Him. Now they would work to trap Him in His teachings so they could accuse Him of a sin worthy of death.

Passover was approaching. Jesus had taught in the temple during the previous Passovers, and the priests expected He would do so again. Word went out. If anyone knew where He was, they were to tell the priests immediately so that they might find cause to arrest Him.

When Jesus appeared along the banks of the Jordan, Satan recognized the incarnation for what it was: heaven's final assault on the kingdom of darkness. So, he mustered his forces to challenge and dispute the Son's right to reign.

The Closed Door

The board had been set. All the pieces were moving inexorably to Jerusalem. It was the fullness of time. The finale to the great clash of the ages was about to break upon the earth. Who would finally rule over the universe? The One who had called creation out of the chaos so it could manifest His image and likeness? Or the one who had usurped Adam's dominion with a subtle lie and had cast the whole creation into despair and death?

Chapter 16
TETELESTAI

If your brother becomes poor and sells part of his property,
then his nearest redeemer shall come and redeem what
his brother has sold.

Leviticus 25:25

"TETELESTAI," JESUS SAID. Then He bowed His head and gave up His spirit (John 19:30). *Tetelestai* is a Greek word used by the priests to signify that the Passover lamb was without spot or blemish. There was nothing more that needed to be added to the sacrifice to perfect it.

Jesus gave back to the Father a life that hadn't been marred by the world. There was no flaw to overlook; no failure to cover up. He had been tested and tried and had triumphed. Creation had been redeemed from death (where it lay) to life (what it was always supposed to have). The Father was forever satisfied.

The Need for a Kinsman Redeemer

In Revelation 5, John the Apostle saw a scroll with writing on both sides, sealed with seven seals, in the Father's right hand. He understood the scroll's significance, for when a Jewish family lost their inheritance or their portion of the land, those losses were listed in a scroll and sealed seven times. Written on the outside of the scroll were the conditions the heirs had to meet to repurchase the land. An angel asked John who was worthy to open the scroll and break its seal.

John knew only a kinsman redeemer could redeem what was lost. In this context, what had been lost was righteousness. If heaven couldn't find a kinsman redeemer to answer to God on the whole issue of righteousness, the scroll would remain closed, and man would be judged and doomed for all eternity.

But man had lost his capacity to answer since his fallen nature makes righteousness impossible. Heaven thoroughly searched throughout man's history, looking for the one man who could qualify as a redeemer. Their search came up empty.

Devastated by the results, John began to weep. An elder approached him and told him to stop crying, for a kinsman redeemer had been found. The Lion of the tribe of Judah, the root of David, had triumphed and was qualified to open the scroll.

John's eyes were opened, and he beheld a Lamb standing as though it had been slain before the throne. A perfect Lamb without spot or blemish, who had taken responsibility for answering to God on the whole issue of man's righteousness.

When Adam fell, God knew man would need a kinsman redeemer to come forth and redeem what man had lost. He also knew this redeemer could never come from Adam or his descendants because Satan, sin, and death totally dominated man and only produced fruits of unrighteousness. So, before God laid the foundation of the world, He secured His solution to man's desperate and dire state by providing for Himself a Lamb. This spotless Lamb approached the Father, took the scroll from His hand, and opened the seals.

Before John had been invited to "come up here" (Revelation 4:1), there had been a momentous event in heaven he had not witnessed. That was when Jesus stood from His throne and declared, "Behold, I have come to do your will, O God, as it is written of me in the scroll of the book" (Hebrews 10:7).

For He knew there had to be a man who would voluntarily empty himself of his rights to live his life in self-interest just like everyone else did. The earth was drowning in these types of men. What was needed was a man who would live for God alone and give to God all His rights no matter the cost to his life or reputation. A man who would live the life of voluntary dependence Adam had refused. His coming would illuminate the difference between God's righteousness and man's idea of righteousness.

He offered Himself to God as a sweet-savor offering for the Father's pleasure and satisfaction. Now God would have a man under continuous trial and testing. A man who wouldn't develop a flaw, blemish, spot, or any such thing. This fulfilled the Old Testament type of the Passover lamb.

Four days before the Passover, God required every household to bring a lamb into their home. During this time, they were to inspect the lamb to ensure it had no visible imperfection or deformity to disqualify it from being offered to the Lord. Before Passover began, they took the lamb to the temple and presented it to the priests, who carefully examined it from the tip of its nose to the end of its tail. If the priest found no spot or blemish, he would exclaim over the lamb, *"Tetelestai."*

Jesus' Arrest

From the time Jesus appeared on the banks of the Jordan, the whole universe had been focused on every word He said and every miracle He did. He was the center of attention. Heaven watched from above, while hell watched from below. His coming was the fire of inevitable provocation and didn't allow anyone to remain neutral. Lines were drawn and sides were picked. His baptism unleashed a tremendous antagonism in Judea. The demons and religious spirits that had witnessed the coming of God's Lamb now watched for an opportunity to tempt Him into breaking His union with the Father by acting out in His interest.

The religious leaders opposed His teachings and took counsel on how to entangle Him in His words. They decried His miracles as works of demons. He never faltered. During the four days He spent teaching in the temple before His crucifixion, the scribes and lawyers assaulted Him with subtle questions designed to reveal the slightest faults. All it would take was one. If the priests had uncovered a spot, He would have been disqualified as the Lamb of God. They came up empty-handed. After Jesus ate the Passover meal with His disciples, He told them that the ruler of this world was coming, but Satan had no fingerhold in Him on which to stake his claim, for there was no fault by which Satan could accuse Him (John 14:30).

From the upper room, Jesus went to the garden of Gethsemane to pray (Matthew 26:36-46). Waiting for Him was a cup filled with all the Fall's pain, suffering, and misery. In reality, only Adam knew the terrible consequence of the Fall. Only he knew what it was to have the light go out while he was dragged into a life of slavery by a cruel creature. His descendants didn't know that horror. They were born into a world where Satan, sin, and death had already defeated them before they took their first breath. They lived under the heavy hand of a taskmaster who cared nothing for them. They were born under it and would die under it as well.

But the Son of God knew only union with the Father. Sin had never touched His life. He had never known death or decay. If He chose to drink the cup, the evil and corruption contained in the cup would shatter His union with the Father. He would know the repugnance of sin and the bitterness of death. Every sin ever committed would be laid upon Him. He wouldn't be spared from the depravity of men and the works they did in the dark because those works were evil. He asked His Father if there was another way to fulfill His eternal purpose besides drinking this foul and offensive cup. But even as He asked, He knew there wasn't. The cup had to be emptied of every last drop, for He had come to be obedient to God even unto death on the cross. For Jesus, the cross, in its most profound meaning, was to be separated from God.

The temple guards burst into the garden and arrested Him. It was their hour and the power of darkness. In the early morning, He was tried before the members of the Sanhedrin and found guilty of blasphemy, a sin punishable by death. Since the Jews had no authority to kill anyone, they took Him to Pontius Pilate and ordered the Romans to do it for them. Instead of death, Pilate ordered Jesus to be scourged and then released.

Jesus was tied to a post and beaten from His shoulders to His upper legs. It was a horrendous thing to witness. The Romans made their whips from strips of leather. They added iron balls and pieces of bones to the whip. The balls caused deep bruising to the body and internal organs. The fragments of bone cut deep, exposing muscles and bones. Blood loss was immense. The scourge's punishment was so severe that some prisoners didn't survive.

Scourging would not satisfy the priests. They were out for blood. When Pilate hesitated to condemn an innocent man, they threatened to write Caesar and inform him that Pilate was allowing another king to rule in Judea, which would effectively destroy any political ambition Pilate may have had. He caved into the priests' demands and ordered Jesus to be crucified.

The Crucifixion

The soldiers led Jesus to Golgotha and nailed Him to the patibulum, just as they had done to scores of unfortunate prisoners before Him. They nailed His wrists to the beam with nails seven to nine inches long. The nails severed the major nerves in His hands, causing waves of unrelenting pain up and down His arms. The soldiers used ropes to hoist the patibulum to the large stakes left over from the countless crucifixions they had performed since coming to Judea. As the soldiers lifted the patibulum, Jesus' total weight pulled down on the nails, causing His shoulders and elbows to dislocate. Then the soldiers nailed His ankles to the cross. The long nails severed the major nerves in the ankles, causing Him acute pain.

The Jewish leaders gathered at the site to mock Him. He had shown great power in healing others. So why didn't He use that power now to save Himself? That's what they would do—save themselves. If He demonstrated His power by coming down off the cross, they would give His teachings a fresh listen. Jesus recognized the voice of the tempter in the crowd's scorn. Satan had used the same arguments in the wilderness. Their insults continued the long six hours He hung there. Still, no spot or blemish was uncovered.

The weight of His body pulled Him down, making it difficult for Him to breathe. His lungs were full of air, but His diaphragm could only expel that air if He pushed against the nails and raised His body long enough to exhale. It was exhausting. He was slowly suffocating to death. Carbon dioxide built up in His blood. His heart beat faster in an attempt to circulate oxygen through His body. His capillaries leaked a watery fluid that built up around His heart. It was a slow, painful death of blood loss, exhaustion, suffocation, and organ failure.

In the sixth hour, God poured His wrath out on Him. Every sin was judged. If those present on Golgotha could have seen in the Spirit, they would have seen a diorama of all man's wickedness: Adam eating from the tree of the knowledge of good and evil, Cain killing Abel, Jacob lying to Isaac, Joseph's brothers selling him into slavery, Israel refusing to go up into the land, Saul disobeying the Lord's command, David sinning with Bathsheba, Israel worshiping idols, the remnant refusing to rebuild the city, Herod the Great killing all the children in Bethlehem and the surrounding areas to wipe out the Messiah, Herod Antipas giving the order to have John the Baptist beheaded, the Sanhedrin handing their Messiah over to the Romans, and the soldiers nailing Him to the cross. Those present would also have seen man's utter and complete depravity and the unspeakable crimes against humanity that were still to occur. What they witnessed would surely have horrified them and broken their hearts. God laid upon the Lamb every sin committed by every man who would ever live.

The skies turned black as the sun went into hiding. The winds began to whip up, and the cold rain fell. Jesus drank fully of the cup. As He drained the last drop, He lost union with the Father, tasting sin's true and awful reality. He knew sin had utterly separated Him from God just like it had Adam. Just as it had all of Adam's descendants. At that moment, He cried out that God had forsaken Him. The cup He drank was bitter. What it meant for Him, of all men, to drink it! What a spiritual price He paid because it had to be drunk! His heart broke under the terribleness of it all.

In the spiritual realm, time stopped and then slowly folded back on itself, enveloping every minute of every day of every century man would live. This folding caught up the entire creation and dragged it to Golgotha so God could judge it. Every man was present, accounted for, and taken into the Lamb's bosom. When Jesus died, they would die with Him.

Jesus was growing weaker. Satan summoned death to Golgotha. For the wages of sin is death, and by accepting all of man's sins, Jesus would have to die, just like every other man before Him had died. But Satan had misread the situation. He believed death had finally triumphed over life and his darkness had snuffed out the light. The Lamb would lie in a grave and return to the dust from which He had been made, just like Adam had done before Him. But unlike Adam, the sin that separated Him from God was not His own. Even as He was made to be sin and suffer the complete consequence of sin, He was sinless. He survived the ninth hour. He survived the wrath that came to rest on Him. No man or demon would take His life. He would lay it down. His Father had given Him that authority.

Death came closer, savoring the moment when it would claim its victim. In the spiritual realm, everything that had been taken into the Son of

God's bosom would be judged, repudiated, and done away with forever. The closed door and the barred way were the next to the last to disappear. When they were swallowed up in His suffering, Jesus cried out, "*Tetelestai.*"

It is Perfect

The sacrifice was perfect. A man had fulfilled God's righteous requirements. There was no fault. There was no blemish. No one could accuse Him of sin. Sin was judged once and for all. There would be no need for any more sacrifices. The Lamb on God's altar was perfect. He poured His blood out for the remission of sin. Nothing more could be added. Nothing could ever be taken away. Sin was defeated. Man as a race, as Adam's descendants, was dead in Christ and would be buried with Him in a borrowed tomb.

Death was coming to take the life of an innocent man. Death came, not understanding that it was about to be swallowed up in His death. His death is the only power upon this earth that can kill death. When Jesus breathed His last, a tremendous power went out into the earth commensurate with what had been accomplished.

As the Lord committed His spirit into the Father's hands, lowered His head, and died, Satan believed he had won a great victory. But he didn't understand the Lamb. He didn't understand the power the Lamb's blood would have once it had been shed. Adam had been judged and crucified in Christ. That fateful moment when he ate of the tree of the knowledge of good and evil was crucified in Christ. The whole of creation was crucified in Christ. You were crucified in Christ. Your old man, with all his blindness, failures, and weaknesses, died with Him on the cross. He canceled the record of the debt that stood against you with all its legal demands and set it aside by nailing it to His cross.

A great earthquake shook Jerusalem. The priests in the temple witnessed the curtain that separated the Holy Place from the Holy of Holies tear apart as if some hand had reached down from the heavens and ripped it in two. The way had been opened, never to be closed again. It was true that man could now enter the Holy of Holies, but it was equally true that God was no longer trapped behind a curtain because of the demands of holiness.

Man had been made righteous, not with his righteousness, but with God's righteousness. Man's accuser lost all ground on which to accuse man.

But there was still more to come.

Chapter 17
THE POWER OF AN EMPTY TOMB

He disarmed the rulers and authorities and put them to
open shame, by triumphing over them in him.

Colossians 2:15

"HE IS NOT for he has risen, as he said" (Matthew 28:6). The tomb was empty. The cherubim put down their flaming swords signifying the way to the tree of life was no longer guarded. The door swung open never to close again. Nothing would ever be the same.

The Empty Tomb

The garden was quiet in the early morning light. Mary Magdalene and Mary, Cleopas's mother, walked down the path to the tomb (Matthew 28:1-10). They carried herbs and spices to anoint Jesus' body in accordance with the burial ritual. Two days before, Joseph of Arimathea had claimed Jesus' body when the Roman soldiers took Him down from the cross. He had his servants carry the body to a nearby garden with a newly cut stone tomb. Both Marys had followed the servants in hopes they could anoint His body before sunset. Nicodemus was waiting at the tomb, surrounded by large baskets filled with myrrh and aloe. Joseph didn't seem surprised to see him.

Joseph ordered the servants to carry the body into the tomb and lay it on a stone table. The servants exited, gathered the heavy baskets, and brought them into the tomb. Silently, the woman stood at the door and watched the two priests quickly bind His body in linen cloths and spices. When the priests finished, the women tried to enter, but Joseph forbade it. There wasn't enough time. The Sabbath was approaching. The servants rolled a large stone across the tomb's entrance to seal it. The two women would have to wait until after the Sabbath.

Now, as soon as the night gave way to light, the woman gathered their spices and headed to the garden. They didn't know who would roll away the stone for them, but it didn't matter. They would leave that to God.

As they drew closer, they saw a small platoon of soldiers huddled around a fire, trying to stay warm. Why were the Romans interested in Jesus' tomb? Did it have something to do with the priests' fear that His disciples might steal His body to make it appear He had risen from the dead? The women didn't know the answers, and they didn't care. The Romans were a godsend. Perhaps the women could convince one of them to help with the stone.

Suddenly, the ground began to shake. They fell to their knees, grasping the expensive spices to their breasts. An angel descended from heaven. The soldiers took one look at him and fainted. Without effort, the angel rolled back the stone and sat upon it. He was shining bright, and his clothes were white as the snow atop Mount Hermon.

The angel spoke to the women, calming their fears. "I know you seek Jesus who was crucified," he said. "He is not here, for He has risen." The angel disappeared from the top of the stone and reappeared at the tomb's door. He pointed inside. "Come, see the place where He lay." The women entered the tomb and saw the empty grave clothes on the stone table. They began to weep. Who could have stolen His body with the Romans standing guard? The angel spoke again. "Go quickly and tell His disciples that He has risen from the dead."

Christ's Complete Victory

This empty tomb signaled God's complete and utter victory over His enemy. In one glorious moment, the Father raised His Son from the dead, and there was nothing Satan, death, sin, or this world could do to stop Him. He had judged Satan in Christ and destroyed his ability to keep man in death and darkness any longer. Sonship had triumphed. The question of who would rule over the universe had been settled forever. God was the victor. Satan, the vanquished. By His death and resurrection, Jesus had stripped the power and authority Satan won in the aftermath of the Fall and regained the dominion Adam had lost in the garden. His resurrection life would become the most incredible force this world would ever know.

The eternal Heir had come into His inheritance. For by Him, all things were created and existed as His possession (Colossians 1:16–17). Even after His inheritance fell into enemy hands to be corrupted and dominated by sin and death, He didn't lose ownership of creation. When the fullness of time arrived, the Son of God, the Father's Heir, came to earth to seek and save what had been lost: the image and likeness man had been predestined to possess. The power of the empty tomb continuously proclaims that He has redeemed His inheritance, and the works of His hands will bear His image and likeness for all eternity.

For the Heir has triumphed mightily! The Son has despoiled and plundered! The Lamb has made an open show of His enemies by overthrowing Satan's throne and sealing his destruction. The kingdom of darkness' annihilation and humiliation are forever on display. Satan can't hide the fact that he has been rendered powerless. He can lie about it but can't deny that his power to keep men imprisoned in sins and lies has been obliterated. He can only stand by and helplessly watch as Christ empties his prisons, plunders his kingdom, and brings his treasures out of his house (Matthew 12:29). The nations that were once his to dispose of as he willed have now become the kingdoms of the Lord and His Christ.

At first, Satan was confused. He didn't know how or why he had been so thoroughly defeated. The priests had laid a lifeless body in the tomb. By all accounts, he should have been the victor and God the vanquished. The moment the Son drew His last breath, Satan's fallen world order should have been established forever. All men must die in Adam, for even the Son of God had died united with Adam in sin. After all, there was no coming back from death. Hadn't history proven this time and time again? Death always won.

Then came the horrific moment that caught the kingdom of darkness by surprise. The Spirit of Holiness entered the tomb and raised Jesus of Nazareth from the dead to never die again. And with His resurrection, He loosed a new law to govern a new creation that now lived upon the earth. In Christ, all men shall be made alive. His resurrection had completely rendered death null and void.

The Power of an Empty Tomb

No Condemnation in Christ

When Christ nailed the whole list of ordinances that stood against you to the cross, He ripped the ground out from underneath sin and robbed the demons of their strength. Satan must have some basis on which to make his power felt because his power doesn't exist unless he has something he can use to accuse you of some sin or fault. He uses those accusations to lash, drive, and harass you. Throughout history, Satan has constantly told men that God was against them because they couldn't do the "Thou shalts" and stop doing the "Thou shalt nots." This is why Christianity isn't a set of rules, rituals, and traditions passed down through generations.

If Christianity consisted of these things, then the Father has undone the victory of the cross and tomb and reopened the door for Satan to regain possession of the Heir's inheritance. The Father clothes you in His righteousness and welcomes you into His presence based solely on His Son's victory. There is nothing you can add to what Christ has accomplished. Neither is there anything you can do to invalidate His victory. From the moment Jesus committed His spirit into the Father's hands, God regarded your sin as being put away, forever silencing Satan's accusing voice in heaven. Satan can no longer bring any charge against you and demand death as His payment, for God justifies you. If God is for you, who can be against you?

There is only one who is against you. The same one who has been against you for as long as you've lived. A liar and the lies he tells. He wants nothing more than to put you on the ground of works righteousness, where your behavior becomes how you are accepted or not accepted before the Father. He uses this time-tested trope over and over again because it works. He trained your worldview to recognize it and accept it. He doesn't mind if you hear the good news that the Father raised Jesus from the dead apart from Adam. He doesn't care if you sing songs about it and talk about it with your friends. He does care and brings his power to deceive and persuade against you if you dare to believe it. If you give him a way in, he will accuse you of your shortcomings and condemn you for your lack.

The spirit of condemnation always brings about an instant arrest. You will go no further. You're stopped short of all the Father has for you.

Everything in your life becomes blighted, and the eternal fruit you were appointed to bear withers and dies.

But in Christ, there is no condemnation (Romans 8:1). For the law of the Spirit of life has set you free from the law of sin and death. The life Christ gives you when you are born again is His resurrection life that conquers death. Christ has placed you in the superior position over sin and death's dominion. The Father sent the Holy Spirit to teach you the power of the empty tomb. You live in the utter triumph of Christ's resurrection. Death can no longer encroach upon you to deceive you back into its grip. You now live by His life as He knows and lives it seated at the Father's right hand. Death cannot intrude upon His life. The same is true for you. You have been brought into a newness of life that no longer answers to this world system but to God alone. This is image and likeness—the inward revelation of the risen Son of God and His purpose for your life.

All there is to do now is believe—in justification, righteousness, His power over sin and *self*, sonship, and image and likeness. Your future is bright.

Part 3

BELIEVE

Chapter 18
JUSTIFICATION
It is God who justifies.

Romans 8:33

WHY ARE SO many of the Lord's people harassed and tormented by the Accuser, causing them to turn their eyes inward in self-analysis? Why are they constantly looking for the one good thing in themselves they can present to the Lord that will make them acceptable to Him? Especially since all introspection will uncover is the 101 things they did wrong today. As the list of wrongs grows, the Accuser belittles and berates the well-meaning Christian, bringing them under condemnation. Satan has become their master once more, for he has convinced them they are less than who Christ says they are.

The answer to the questions is a simple one. The Lord's people are harassed and tormented because they don't understand that Christ answered to the Father on their behalf in all He will ever require of them. They waste countless years poking around, trying to find something in themselves that will answer to God's righteous requirements. While they do so, they are harassed, plagued, and beggared by their failures, weaknesses, and all the wrongs they have done. They are so obsessed and occupied with their lives that the great truth of salvation no longer impacts their thinking.

Their life isn't about them, whether good or bad. It's about another life, and that other life has become the only way back to the Father. That's why Christ's death and resurrection are the only proof the Father gives His children that their sins have been set aside forever.

New Creations in Christ

When Adam ate the fruit of the tree of the knowledge of good and evil, he did so believing he could establish a government separate from God's commandments. What he discovered was he had been imprisoned and enslaved by a foreign power that had invaded his body and now ruled over him with an iron fist. That foreign power is called Sin. Fallen man obeys Sin's autocratic edicts because he has no choice.

The law of Satan's kingdom is the law of sin and death. This law requires the death of any man who sins (man's refusal to seek God and make His glory his supreme object). Sin has the legal right to demand your death if you commit even one. Except Sin's legal authority doesn't end at your natural death. Sin's interest can only be truly satisfied when you suffer the second death and are thrown into the lake of fire with the rest of God's enemies (Revelation 20:15). There is no reprieve. Sin demands and expects God to blot you from the universe.

Then Christ appeared and destroyed all of Satan's work, including Sin's complete mastery over you. Satan will never be more defeated than he was when Jesus rose from the dead. God united you in Christ, so you died with Him when He died. By joining you with Him in death, Adam's nature, which Paul calls the old man, was buried with Him in that borrowed tomb.

When God raised Christ from the dead, He also united you with Christ in the power of His resurrection. He left the old man in the tomb, which means God raised you with Christ, liberating you from Sin's rule because Sin can only legally exercise his jurisdiction over the old man. The resurrected you is a new creation, which Paul calls the new man. This new man is alive to God and walks in the newness of life. I heard a teacher say that the new creation is not a tadpole that turned into a frog because this is evolution; he taught that the tadpole had turned into a canary. The new creation is a miracle, a new species on the earth. He no longer lives under Sin's power.

By your union with Christ in His death and resurrection, God has declared that He has permanently removed the ground upon which Sin demanded your eternal death in the lake of fire. Justification is more than the forgiveness of sins, though God has forgiven your sins. The definition of forgiveness is the cancellation of something owed. But justification means punishment is no longer possible because you haven't committed any crime. You stand in the garden again, but this time you've eaten the fruit of the tree of life and triumphed in Christ over the enemy.

God has justified you from your sins' criminality and the accompanying guilt by removing Sin's legal claim against you. Because the old man died in Christ, Satan can no longer condemn you for your sins. In the new man, God has broken your association with Adam. The old man who knew nothing but the law of sin and death is dead and buried, so walk away and leave him dead and buried.

Because you're justified, the Father has declared you righteous in Christ Jesus, and nothing in this world, or in you, for that matter, can make you unrighteous. In Him, God has set aside your impurity. Righteousness no longer ebbs and flows depending on how you feel you performed today. The result of the righteousness that comes from being justified is that even on your worse day, you stand before Him holy, blameless, and above reproach.

God united you with Christ in His crucifixion to render the body of sin inactive. You're dead in Christ, and Sin has no ownership claim on the new man, who belongs exclusively to God. Christ now becomes your example. He died to Sin once and for all. Since He has died to Sin, you now must also, by faith, consider your *self* dead to Sin.

Ruling Over Sin

Now that you've considered your *self* dead to Sin, you mustn't allow it to reign in your mortal body. Many Christians don't believe this is possible because they have tried to stop "sinning" only to fail repeatedly. They fail because you can't pluck out sin or eradicate it by your will. You have to die to it and bring in another nature in which there is no sin. Christ didn't rehabilitate your character or reform your behavior. He executed you by uniting you in His death, where you died to Sin, then joined you to Him in His resurrection, where Sin has been rendered powerless.

How did God counsel Cain in Genesis 4? He warned Cain that Sin was crouching at the door, ready to pounce and take him captive, but Cain must rule over it. *Must* is a modal verb that expresses duty. It was Cain's duty to rule over Sin. At that moment, Cain was still in control of his actions. Yet, he didn't heed God's counsel. He permitted his anger to fester, allowing Sin to exercise its dominance. There came a point when Cain was no longer in control. He killed his brother and suffered the consequence of his actions.

You must not allow Sin to reign. If you do, you'll have no choice but to obey its passions. Sin will gladly rule over you if you give into Sin or believe you've no choice but to sin because you're human and have a sinful nature. Sin reigns wherever it is permitted to reign.

You'll live in Cain's reality if you don't rule over Sin. Sin will always be at the door, present, crouching, waiting to devour, and you'll always be too human to resist its desires. But if you will, by faith, apprehend that Christ's resurrection has rendered the body of sin inactive, you'll no longer have to do its bidding. It can crouch at the door all it wants, for Christ now lives in you and has complete authority over the powers and rulers of darkness. He hasn't left you a life where you have no choice but to sin even when you don't want to. He has given you good ground to stand on. His death has put away the man who could never reign, to make room for the man who can.

Who Are You?

After the Fall, men took on Sin's identity. They became sinners and behaved as such because they had no choice. Sin reigned over their minds, wills, and emotions. But in the new man, Christ reigns by an incorruptible life. Sin is no longer your identity. You've become a son.

Christ's sacrifice has the incredible power to perfect (or make mature) all those Christ sanctifies. The definition of sanctification is the action of making one holy or declaring something holy. We are being sanctified, which means God is setting us apart as holy so we belong exclusively to the Lord. He sets you apart so you can always choose the good and refuse the evil. The Father has safeguarded righteousness in Christ. In Him, righteousness remains incorruptible and indestructible. The Father then gives you Christ as your answer to all things pertaining to life and godliness.

Let me reiterate this because I know you've heard countless times (too many to count) that as long as you're alive, saved or not, you'll sin because you're human. Even as a Christian, your nature is to sin, and Sin is always waiting to raise its ugly head and drag you where you don't want to go. This false teaching makes the correlation that because you have the ability to sin, that ability is your true identity even after you've been born again.

Stop identifying yourself with the Fall. Start identifying yourself with the resurrection. Christ does. Don't accept this false teaching and live under Sin's constant power and death. You have one teacher, and He says He united you in His death so that He could permanently break Sin's power in you. Your nature is no longer sinful. You have His nature by the new birth.

Yeah, but . . . (fill in the appropriate excuse here).

Do you believe Christ's death and resurrection are so ineffectual that they couldn't fully deliver you from Sin's power? That somehow, when it comes to you, Sin is stronger than Christ? Don't allow life to speak louder than His voice. That is why you're having so much trouble with Sin. You've accepted the teaching that you're still Sin's slave and will only be delivered from its power when you go to heaven. Today, Christ proclaims you no longer have to present your body to Sin and be forced to serve it. He has set you free so you can present your body to righteousness and produce fruits of holiness.

God's sons bear His righteousness, which is greater than Sin's power. If you will put off the identity of a sinner and put on the identity of a son, you'll realize Sin is a defeated foe. Christ saved you from your sins. He didn't save you in your sins.

Don't be afraid to proclaim that you live by the Spirit, not by the flesh. Don't be afraid to declare that Christ has made you righteous. After all, He isn't afraid to declare His righteousness over you. Allow this declaration to become more than words. Let it become the truth you live by and the ground you walk on. Read Romans 6 and count the number of times Paul writes that Christ has freed you from Sin.

Now, that doesn't mean you can't commit an act of sin if you yield yourself to Sin. Open the door just like Cain did, and Sin will devour you. Even if you falter and open the door, that act doesn't diminish the truth that He has freed you from Sin. You can choose to walk in His righteousness and mature in Him so that the sins that so easily beset you today will be a thing of the past tomorrow. What was weak will become strong because His life works in you to produce fruits of holiness.

Am I saying I'm perfect and I don't sin? I'm asked that question constantly when I teach Romans 6. That question exposes the worldview that keeps many Christians bound in the flesh. Why does it come up? Why don't Christians rejoice when they hear the good news of His victory over Sin? Why do they consistently confirm and qualify Sin as their lord and not Christ? They ask that question because they live with the sin consciousness they've heard about their entire lives. They look at their lives through sin's lenses instead of His righteousness.

No, I'm not saying I'm perfect and don't sin. I'm saying Sin no longer forces me to do its will because I'm *just* a sinner saved by grace. I took Romans 6 to heart and made it the foundation of my life. My old man was crucified with Him so that the body of sin might be brought to nothing so that I am no longer enslaved to Sin (Romans 6:6). And if I stumble, the truth of Romans 6:6 doesn't evaporate into thin air. I go to my Advocate in those moments, and His blood washes me clean. Then I pick up where I left off and continue to pursue His image and likeness with every fiber of my being.

You may be thinking, *Yes, but didn't Paul write in Romans 7 that he is a wretched man because the law of sin and death still reigns in his mortal body, making him Sin's captive?* Well, does he actually say that? Let's take a look at Romans 7.

Chapter 19
THE TROUBLE WITH ROMANS 7

Wretched man that I am! Who will deliver me
from this body of death?

Romans 7:24

IN BETWEEN ROMANS 6, where Paul declared Sin no longer has dominion over him, and Romans 8, where he writes that the law of the Spirit of life has set him free in Christ Jesus from the law of sin and death, is Romans 7, where he seems to contradict everything he wrote in chapter 6, and everything he will write in chapter 8. In chapter 7, Paul paints a picture of a man who can never do right no matter how badly he wants to because he is captive to the very sin Christ died for once and for all (Romans 6:10). So, an examination of Romans 7 is in order, for either chapters 6 and 8 are true, or chapter 7 is.

Works Righteousness versus Christ's Righteousness

In AD 49, Rome's religious centers were divided into three different parties. Most of Rome's citizens were pagan, worshiping at the altars of false gods. These gods reigned over every aspect of Roman life, and the people offered sacrifices to appease and mollify the gods. There were also Jews in Rome who kept the law and the traditions of their fathers. They were kindred souls to the Jews in Jerusalem. A new religion had recently risen, consisting of people who worshiped and followed Jesus, the Messiah.

Most Jews who believed in Jesus also believed that the law and the traditions needed to be followed and kept—that Christ may rule and reign in heaven, but here on earth man must still keep the law if he wants God to consider him righteous enough to enter heaven. Christ's appearance did bring good news to the relationship between God and man. His death and resurrection meant that if a Christian stumbled and fell, Christ would intervene on his behalf and cleanse him of his sins.

Paul's understanding of the gospel was fundamentally different. He didn't preach righteousness based on a person's ability to faithfully keep the law and do other good works so they could be acceptable to God. Instead, he preached a righteousness apart from the law, where God saved a person and considered them righteous if they confessed with their mouth that Jesus is Lord and believed in their heart that God raised Him from the dead (Romans 10:9). Paul made the immensity of what Christ accomplished on the cross the centerpiece of what God was doing on the earth. Faith in Christ alone was all God required for righteousness.

This disagreement over what constituted righteousness wasn't contained in the synagogues or the churches. It led to disturbances in the streets, which quickly came to the attention of the Roman officials. To restore order and maintain peace, Emperor Claudius ordered every Jew banished from Rome. He didn't discriminate between the Jews who didn't believe in Christ and the Jews who did. If you were Jewish, the Romans forced you to leave the city. That's how Aquila and Priscilla ended up in Corinth while Paul was there (Acts 18:2).

Once the Romans banished the Jews from the city, believers no longer preached works righteousness because those coming to salvation had never heard of the Law of Moses. Faith and righteousness were established on Christ alone. When Claudius died five years later, his edict died with him. The Romans announced the Jews would be allowed to return to the city. Paul, anticipating that Jewish believers would insist that gentile believers keep the law as the means of righteousness, penned the epistle to the Romans. For Paul knew that the doctrine of works righteousness had done great harm to the integrity and purity of the gospel.

As Paul established churches in Asia Minor, a group of men followed after him. These were the Judaizers, whom I wrote briefly about in chapter 14. Whenever Paul left a city or a region, the Judaizers came into the churches and taught that Paul's gospel of righteousness through faith alone was a false teaching. Believers could only be accepted by God if they kept the law and the fathers' traditions and were circumcised. In their preaching and doctrine, the Judaizers put Christ and the law on the same level.

Paul was in Antioch when he received a letter from the believers in Galatia asking him why he had preached an incomplete gospel. Why hadn't he taught them that they had to be circumcised or keep the Law of Moses to be righteous before God? Paul recognized the Judaizers' teaching as a snare to enslave the gentiles into a compromised gospel that could never provide transformation. More importantly, the Judaizers' theology negated the death and resurrection of Jesus Christ as the sole means of justification and righteousness.

Either Paul was correct that Christ's finished work was all-sufficient, or the Judaizers were correct, and Christ's death and resurrection weren't as perfect as Paul believed, making circumcision and keeping the law necessary to complete a believer's salvation. Paul went to Jerusalem to meet with the church's leadership to decide once and for all what the gospel's actual message should be. This meeting took place in Acts 15.

Paul argued that a believer, whether Jew or gentile, is complete in Christ. Jesus' blood washed them clean, and His death and resurrection satisfied God forever on the issue of sin and righteousness. When Paul finished speaking, members of the party of the Pharisees argued that Jews and gentiles could only be made acceptable to God if they were circumcised and kept the law.

Peter spoke next. He told the council members that when God sent him to preach the gospel to Cornelius's household (Acts 10), God made no distinction between Jew and gentile. He filled the gentiles with the Holy Spirit even before he had finished sharing the gospel, cleansing their hearts in the same manner he had cleansed the hearts of Jewish believers. If God didn't make a distinction, then why should they?

As to the law, Peter asked all those present why they should burden the gentiles with a yoke (the law) that the Jews had been unable to bear. True righteousness is rooted and grounded in the truth that believers are saved by faith in Christ's finished work and not by keeping the law. Paul and Barnabas then recounted all the signs and wonders God was doing among the gentiles as proof that what Peter had spoken was true. God was saving the gentiles by grace through faith.

James, the Lord's brother, had the final word. He said God was raising up the tabernacle of David where, in the past, God welcomed Jews and gentiles to enter and worship Him. Therefore, he believed that the gentiles shouldn't be troubled with the doctrine of circumcision and keeping the law. All the council would ask of these new believers was that they abstain from eating things polluted by idols, from sexual immorality, and from eating meat that still contained blood.

Old Testament Types

Paul returned to Antioch, wrote the Galatians, and explained that he hadn't taught them the law and circumcision because they wouldn't have been able to keep the law. It would have become a yoke around their necks. To explain the differences between his teaching and the Judaizers' teaching, Paul used Abraham's two sons: Ishmael by Hagar, the slave woman, and Isaac by Sarah, the free woman.

The slave woman's son was born only because Abraham and Sarah devised a natural solution to fulfill God's promise. The free woman's son was born when God fulfilled the promise He made twenty-five years earlier.

Sarah was barren when God promised to make Abraham the father of many nations. Unless God performed a miracle, there was no way Sarah would ever be able to bear a child. As the years passed and God delayed fulfilling His promise, Sarah convinced Abraham that the only way for him to have the promised son was to have a child with her maid Hagar. She promised to adopt the child and raise him as her own.

The plan went haywire immediately. Hagar gloried in her pregnancy and treated Sarah with contempt, while Sarah, consumed with jealousy, made Hagar's life miserable. Under those circumstances, Ishmael could never become Sarah's son. All he could become was a constant reminder of her barrenness.

Hagar and Ishmael corresponded to the Jerusalem that sent the Judaizers to confound Paul's gospel of grace and freedom. Hagar was Sarah's slave, which meant Ishmael was the son of a slave. Paul used mother and son to teach the gentiles that circumcision, the law, and Israel's traditions were the rudimentary doctrines of slavery. For Ishmael had been born due to Sarah's barrenness. His birth didn't suddenly overcome this insurmountable obstacle. The door to God was shut. Circumcision, the law, and Israel's traditions could not force the door open.

Paul implored the Galatians not to go backward, for nothing was waiting for them but slavery. The Judaizers' teaching wasn't from the Lord because works righteousness was the opposite of the gospel's message. Righteousness by faith in Christ alone was a call to freedom from the self-centeredness that kept them in bondage to Sin.

Sarah and Isaac represented a Jerusalem also. The heavenly Jerusalem only knows freedom because it exists in the pure light of God's undiminished glory. Sin and death cannot touch it, for the holiness of the Lord will never permit sin and death to enter.

All those who are born again belong to the New Jerusalem and share in her freedom. God had promised Abraham a son, and even though Abraham was old, he believed God could give life to the dead and call into existence the things that do not exist (Romans 4:17). Sarah had a son when she was ninety-one years old, well beyond the childbearing age. Paul compared the gentiles to Isaac, who was born of the promise, born of faith.

The Judaizers vehemently objected to the freedom contained in Paul's message. They were afraid that the gentiles would use this newfound freedom as justification to continue their sinful lifestyles. They insisted the gentiles needed the law to curtail their previous bad behavior and to enforce godly behavior upon them. Without the law, how would these former pagans ever learn what it took to please God?

Paul taught that the purpose of the freedom given to Christians was not so they could indulge the flesh. In God's eyes, freedom served a much higher purpose. It was to free His children from the selfishness that prevented them from walking in love. The whole righteousness of the law could be summed up in two commandments: to love the Lord with all your heart, soul, and mind, and to love your neighbor as yourself (Matthew 22:38–39). The gospel sets believers free to manifest His love, which is the ultimate freedom.

There will always be a conflict between Ishmael and Isaac. When Abraham made a great feast celebrating the day Isaac was weaned, Ishmael laughed at his half brother and persecuted him. Sarah was furious and insisted Abraham send Hagar and Ishmael away. "For the son of this slave woman shall not be heir with my son Isaac" (Genesis 21:10). Sarah's words were prophetic. They summed up the differences between two races, economies, and powerful forces—life and death. The slave is born, lives, and dies a slave. He cannot inherit life, only death. The son is alive and will never taste death.

To Those Who Know the Law

Paul's great letter to the Romans was written to both the gentile members of the churches and the Jewish believers now returning to the city. These Jewish believers would find the church radically different. Before Claudius' edict, they were the majority and the gentiles the minority. Now, the reverse was true. Paul didn't want the Jewish believers to entangle the gentiles into keeping the law as the means of righteousness.

Paul included both Jewish and Gentile believers when he wrote chapter 6. Their union with Christ in a death like His freed them from Sin. What did Paul mean by "a death like His"? When Christ died to Sin, He did so once and for all, which means that every Christian needs to reckon themselves dead to Sin the same way—once and for all.

Paul specifically wrote chapter 7 for those who knew the law. What Paul wrote he didn't write to the church as a whole, but to the Jewish believers who believed that they still had to keep the law to be righteous in God's eyes. He wrote in verse 1: "Or Do you not know, brothers—*for I am speaking to those who know the law*—that the law is binding on a person only as long as he lives?"

Paul told the Jewish believers that just as they died to Sin when Christ died, they also died to the law, which is only valid while people are alive. Once they died, they were free from the law which bound them. He used the relationship between a husband and wife to illustrate his point. As long as the husband lives, the wife is married to him. If he dies, then she is no longer his wife. She is free from the law that bound them together.

The same is true with those who knew the law. While they lived as Jews, they were expected to keep the whole law. But if they died in Christ, they would be free from the law. That's what happened when they became believers. They died to the old man's responsibilities and penalties under the law. They became alive to God, who requires faith in Christ's finished work as the foundation of salvation, justification, and sanctification. Grace is aligned with faith and not with works righteousness.

Paul anticipated the Jewish believers' next question: Is the law sin? Of course not, he wrote. The law was God's answer to the Fall. It reestablished God's good on the earth and gave men hope that God still expected His eternal purpose to be fulfilled in His creation.

Man had to be freed from the law because the law couldn't give back to man what had been lost in the Fall. It couldn't restore image and likeness. In itself, the law was not an instrument of change. God gave Israel the law to show them how impotent they were in their fallen state on the whole issue of righteousness. It successfully exposed their weaknesses and proved their captivity to Sin. The more they endeavored to keep the law, the more they were conscious of the death working in them. The law didn't save them but condemned them and brought them under God's wrath. Grace and truth through Jesus Christ succeeded where the law failed.

Set Free from the Condemnation of the Law

This reality was what Paul was writing about in Romans 7. He told the Jewish believers that it was only because of the law that he came to know what God expected of him. He used the commandment of coveting to illustrate his point. The definition of *covet* is to yearn or desire something. Paul wrote that the law gave him a name to call this yearning within him. But the law also told him that coveting was sinful and he shouldn't do it. So he tried to stop. When he did, a greater truth was revealed. He couldn't stop coveting. It wasn't a matter of willpower. Something else greater than his will was operating in him. Paul called it sin in the flesh, which had complete dominion over him.

From his failure to stop coveting, Paul learned two things. First, he realized that he had to live or abide by everything written to keep the law as God intended. Second, he learned that if he was guilty of breaking one commandment, he was guilty of breaking them all. That's when Paul realized that the law couldn't save him. It could only condemn him. Whereas the law taught him right from wrong, he found he was dominated by Sin dwelling in his flesh. Sin prevented him from doing the good he wanted to do.

What a horrible place to find oneself. Paul described that place when he wrote, "Wretched man that I am! Who will deliver me from this body of death?" (Romans 7:24). Paul didn't write these words in defeat and resignation. He wrote them from faith in the life of Christ by which he now lived. For Christ's life had thoroughly triumphed over the Sin that worked death in him. He was now dead to Sin and the law. He was alive to God, and his faith in Christ's finished work had been counted as righteousness.

The gospel is the good news of God's righteousness, clothing you through grace by faith. It doesn't confound and frustrate you by giving you a law you can't keep. Instead, the gospel gives you Christ. If you believe the gospel, God reckons you righteous for eternity. The law no longer has any authority over you because you no longer live under its sphere of influence. You have been set free from the law. Once and for all.

Chapter 20
RIGHTEOUSNESS

In the presence of the God in whom he believed, who
gives life to the dead and calls into existence
the things that do not exist.

Romans 4:17

MAN HAS CONTESTED what makes him righteous before the Lord since the beginning. Is righteousness found in Christ alone? Or is righteousness found in Christ and all the things we add to Christ in order to feel better about ourselves? How we answer the questions determine the peace in which we live. If Christ died for God, and God is satisfied with Christ, then we are at peace with God. But if righteousness is something that we still must secure by our works, then we will never know true peace, for there is no way our works will ever be perfect enough to satisfy God.

Paul's Understanding of the Gospel

In his epistle to the Romans, Paul wrote that he was not ashamed of the gospel for it is the power of God for salvation to everyone who believes (1:16). In a legalistic world where all religious systems were rooted and grounded in works righteousness, Paul was not ashamed to preach that man is made righteous based solely on faith in Christ's finished work. Man plays no part in his standing before God because he is spiritually bankrupt. There is nothing he can do to make himself acceptable. He needs a Savior—a man God will accept on his behalf. Christ died for God, and God is wholly and forever satisfied with Christ.

For his preaching, Paul was persecuted, was beaten on numerous occasions, was stoned and left for dead, was shipwrecked three times, spent a night and a day adrift at sea, imprisoned in Caesarea and Rome, and, at the end of his life, was imprisoned again and martyred. And after all that, he didn't compromise his message. He continued to preach grace through faith in the finished work of Christ alone.

Paul could have easily stopped the beatings and the imprisonments by compromising the gospel and preaching works righteousness. He would have gained the religious world's approval if he had done so. He refused. God had revealed the Son in him, and this revelation of all the Son had accomplished for both God and man became the gospel God called him to preach to the gentile world (Galatians 1:16).

The Son of God ruling and reigning in heaven was the same Son who now ruled and reigned in the apostle. The union between God and man didn't diminish Christ in His glory. Quite the contrary. Christ's indwelling life brought God's righteousness, allowing Paul to live before the Father as if Adam had never eaten of the tree of the knowledge of good and evil. Paul continued to preach the gospel and suffer the persecution, which he described in 2 Corinthians 4:17, as light momentary afflictions that were preparing him for him an eternal weight of glory beyond all comparison.

Paul's understanding of the gospel is still under attack today. I've heard many preachers and teachers instruct believers to reckon themselves dead to Sin, but in the same sermon, they preach and teach us we're imperfect and will always be prone to sin. This contradictory message provides the flesh with the perfect excuse to sin. Think about it. If you've been taught that your whole Christian experience will be one of sin, failure, and weakness, why are you surprised when you sin, fail, and are weak? Worldly wisdom has permeated the gospel and slowly transformed it. Now Christians study fallen man to understand themselves as God's sons. The tragic result of such a study is that our identity can never change from who we were before we were saved.

The Bible tells us to put off the old man and put on the new man so we're no longer consumed by our past (Colossians 3:9-10). The new man is dead to all the old man's mistakes, lies, regrets, emotions, failures, and weaknesses. He is alive to God, who sees him as a son loved before the foundation of the world. And if you read that sentence and think, *Yeah, but*

. . . then you have yet to see the full impact of the gospel upon your life. It's not about you and never has been. It's about all Jesus accomplished when He died. He redeemed God's eternal purpose so you can know the Father's will and walk in the fullness of life.

Righteousness through Faith Alone

Righteousness through faith alone was the reason Paul confronted Peter at Antioch (Galatians 2:11-14). When Peter visited the church, he knew that most of its membership was comprised of gentile believers. He worshiped and ate with the gentiles on the uniting ground of Christ. When a party of men came from James, Peter withdrew from the gentiles because he feared what the circumcision party might say about him if they found him fellowshipping with them.

When Peter separated himself because the law stated that being in the company of gentiles made him unclean, other Jewish believers did the same. After Barnabas separated himself from the people he had known for years, Paul knew he had to act. He couldn't allow the churches to be segregated into two distinct classes made righteous by two different means. Paul stood to defend the gospel and not put Peter in his place. Significant damage was being done to the gospel's integrity. Either it is Christ alone, or it is Christ plus whatever else men attach to Christ to be righteous.

Any law, whether it be the Law of Moses or all the laws we impose upon ourselves because we think we must do them to please God, is a trap conceived in hell. For what is the strength of the principalities and powers of darkness arrayed against you? It's the whole range of laws, whether imposed externally or internally. The law becomes Satan's playground. It's the source of his strength, confidence, and ability to accuse and condemn God's sons. He becomes helpless and powerless if that ground is broken up and taken away through faith.

When Christ rose from the dead, He removed the ordinances against you and put away the legal demands so Satan would have nothing to stand upon. If there are no more ordinances, if righteousness is by grace through faith, if no one can accuse a son before the Father, for the Father has justified His sons forever, how does Satan ever regain control over you?

He does so by restoring the ground Christ removed. He brings back the ordinances and your weaknesses in the face of them. He convinces you that keeping the law (even self-imposed ones) is necessary to be acceptable to God. You aren't to fight this fight. You don't need to. Christ has already fought it and won such a resounding victory that the powers of darkness have been shattered. But only if you believe it to be so. For if you hint that Christ's finished work is lacking and you must make up the difference by obeying laws, then Satan will make a mess of your life.

Let me draw a clear line here. Most Christians believe Christ's finished work was significant enough to secure heaven for them when they die. Paul didn't withstand Peter at Antioch over this doctrine. He withstood Peter because Peter declared that the Christian life is lived by keeping the law, and Christ's undiminished life in believers lacks the power to ultimately deliver them from who they were in Adam. There is an enormous difference between believing Christ saved you for heaven and believing that His tremendous victory over sin and death raised you up as a new creation, a son who no longer has any association with Adam.

Please don't allow yourself to believe that you must remain in prison because it is your destiny to continually bear the consequences and punishments for the old man's deeds. Your prison isn't the benevolent prison from *The Andy Griffith Show*, where Otis locked himself up every Friday night and let himself out after he sobered up. The prison you find yourself in is bleeding you of the life He gave you when you were saved. The Lord has blown your cell door off its hinges. So why remain? You are justified.

According to the gospel, you have never committed the crime you believe imprisons you for this life. Come out of the darkness and into the light! Christ has finished His work. All He asks is that you believe Him. If you can't because you're overcome with guilt, shame, and grief, go before Him and stay there until He reveals the truth to you, for it is the Father's good pleasure to give you the kingdom.

If unbelief was Adam's downfall, allow faith, even if it is as small as a mustard seed, to destroy Satan's work against you. Christ has freed you to walk in the fullness of image and likeness. Don't let Satan rob you of the life Jesus paid for you to have.

Abraham's Faith

Paul battled against the law's encroachment into the gospel by using Abraham's life as proof that righteousness comes through faith, not works. I could write many chapters on Abraham, for God revealed so much about His eternal purpose through Abraham's life. Instead, I want to focus on God's promise to Abraham that he would have a son. As I briefly wrote in the previous chapter, Sarah's barrenness stood in the way of Abraham becoming the father of the promised son.

When God appeared to Abraham in Ur, He promised Abraham He would make him a father and the father of many nations (Genesis 12). Then God did an unexpected thing. He went away and took years to fulfill His promise. God will always do what He promises, but God extended Abraham in faith to gain His eternal purpose. It is the divine way of delay and contradiction. Delay reveals what's in your heart. Just how much of the things of God you want for your own sake to make a name for yourself. The same was true with Abraham. God's delay revealed much about Abraham's heart, both good and bad.

As the years passed without the promised son, Abraham and Sarah finally gave into the reasoning of their fears. Fear will always give you a way out of the circumstance that caused you to be afraid in the first place. To them, the solution to the problem seemed so rational. Sarah told Abraham that if he slept with her handmaid, she would adopt the child as her own, and they would fulfill God's promise. Abraham agreed.

He was eighty-six years old when Ishmael was born. Thirteen years later, God appeared to him and reconfirmed the covenant to make him the father of many nations. Abraham and his descendants would bear the mark of God's covenant in their flesh. Every male throughout the generations, whether born or brought into the household, would be circumcised. God changed Sarah's name from Sarai to Sarah at this time, for she would have a son and become the mother of many nations.

This time when Abraham heard the promise, he laughed. God had come, but He had come too late. Abraham offered up the only solution he had to this impossible problem. He implored the Lord to allow Ishmael to live before Him as the promised son (Genesis 17:18). But Ishmael couldn't live before the Lord. For the way was forever barred to Ishmael since he was the product of the old man.

Abraham offered Ishmael as the answer to God's promise because he had reached the limits of his faith. Even if he wanted to believe, his thinking now constrained him. He couldn't see how God could do as He promised. Both he and Sarah were simply too old.

Yet, the obstacle to having a son had never really been their ages, but Sarah's barrenness. And even though Sarah was barren, Abraham left everything behind to go to a country that God would only reveal once the journey began. He went because God had commanded him, and he believed. His leaving proved everything. He would go to this undiscovered country and become the father of many nations. He always knew Sarah's barrenness was the true hindrance to God fulfilling His promise, but he went out believing anyway.

The only way Sarah was going to have a child was for God to raise the dead and call those things into existence that did not exist. Abraham may have laughed and offered Ishmael as a substitute, but these two things were not indicative of the strength of his faith. He left Ur and stayed in Canaan. He left believing and stayed believing that God would keep His promise and bring forth life where only death existed.

In light of Abraham's faith, what did God do? Three things in this order: He counted Abraham's faith as righteousness. He established a covenant with Abraham and his descendants. He gave Abraham circumcision as a sign of that covenant.

Paul argued that when God made His covenant with Abraham, He did so absent the law. God wouldn't give the law to Israel until 430 years later, and when He did, it didn't void His promise to Abraham. The law doesn't have the power to annul the covenant. Covenants don't work that way. Once established, no one can add to them or subtract from them. The giving of the law didn't mean God had changed His mind on the means of righteousness. Righteousness only comes by faith in God's immutable promise.

God's Covenant with Us

God has made a new covenant with His Son, and we are the recipients of that covenant, just as Abraham was the benefactor of the covenant God made with Himself (Genesis 15:17). Abraham believed in God, and God declared Abraham righteous. Abraham could do nothing to add to the promise or subtract from it. All he could do was believe the impossible. God would be able to raise the dead (Sarah's womb) and call those things (Isaac) that were not into existence.

The new covenant operates the same way. You believe God can raise the dead, but in your case, God can raise up a son of God where there once was only a son of Adam. When God raised you from the dead, He raised up an entirely new man whose identity no longer belongs to the past but to God alone. He called a new creation into existence whom He ordained to be conformed to the image of its Creator (Colossians 3:10).

Paul wrote that all Abraham did was believe and God declared him righteous (Romans 4:9). The same is true with believers, whether Jew or gentile. Whosoever believes, God declares him righteous. The belief is all God requires. Isaac was proof of God's resurrection power. The new birth is also proof of the same power.

Your faith is in believing His truth, and your fight of faith is in maintaining the life He has produced in you. Can you see the correlation between Abraham and yourself? Can you see that the simple prayer you uttered when you were born again was the same as Abraham's when he was leaving Ur? The same challenges that Abraham faced, you also face. You're on a journey to a new land and are hindered by the same problem Abraham faced—barrenness. You believe the same things as Abraham—that God can bring life where there was only death and call those things that don't exist into existence. That only God can answer for His promise. By giving you the same faith as Abraham, He has brought you into Abraham's household, where faith is counted as righteousness.

God didn't give Abraham a law to keep. Paul argued that God didn't give believers in Christ a new law to keep either, except to love one another as He loves them. Abraham's righteousness and the believer's righteousness are the same. The gospel isn't complicated, but that doesn't mean it's powerless. For it is the power of God unto salvation to everyone who believes (Roman 1:16).

Chapter 21
WHO YOU ARE IN HIM

Even as he chose us in him before the foundation of the world, that we should be holy and blameless before him.

Ephesians 1:4

WE HAVE BEEN justified. We have been freed from the power of sin. We have been made the righteousness of God (2 Corinthians 5:21). No longer are we enslaved to worldly wisdom and the worldviews it trained. We've been unchained from all the voices and false teachers that have kept us imprisoned in a kingdom that thrives on darkness. God has placed us in Christ so He can be the one who teaches us what to think and then how to think about it. In Christ, we've been liberated to pursue image and likeness without limitations or hindrances. Our horizons have truly become eternal ones.

The Blood of the Lamb

Forty days after His resurrection, Jesus gathered His disciples on the Mount of Olives and instructed them not to leave Jerusalem until they received the promise of the Holy Spirit (Acts 1). Once the Spirit came, they were to take the gospel to Judea, Samaria, and to the end of the earth (v. 8). When He finished speaking, He was lifted into the sky. The disciples watched Him ascend until a cloud hid Him from view. Two angels appeared beside them and asked them why they kept looking up. Jesus would return to earth the same way He had ascended into heaven.

It would have been impossible for Jesus to have ascended if He had not perfectly accomplished the work He came to do. If He had faltered just once, heaven would have been closed to Him. But the Father declared His offering *tetelestai*. This means your salvation is forever settled. It's yours, full and complete. You're as perfect as you'll ever be, for Christ entered not into a man-made temple but into heaven to appear before God on your behalf. His blood was more potent than all the blood of goats and bulls poured out on the Altar of Sacrifice, for His blood purified your conscience from dead works to serve the living God (Hebrews 9:14). Sin no longer separates you from God in heaven. The blood of the Lamb has permanently opened the door and the way.

Identity in Christ

Your identity begins and ends in Christ. God's power now ensures your progress toward image and likeness. Every spiritual and Christly virtue you possess as a result of the new birth is being brought to maturity so you're not just a theoretical and dogmatic Christian, but a real one, spiritually responsible and accountable, with the root of His life within you. Conformity is what governs His work. But it is His work and not yours. You'll fall short of Christ's image and likeness if you resort to your thoughts, ideas, opinions, and resources.

Scripture tells us that Christ is seated in heaven (Colossians 3:1). Sitting means ruling, reigning, and resting. In Christ, God now has His perfect Man according to His original thought, and in that Man, all those who believe in Him are represented in perfection and fullness. His throne is eternal. His power and authority have no end. His will and purpose will never cease. A scepter of righteousness has become the scepter of His kingdom.

Christ is the dominant authority over all the powers of darkness. He has all the power. The demons, including Satan, have none. He rules over them; they don't rule over Him. Right now in heaven, He is working to bring all His enemies under His feet. The last of these enemies will be death (the penalty for sin). It is inevitable. Christ will place His foot on death's neck—the sign of complete and absolute victory.

Christ's kingdom isn't confined to heaven but has been put into every believer, so His ruling, reigning, and resting can be revealed as more powerful than the darkness, sin, and death that still rule in the hearts of fallen men. In Christ, His victory is your victory. The apostles turned the world upside down because their gospel wasn't confined to words alone. God did signs and wonders to prove that Christ had conquered death and governed with full authority over the kingdom of darkness. The kingdom of God should be constantly expanding everywhere His children are. It's not a kingdom of weakness or a domain for some distant day. Right now, the Christ ruling and reigning in heaven is the same Christ dwelling on the inside of you.

You are to be governed by glory just as Christ is governed by glory. If you desire to live in Christ's fullness, then the Father must occupy the same place in you that He has in Christ. For it is in Christ that all the fullness of God was pleased to dwell (Colossians 1:19). Jesus, as perfected man, is the exact copy of the Father. Divine majesty and divine purpose dwelling in a man—who He is, what He is, what He desires, His satisfaction, His joy, His truth, His life, the list keeps going. God is permanently housed in Christ Jesus, the Son of Man. And in His church, His body, Christ is also permanently housed.

There is a union between the Father and the Son and the Son and His church. Union isn't an experience. It's a position given to all believers by Christ. This union happened the moment you were born again and is represented in the New Testament by the phrase "in Christ." There is no more controversy between heaven and you. In Christ, the Father has reconciled you who was once alienated and hostile to God and made peace through the blood. The Father has put you before the public and declared that you are His son without blemish and unable to be accused or criticized by anyone. His Son redeemed everything in you that contradicted the union He created you for.

If you want to mature in the Lord, you must accept that you are dead to everything from the world and Adam. There is nothing in this world that you can rely on to either possess or augment the kingdom. God has judged the world and has done away with it. You can't serve Him by using what He has rejected. You can never come to life until you repudiate what God has repudiated. If you ignore this fact, your spiritual life will know lack and eventually come to a point where there is no further progress. That is the nature of spiritual death. It is vanity, never coming to the fullness God intended you to have.

Life Begins and Ends in Christ

After the triumph at Jericho, the children of Israel suffered a defeat at Ai (Joshua 7). Joshua cried out to God, asking why the army suffered such a sudden reversal. God told Joshua there was sin in the camp, which brought about their arrest. Achan from the tribe of Judah had stolen some gold and silver, which had been consecrated as holy to the Lord before Jericho fell. Achan had taken what belonged to God and sought to use it for his advantage. The flesh always does this. It takes what belongs to God alone and tries to use it for its own sake.

Achan had also stolen a cloak from the land of Shinar. Genesis 11 tells us that after the flood, Nimrod gathered men in Shinar to make a name for themselves, separate from God, and build a strong tower able to withstand God's judgment in the future. Babylon is part of a spiritual order that has always been antagonistic to God. It is worship energized by the god of this world, usurping God's place as God. The judgment of both Nimrod and Achan reveals that God has first rights, and the flesh must not appropriate what belongs to Him alone.

Works righteousness is a worldly construct that is the basis of many religions. False gods are only appeased and mollified by what humans do in their names. Christianity is different. It rejects the world's understanding of how to appease a god and unequivocally states that since your life begins and ends in Christ, everything pertaining to life must come from God alone.

Those who God uses the most are those who trust Him the most. Trust Him for what? Salvation, justification, righteousness, sanctification, and image and likeness. Your devotion to Christ must include the willingness to pay the price necessary to restore God's testimony upon the earth.

Your life is the evidence God provides to those in heaven, on earth, and under the earth that Christ has risen from the dead and has been seated high above His enemies. This is the reason why the Father put you in Christ. Through your life, the Father proves over and over again that He has given His Son a name above every other name that is named. At the name of Jesus, every knee shall bow and every tongue confess that Jesus is Lord to the glory of the Father (Philippians 2:9-11). This bowing of the knee is not an end-times event. It has been happening since He ascended into heaven and was received as absolute Lord with all authority.

163

Christ divested Himself of His godly dignity when He descended to an inferior condition by taking upon Himself the form of a servant to model sonship so you could see and know what God expects from you. He didn't descend as far as you had fallen. For fallen man is the true definition of an inferior condition. All that fallen man holds dear (namely his worry and anxiety over the outcome of his life) proves he lives from an inferior position of great futility. Christ exalted in heaven is the superior position. Christ's victory in you and through you is the superior position. Whenever you insist on your way, you fall back into an inferior position and become conquered instead of a conqueror.

Christ chose to empty Himself of His rights and become God's servant, serving both God and man. He served God by providing Him a life by which the Father could manifest His glory. Jesus put the kingdom of darkness to flight with just a word, and men were saved and redeemed according to God's eternal purpose. He served man by proving that God would willingly unite Himself with man to accomplish His will. This is His testimony, and now it has become your testimony.

Grace through Faith

Wherever there is an incomplete picture of God's grace, there will be an incomplete testimony. Grace is the gift God gave you when you first believed. For grace is what you needed so God can bring you into the fullness of sonship. Grace is more than undeserved merit whose sole purpose is to forgive you repeatedly for your sins. It isn't a permission slip that overlooks your behavior. Grace is empowerment.

In Christ, God has freely given you His transformative power that overcomes every obstacle standing in the way of His great purpose. He is willing to use the same power He used to create the heavens and the earth to transform you into His image and likeness.

Paul wrote in Ephesians 2:8 that we are saved by grace through faith. If you apply faith to the truth of what He says about you, the Holy Spirit uses grace to take that truth and make it your reality. It's no longer you trying to become. Try to become, and all your trying will only reveal your spiritual poverty. It's grace that reproduces the Son in your life. For example, you aren't trying to love impossibly unlovable people because you're supposed to. No, you're becoming love, and no one is impossible to love.

Faith is the perspective by which you now live your life. It's the understanding of who you are now that He has come. Faith is always looking for a place where the risen, ruling, and reigning Christ in heaven can be revealed on earth. The purpose of God in Christ is to bring men to the throne and to His perfect Man to prove once and for all that He is Lord. Because you're in Christ, the Father has given you the pleasure, honor, and responsibility to bear His testimony of His Lordship and turn the world upside down once more.

If you don't believe this is possible, you have yet to catch sight of the risen Lord seated on His throne and dwelling in you. Having light is one thing, but how you live in that light is more important. Are you obeying all that the light has shown you, or are you still anxious over the outcome of your life? Are you becoming what He died for you to become, or are you discounting the importance of this great truth so you can remain alive to yourself? Jesus prayed God's will be done on earth as it is in heaven (Matthew 6:10). This doesn't have to do solely with God's power but also with God's heart toward you and His purpose to redeem not just man but the whole of His creation to image and likeness.

You are in Christ. This is the truth God has spoken over your life. You are in Christ, and in all His fullness. Because He lacks nothing, neither do you. For not only are you in Christ, but Christ is in you also. I'll explore this truth in the next chapter.

Chapter 22
WHO HE IS IN YOU

"If anyone loves me, he will keep my word, and my Father will love him, and we will come to him and make our home with him."

John 14:23

IN JOHN 8:29, Jesus declared this truth about the way He chose to live His life. "I always do the things that are pleasing to Him." So let me ask you a question. Did you read Jesus' statement and wince—even just a little? Does doing the things that are pleasing to the Father seem like a hit and miss proposition in your life? Are there days you triumph in the doing and days when you fail miserably? Do the days of failure outnumber the days of triumph? Be honest.

If you answered yes to the last questions, then you have yet to grasp the reason Christ has made His home in you. He doesn't come to dwell in you to be limited and pent-up. He lives in you as the ruling and reigning King of heaven to secure His image and likeness in you. His life is the power at work in you to both will and work for His good pleasure (Philippians 2:13).

Moses Pleads for God's Presence

Moses lay face down in the Tent of Meeting, interceding for the people and himself. He hadn't asked to be a deliverer. He hadn't asked to meet with God in a bush that burned but wasn't consumed. It was never his dream to be a leader of a people who didn't want to follow him. He had tried everything he could to escape the call, but God had dismissed his concerns and sent him to Egypt anyway. As the fire in the bush slowly extinguished,

166

Moses only knew a few things. He was to tell the people that God had come down to deliver them; that Pharaoh was to let God's people go; and when they were free, he was to bring them to Mount Sinai, where God would be waiting for them.

Even when he was on his way to Egypt, he still didn't want to go. He was a fugitive from Egyptian justice. If he returned, the Egyptians would make him pay for his crime with his life. He was also a shepherd, an occupation the Egyptians despised. Pharaoh would never listen to him. After all, Pharaoh was a god—the son of Ra, the greatest of Egyptian gods. Then God said He would make him a god to Pharaoh and force the great king to listen to a fugitive and shepherd's words.

It had been a struggle to get the people to Sinai, for they had made it clear from day one that, while they liked the idea of leaving Egypt for their own land, they didn't actually want to make the journey. Every step of the way had been filled with fear-riddled complaints. Finally, they arrived, and God was faithful to His word. He was waiting for them at Sinai.

Moses spent days in the Lord's presence, listening to His desire to dwell among His people. It was for this purpose He had brought them out of Egypt, and it was for this purpose He was bringing them into the Promised Land. The Lord had given Moses plans for a tabernacle where He would dwell and a law for the people to obey.

Then came the jarring news that the people had created a new god to lead them into the land. It was an utter betrayal of all the Lord had done for them. Moses hurried from God's presence. What he saw in the camp angered him. The people had broken loose and were worshiping a golden calf. He dealt with all he saw and withdrew to the Tent of Meeting to intercede on the people's behalf, for God had been clear that He intended to destroy them because of this great sin.

As Moses lay on the cool sand and wept, he knew he hadn't risked his life to return to Egypt to have it end like this. God would no longer go up with them into the land. Instead, He would send His angel before them. Moses didn't want to be led by an angel. He needed God to go up with them, for he didn't know how to lead these stubborn and stiff-necked people. He had barely gotten them this far.

The revelation he received at the burning bush was no longer enough. If he was going to make it through another day, he needed a more profound revelation of who God was for the people. If the remarkable story of their exodus ended without God's presence, then he had failed everyone. So he prayed and wept for forty days until God told him to return to Mount Sinai, where He would have all His goodness pass before him. It was enough. As God passed by and proclaimed His goodness, Moses knew He would forgive the people and go up before them as they journeyed to the Promised Land.

God's Presence in Us

God now reveals His goodness in His Son. The finished work of Christ allows the Father to do what He has always purposed to do. To reveal His Son on the inside of every believer, which means the ruling and reigning Lord of heaven is now dwelling on the inside of you. He didn't strip off His power when He consciously decided to reside within you. He came without measure. You are His temple, which is the dwelling place of His glory.

His purpose for you is more than you can imagine, for His plans are immense. Paul summed up those plans when he wrote that Christ in you is the hope of glory (Colossians 1:27). This little phrase is a mighty and powerful expression of God's eternal purpose. Christ in you, the hope of glory, wraps up the whole impetus of your Christian experience. The Father's purpose in creation has always been Christ dwelling and living in fullness and without measure in man and, through His indwelling life, filling the earth with His glory. The Fall may have interrupted His purpose, but the Fall could never defeat it. God gave the world the nation of Israel as a picture of His intense desire to dwell in and with His people. He has always sought a dwelling place where He would be welcomed and live unhindered.

In today's vernacular, you mainly use hope to express a wish to ward off a failure you suspect is coming. You usually say, "I hope so," when you don't expect to receive what you've asked. You cross your fingers and hope that somehow, someway, things will work out. Biblical hope is not a fingers-crossed somehow, someway wish. Biblical hope is founded on trust in the God who promises. Your faith is rooted and grounded in hope. Christ in you is God's answer that you'll know and live in the fullness of image and likeness. He came to make His home in you because it is the best way He can communicate who Christ is to be in you.

Your life as a son is determined by how great the revelation of Christ is in you. You're the one who makes that determination. He has come in fullness. Will you meet Him in your inner life and believe Him for fullness? For if you will be absolute with the Lord, He will be absolute with you. If you are careless with the things of the Lord, then you will be straitened and never come to know all God has for you.

In heaven, Christ is revealed as central and supreme to what God is doing on the earth. His commands are obeyed without question or negotiation. All heaven hangs on His every word. The same must be true with you. He is the Lord, and He is central and supreme in you. He expects His word to be obeyed without question or negotiation. He is the only Lord in your temple (there can't be competing lords), which means you have agreed to a great and powerful exchange. He hides your life in Him, and He becomes the life by which you now live. Christ is your one teacher, and He chooses to educate you in the school of His sufferings.

Scripture tells us that the Father found it appropriate that Christ, the founder of our salvation, should be made perfect through suffering (Hebrews 2:10). Christ was spotless. Still, God brought out His nature in clarity and perfection through suffering. He didn't just suffer on the cross. His suffering came by not giving in to His self-interest when confronted with losing His reputation and stature.

Christ's sufferings embrace an entire realm you'll have no part or share of. They belong exclusively to Him. God doesn't call you to partner in the atoning suffering of Christ. You don't atone for your sins or suffer for salvation. Your participation in His sufferings is for the drawing out of His life within you, the hope of glory. You also share in His sufferings for your vocation. These types of suffering, though, have numerous forms and aspects.

We Must Be Emptied of *Self*

The Lord deals with you in this manner because He wants His nature and life within you to be brought out in the same spotless perfection as Christ's. Suffering has always been the way of fruitfulness because of its ability to expose the machinations of the *self*. Paul recognized that sharing in Christ's sufferings and becoming like Him in His death were the only means by which he could attain the resurrection from the dead (Philippians 3:10–11).

The Holy Spirit introduces the inward cross into our lives, which is how He empties us of *self*, where all our considerations for reputation, position, honor, ambition, and everything else that belongs to the old man is housed. These things may reside in the *self*, but they must be set aside so Christ can reign. The Holy Spirit recognizes that the *self* and its worldview are the obstacles to Christ receiving all He died to possess. He knows your worldview will adapt and deceive you so the *self* can survive and defraud the Son of His glory. Your worldview will even give ground along the periphery but will wage all-out war when the Holy Spirit demands that *self* give way to the greater life now residing inside.

That's why all suffering is trying to the *self*. It must be taught to put on the new man. The *self* finds the school of His suffering irksome because it's always dictated what it wants and needs. Now, the Lord has come, and the *self* must learn to be emptied, denied, and become obedient to another's purpose and will. The Lord isn't going to minister to your selfishness. The only way God's purpose will be established in you is through travail and anguish.

But there is a great purpose in your travail and anguish. When Christ, who is your life, appears, you'll also appear with Him in glory (Colossians 3:4). This is your end, so this is where your focus needs to remain. Your job is to stay in the game no matter how much your *self* whines in protest. You're being transformed, and the Holy Spirit fully believes in His ability to mature you into a son. The abiding fruit Christ appointed you to bear will only remain if it comes from a crucified life (John 15:16).

Christ in Us

Now, you do have a choice to make because there is always a choice to be made. You can hear His word for your life and obey, or you can have another idea of how your life should be and keep living the way you always have. You can incorporate Christ into your life, which means He is only Lord when you need Him to be. You can fill His temple with this world's clutter, and the world will overwhelm you until it forces you to cry out to the Lord for deliverance from all your selfish choices.

You may live like that, and there will be mercy in your time of need, but that is not sonship. Your ideas on what your life should be are the old man dominating the new man. It always ends the same way. You are frustrated and disappointed that all your dreams and hopes (fingers-crossed, somehow, someway hopes) are in ruins. Your life will be a losing battle against an enemy who will destroy you because you have chosen to fight him on his killing ground.

Or you can choose God's eternal purpose and pursue His will for your life with the same passion and determination you're chasing all the other things that will ultimately kill you. Christ in you is life-changing. His finished work leads to this one thing: the fullness of God coming and dwelling in you. It's worth repeating. God created the heavens and earth so He could come and dwell in a people who would welcome Him. It is so intimate and personal. He wants to be your Father, and He wants you to be His son upon the earth. What does a son upon the earth look like? He looks just like Jesus, whose reply to Philip in John 14 sums up the meaning of image and likeness. Philip asked Jesus to show them the Father so they could believe. Jesus answered, "Have I been so long with you, and you still do not know Me, Philip?" (vv. 8–9).

Now that is a huge statement, but it is a true statement nonetheless. Christ in you is the hope that God's glory, the fullness of His presence, might be made known to everyone who comes in contact with you. You may have read that statement and your heart sank because it's not the truth you're living. The good news is that it may not be the truth you're living right now, but it can be. All you have to do is choose Him. No more negotiating His revealed will for your life because you want what you want. No more defining your life by your needs, wants, fears, and desires. It's all or nothing. There is no middle ground in God.

Why is the Holy Spirit so insistent that you put on the new man in fullness and not just in the parts you find convenient? Because He knows an ill-defined Christ in your life is the source of all your weaknesses, failures, and disappointments. Christ can't be unformed. He can't be a Christ without features. Don't settle for anything less than the full measure of Christ. Don't let life speak louder than His truth.

God didn't create you to be an independent authority. The Fall's destruction can be summed up when Satan convinced Adam he could establish his government and decide what was right and wrong for him. All he had to do was find the courage to throw off the Son's kingdom. Satan's lie has lost none of its allure through the ages. All you have to do is look around. This lie is the source of all the evil in the world. Never once has it been the source of good.

Christ in you is God's mighty victory over the lie that came into the universe and brought with it death, schism, division, and disintegration. His life in you is the Father uniting all that has been divided. If you can recognize it, you'll see how divided your life is, for you give yourself away in pieces. There is a piece of you for work, a piece of you for family, and a piece of you for God. You even keep a piece for yourself, which no one else is entitled to. You live in a constant state of war against the forces arrayed against you, demanding their piece until nothing remains.

The busyness this world demands distracts from the truth that Christ in you is the unification of all those pieces. Now there is only Christ. There is only Christ for work. There is only Christ for family. There is only Christ for God. There is only Christ for you. Don't allow the world to tell you that individualism is a prize to be desired. He has brought you from being a part to being unified into His glorious whole—the fullness of His expression on the earth.

On the Outside Looking In

Moses would find himself lying on his face in the Tent of Meeting again when the people refused to go up into the land because they saw the giants. Like before, Moses knew it wasn't supposed to end like this: a people disqualified because they couldn't see all God had done on their behalf. Now, they would have to go into the wilderness to die.

His anger and impatience with the people erupted at Meribah (Numbers 20). The people accused him of not caring that they were about to die of thirst. God told him to speak to the rock and command it to yield water so the people and their cattle could drink. Instead, he struck the rock and railed against the people's constant rebellion. His disobedience cost him the land. At the end of his life, God took him to a mountain where he could see the land he had fought so hard to bring the people to. He died on the outside looking into something that should have been his but wasn't. As he viewed the land, he knew his life wasn't supposed to end up in defeat.

The same is true for you and me. We could wind up on the outside, looking in because we couldn't see the wondrous vistas stretching out before us. Paul didn't want the same to happen to him. That's why he gladly suffered the loss of all things (his position and reputation) and counted them as rubbish so that he might gain Christ and be found in Him (Philippians 3:8). Christ in you is not mere theology. It is something that must be entered into. Satan will fight to keep you on the outside looking in. Don't let him. Instead, allow Christ in you to be your hope of glory.

Chapter 23
EITHER . . . OR . . .

*If all your thinking has led you to this point, perhaps it's time
to have another thought.*

Graham Cooke

THERE CAN BE no maturity or growth in the Spirit until we cross a true spiritual Rubicon. We have to choose, once and for all, who we are as Christians. Are we defined by our failures, weaknesses, limitations, and immaturity? Are we broken, sinful wretches with no real hope of being anything more until we get to heaven? Are we the same people we were before we were saved except now we pray, go to church, and read our Bibles?

Or are we defined by who Jesus says we are? He tells us we must look to who Adam was before he ate of the tree to understand are true identity. This was the purpose of His redemptive work: to give back to us the life and destiny we had before Satan entered the garden. Jesus' death and resurrection erased all the destructive force and power of the Fall so we can know the freedom and intimacy Adam experienced before he was deceived.

We need to stop defining ourselves by our conditions (the weaknesses and failures we see in our lives) and start defining ourselves as God defines us. He calls us to be sons, which means we don't just enjoy the benefits of sonship but shoulder sonship's responsibilities as well. He expects us to grow in the knowledge of the Son of God so we can be mature men and women whose lives express the measure of the stature of the fullness of Christ (Ephesians 4:13). What He doesn't want is for us to be humble braggarts of our weaknesses and sins. He receives no glory when His children live as if they are *just* sinners saved by grace held captive by a sin nature that no longer exists.

The Priests' Faulty Worldview

The root of the priests' opposition to Jesus was based on their worldview. They believed God had appointed them to guard the integrity of His truth, which made them exceedingly zealous in upholding their duty. When a new rabbi appeared on the scene, they would examine him thoroughly. The only problem was their examinations were fear-based. They had already predetermined that they wouldn't allow a challenger to emerge who could threaten their power or position. So they probed until they uncovered a fault. When they did, they denounced the rabbi as a heretic and warned the people not to listen to him.

Throughout the Gospels, the priests desperately tried to uncover such a fault in Jesus. They always emerged from their debates with Him a little worse for wear. They had no answer for His wisdom. There were times He refused to engage them in conversation. He didn't take up the priests' worldview unless He was contrasting it to kingdom reality. He turned their questions back on them, leaving them flabbergasted, for they knew if they answered truthfully, they would be the ones discredited. He wasn't interested in the day's politics. He wasn't ignorant of them. He wasn't engaged in them to their level. For politics do make strange bedfellows, and the Romans were just as responsible for keeping the priests in their position as was their calling to preserve Israel's law and traditions.

The crowds around Jesus continued to grow, and the priests could feel control slipping through their fingers. When the people began to speculate whether Jesus was the long-awaited Messiah, the Son of David, the priests knew they couldn't risk such a belief taking hold in the land. If the Romans considered Jesus a threat, they would raze Israel to the ground just like they had done to other rebellious nations.

After Jesus healed a man who was blind and mute, the people eagerly reignited their belief that He was the Messiah (Matthew 12). The nearby priests scoffed at the notion and informed the crowds that Beelzebub, the prince of demons, gave Jesus the power to cast out demons.

Either . . . Or . . .

When Jesus heard what the priests said, He asked them some obvious questions. What would Satan have to gain by dividing his kingdom? How could he withstand such a division? The priests refused to answer, so Jesus answered for them. Of course Satan had nothing to gain. He was a strong man ruling over a vast kingdom. He exerted his power to keep his empire intact and under his dominion. The only way Satan's kingdom could be plundered and his treasures brought out of his house was if someone stronger than him entered his realm and bound him.

Jesus asked the priests to make a judgment. Was casting out demons a good thing or a bad thing? He told them to either make the tree good and its fruit good or make the tree bad and its fruit bad (Matthew 12:33). How they perceived the tree would determine the quality of the fruit. If they decided that casting out a demon was good, He did so by God's power. But if they decided that casting out a demon was bad, then He did so by Satan's power.

The priests refused to answer because they perceived a trap. If they decided that casting out the demon was good, they would reinforce the crowd's belief that Jesus was the Messiah. It would be easier not to answer and allow the masses to doubt the source of His power.

Rejecting Spiritual Poverty

For most of my Christian life, I lived in a state of spiritual poverty because my life wasn't commensurate with what I read in the Bible. If I was asked whether I was justified and Christ's finished work made me righteous, I would have answered yes. If I was asked whether I was in Christ, Christ was in me, and His indwelling life was the hope of glory, I would have answered yes. My theology wasn't my problem. My problem was that I failed to live up to what I knew was true. I was straitened. I knew it, and that knowledge tormented me. I couldn't understand why I was so helpless to live up to those sacred doctrines. Each day I woke determined to be kind, demonstrate self-control, and show gentleness in my interactions with others. My determination didn't make any difference. By mid-morning, I was the same person I had been yesterday.

I redoubled my efforts to do all the pastors and preachers told me to do to be a more successful Christian. I studied more, prayed more, worshiped more, gave more, served more, and while there were changes in my life's periphery, nothing changed at my core. I couldn't understand why. Wasn't I doing everything I was supposed to do? It seemed unfair that I had to remain that wretched man Paul wrote about in Romans 7 when I didn't want to be.

My self-flagellation proved my worldview was in control of my spiritual life. The Father may have called me a son, but His truth had been invalidated by the lies I believed about myself. I couldn't overlook my mounting failures regarding spiritual things, and my worldview was only too eager to confirm that God would only accept me if I were perfect. But I wasn't perfect. I proved that every day. Every time I failed, my worldview quickly reminded me that God didn't love me because I was spiritually bankrupt.

I knew my worldview was telling me the truth. If I couldn't measure up to my standard of how a Christian should behave, how could I measure up to God's high standard? My belief that God didn't love me broke my heart and gave me no hope of being like Jesus. My worldview used my brokenness to etch my identity in stone. I believed I was worthless, so God deemed me unworthy of His love. All I had left were tears and sorrow.

But those tears and sorrow over the sinfulness of my behavior proved that the Holy Spirit was at work in me. Once upon a time, I would have sinned without guilt, condemnation, or shame. My bad behavior wouldn't have registered a blip on my heart's radar. But now, every time I failed, I cared deeply. My tears and sorrow were proof of how much I cared. Those same tears and sorrow were also proof that His grace was trying to mature me into a son, but my inability to accept what His finished work had accomplished on my behalf caused me to be uncooperative with His grace.

Tears and sorrow will never produce life. It was only after I changed my thinking and believed what He said about me did grace begin transforming me into image and likeness. I understood that all my sinful behavior had a single root. I never reckoned the old man dead. I permitted him to do whatever he wanted whenever he wanted. Sin was crouching at the door, and I never mastered it because 1) I didn't know I was supposed to, and 2) I didn't know how. When I behaved in a manner that wasn't Christlike, I reacted not as a son who had been redeemed and justified. Instead, I responded like Adam in the garden. I beheld my nakedness and used my tears and sorrow as leaves to cover my mortification.

Either . . . Or . . .

The Lens of Your Worldview

You aren't Adam running and hiding from God because you're naked and scared of what God will say when He finds you. Your worldview may tell you that's who you are, but your worldview is a villain. You are a much-loved son who has been cleansed and clothed in His righteousness. The Lord has extended grace to you. If you believe things about yourself based on the current condition of your life, you may very well miss the grace of God that transforms you into the fullness of sonship.

You either view your life through the lens of your worldview or the lens of His truth. If He says He forgives you, do you live as if He has forgiven you, or do you live condemned? If He says He has justified you, do you live justified, or are you burdened with regret? If He says He loves you, do you live loved, or are you insecure about how He feels about you at any given time? Are you allowing your failings and your feelings about those failings to color your perspective?

Your failings are just your temporary condition. They don't tell the truth about God's work in you. That's why you must think as He thinks. You must allow grace to have its perfect work in you. Otherwise, all you'll end up with is a theology and no grace to bring that theology into reality. It's time for you to make a judgment about who you are. Will you make the tree good and its fruit good, or will you make the tree bad and its fruit bad? You may be inclined to answer that you're neither tree because you bear both good and bad fruit. According to Jesus, a tree that bears both good and bad fruit doesn't exist.

But if that tree exists in your thinking, you've been deceived. You're allowing your worldview to exalt your condition over the position you occupy in Christ. You must accept the truth that you aren't the measure of anything. He is. Your condition is just that. It's a temporary, transitory thing. If you have difficulty accepting this truth, when do you ever receive the grace to be who He paid for you to be? When do you ever receive the full measure of the Holy Spirit and His ability to raise up sons in His image and after His likeness? When do you believe that you're an oak of righteousness, the planting of the Lord that He may be glorified (Isaiah 61:3)?

If you allow your worldview to keep you from believing that Jesus made you a good tree, then there's no hope for the fruit. You'll live right where you, halt between two identities, believing you're a hybrid of both. Again, no tree exists that produces both good and bad fruit. How you identify your life—either as a good tree or as a bad tree—will ultimately reveal what you see and believe and what you fail to see and believe.

Christianity is not about what you know. It's about what you see. So, why not stop seeing yourself by your condition and start seeing yourself by your position? If you do this one thing, the Holy Spirit will finally be able to release grace's fullness in your life and begin His work in earnest to bring you to maturity. Then watch how quickly things change.

What glory do you bring the Lord if you live the same way you've always lived? What does your enslavement to sin reveal about the power of His shed blood? What kind of message do you send when you tell the world that you're saved in your sins and not from your sins? He didn't send His Son to die on the cross so you can proclaim you're a Christian yet remain the same.

If this book accomplishes one thing, let it be that I was able to tell you who you are. Let this book inspire you to believe all the Father says about you. If I can convince you to see yourself as a good tree producing good fruit, you'll be able to get up every morning and live not from your condition but in the fullness of your position. You're destined for the throne of God (Revelation 3:21). But only sons can ascend to the throne, for sons are as limitless as the Christ indwelling them.

Either . . . Or . . .

Jesus told the priests to either make the tree good or make the tree bad. How they perceived the tree would determine the identity of the fruit. The priests were too interested in the consequences of proclaiming the fruit good to understand what He was asking them to do. Jesus wasn't saying that the fruit determines what kind of tree you are. That's what we do as Christians. We judge the tree by the type of fruit it produces. No, the tree determines the fruit.

You'll only bear good fruit if you see that His blood makes you a good tree. If you know who you are, your life will reveal it. If you don't know

Either . . . Or . . .

who you are, your life will show that also. If you think you're some weird hybrid tree, you're considering the wrong thing. You're allowing the fruit to identify the tree.

In nature, an apple tree only produces apples. It cannot produce oranges. If an apple tree produced oranges, it would be an orange tree, not an apple tree. The same is true for you. A tree bears fruit after its kind. That's why a good tree can't bear bad fruit, and a bad tree can't bear good fruit. Agree with what God said about you, and you'll produce good fruit that abides. As a man thinketh, so He is (Proverbs 23:7 KJV). If you can believe that Christ's finished work made you a good tree, the fruit will follow because it must, and you'll be amazed at the goodness of God.

Chapter 24
THE NARROW WAY

Blessed are those who mourn, for they shall be comforted.
Matthew 5:4

JESUS SAID THE only way a person could come after Him was to deny their *self*, take up their cross, and follow Him (Matthew 16:24). And ever since He made that statement, the definition of the word deny has been under constant negotiation. *Deny* is defined as the refusal to give or grant, to reject, repulse, or dismiss the influences the *self*, with all its issues, has over your life. The *self* demands the right to sway you toward self-survival every time it thinks it's in danger of not getting its way.

Jesus' command to deny the *self* is a call to freedom from all the hurt, pain, grief, offense, or injustice you have endured in this world. The *self* holds on to these things as a way to define and identify itself as it navigates through life. But Christ crucified and buried the old man (the old you) who suffered those traumatic events, so that another life filled with peace, joy, power over the elemental things of this world, and victory can reign in you instead. The journey to spiritual maturity begins with the denial of *self* so the true you can live as He always intended.

Which Gate Will You Enter?

As Jesus concluded the Sermon on the Mount, He introduced two gates of life His disciples could choose to enter (Matthew 7). The first gate was wide. Its spacious room and the large crowds favoring it made the gate desirable. People entered expecting to find a life of blessing and ease. As they walked down the broad path, they were horrified to discover that the gate hadn't led them to blessings but to misery and the loss of eternal life.

The other gate was narrow. It wasn't easily found, so one had to seek after it if one wished to enter. Unlike the wide gate, the narrow gate led to the absolute fullness of life. Only a few were willing to pay the price necessary to enter. Yet, Jesus told His disciples to choose the narrow gate.

The Greek word *narrow* is defined as one standing before a judge. For a Christian, our Judge is Christ. This judgment will not determine whether or not we enter heaven. That was settled when we believed the gospel. The judgment seat we will appear before is the Bema throne (1 Corinthians 3:12–15). During the first century, the Bema throne was what the champions in a physical contest appeared before to receive the rewards of their victories.

How Are You Building Your Temple?

After Christ returns to earth and establishes His kingdom, believers will appear before Him so He can examine the fruit of their lives. The standard of judgment He will use is His nature. You'll be measured by fire to reveal how much of His image and likeness is in you. Yes, you'll be rewarded for obeying His call on your life, but the standard remains the same. You were created in His image and after His likeness. How well did you build upon that foundation?

What building material did you use? Did you use hay, wood, and stubble? Did you use what was expedient and convenient? Did you allow your *self* and worldview to dictate the building material so they could still govern your life? What do you see when you step back and view the temple you constructed? Do you see Him, or do you see yourself?

Or did you build with gold, silver, and precious stones? Were you a wise master builder who understood the enormity of what you had been called to construct? Did you build your temple based on the Word of God? Did you reject the easy thinking that deceives you into believing it doesn't matter how you build since you were saved and going to heaven? Did you see the Son and realize that He alone was the standard? Did you come into agreement with His thoughts? Did His way become your way, His will become your will, and His eternal purpose become yours?

Christ will apply the purifying fire to both types of temples. Only the temple built to ensure the Father received His satisfaction will survive. No matter the call on your life—whether you are called to a worldwide ministry, to the business world, or to be a father or mother who gave their children a happy childhood and a strong Christian education—the preferred building materials remain the same. They are the costly materials of love, consecration, and revelation. Did you allow the Holy Spirit to accomplish what He had been sent from heaven to do—to take what belongs to Christ and reveal it in you?

The Bema throne of Christ will determine how you'll spend eternity. Viewing your life by the years you spend here on earth is tempting. The world system oppresses you with the hardship of daily living and always gives you something to occupy your time, heart, and emotions. It's wood, hay, and stubble, but the immediacy of life closes your eyes to the more significant issue of eternity.

This life is just a vapor. A drop of water in the vast ocean that makes up eternity. You may live in your physical body for seventy or eighty years, but that is nothing compared to the unlimited eternity you'll dwell in. Your worldview will convince you that this present life is all that matters to deceive you into building for this world only and not for the world to come.

But the world to come is drawing near. It will arrive either when your life comes to its natural conclusion or when Jesus returns in glory. Either way, when it arrives, how will you be found? What will His purifying fire reveal? No matter what else is going on in your life, this is the only question that matters. You will stand before Him and account for how you built your temple. What will you say? What excuse will you give for the building material you chose?

When discussing the Bema throne, I find that many believers grow uneasy. They are concerned with what He will say to them at that moment and uncertain about His reaction because they don't know what God requires of them. One school of thought comes from believers who think that because they prayed a salvation prayer and that prayer entitles them to all the fullness of heaven, it doesn't matter how they live their lives. The other school of thought is the exact opposite. These believers are positive God is keeping a strict count of every sin they commit and every word they utter. They are already doomed in their thinking and convinced He will say,

"Depart from Me, you who work iniquity." Then there are those believers in the middle of the two extremes. They've never considered what eternity will be like—besides their mansion's floor plan and location (whether by a lake, near a mountain, or on a beach). They've given great consideration to that.

Pursuing the Narrow Gate

Jesus told His disciples to live each day knowing they will appear before Him and give an account for their lives. Why did He ask them to live like that? Because it focuses the attention on what matters most. The narrow gate is the only way to the fullness of life here on earth and in the ages to come. The moment you determine you'll enter the narrow gate, you'll discover the only thing that can pass through is Christ. Your *self* and worldview cannot enter in. They don't fit because they're occupied with something other than Christ. They're deciding your life based on what's good for them right now and not on eternity.

Jesus told His disciples that if they would come after Him, they would first have to deny their *selves,* take up their cross, and follow Him (Matthew 16:24). Before you can follow Jesus through the narrow gate, you'll have to deny your *self.* The very *self* that's at work within you to make sure it is governing and not Christ. The last thing the *self* wants is for you to consider going through the narrow gate, for the *self* knows what's at stake. So, the *self* graciously defines self-denial for you.

The most popular definition is this: If God tells me to do A, and I want to do B, I must deny my impulse to do B and do A whether I want to or not. Or self-denial is when I have to perform a task I think is beneath me. The task strikes at my pride, and if I do it, I've denied my *self.* My favorite definition is this one: When I have an overwhelming emotion, I must choke it back and do the opposite. Instead of speaking angrily at someone who just offended me, I swallow my wrathful words and say something nice.

If the above definitions were all Jesus was talking about when He told the disciples to deny their *selves,* then all of us would be building with gold, silver, and precious jewels because we all do those things to some varying degree every day. Self-denial is something entirely different.

Naaman's Faulty Worldview

In 2 Kings 5, we find the story of Naaman. He is the commander of the Syrian army and the king's counselor. He led the Syrians in victories all across the Levant, including the northern kingdom of Israel. After one such victory, He gave his wife a young servant girl who his men had captured as a spoil of war. Naaman was afflicted with leprosy. One day, the young girl lamented to her mistress the lack of prophets in Syria. If only Syria had a prophet like those found in Israel, the prophet could cure her husband of his leprosy.

Naaman's wife told him all the young girl had said. In turn, Naaman told the king, who wrote a letter to Jehoram, Israel's king, asking Jehoram to heal his general. In case the letter wasn't persuasive enough, Naaman also brought a large sum of money with him.

Jehoram read the letter and tore it up in despair. He didn't have the power to heal Naaman, and his relationship with the prophet Elisha was adversarial at best. He took counsel of his fears and believed the Syrians were picking a fight by asking him to do such a thing. Elisha heard about the letter and told the king to send Naaman to him. Naaman arrived at Elisha's house with great fanfare. A servant exited the front door and told Naaman to wash in the Jordan River seven times and the Lord would cleanse him. The servant went back inside and closed the door after him.

Naaman is a type of the natural man. Despite his fame in the region due to his mighty victories, death still worked in him. Because there was death, his fame and prowess on the battlefield couldn't cure him. He had to seek life from another source. Elisha represented God's victory over death. There was life in the servant's words, for God had given them to the prophet.

Naaman was offended to his core when Elisha sent his servant instead of coming himself. He was a great man, and great men don't speak to servants. The prophet should have given him the honor due him, left his house, and healed him. Not only was Naaman offended because of the servant, but he was also offended by the message. If all he had to do to be healed was wash in a river, then he didn't need to travel to Israel. Syria's rivers were far greater than the Jordan. He refused to do as the servant said, and, in his anger, he and his great entourage turned around and headed for home.

Naaman's disease was not his lack. His lack was the offense and anger he displayed when confronted with the full implications of the cross. Elisha had told him how to be healed. But that way was through the narrow gate, and Naaman couldn't go through. He required recognition of who he was and what he had accomplished. He needed Elisha to do something more in line with his high opinion of himself. Naaman felt the sting of being ignored by the prophet, which became a consuming fire. He went away in a great rage.

No one likes to be ignored or not be recognized for their accomplishments. Naaman wasn't that much different from us. He had to learn that if he were going to be healed, he would have to be emptied and have nothing in himself. The cross was being worked in his inner life.

That night, Naaman's servant told him that the prophet's servant had spoken a great word. All Naaman had to do was go to the Jordan and wash. If he did so, he would be healed. It was such a simple thing to do for a great reward. Naaman pondered the servant's words and decided he was correct. He went to the Jordan and dipped seven times. On the seventh time, he came up healed.

Naaman went through a very exhausting test. Did he want to be healed? Or did he want to be flattered and have a great fuss made over him because of who he was in the natural? The choice was up to him. He resented the fact that God wasn't impressed by his stature. God never takes into account who we are in the natural. He ignores the old man and sets him aside. This setting aside of the old man is what the cross represents. Do we really mean business in the matter of resurrection life? Or do we not? If we want to walk in the full measure of the Son, we'll need to take up our cross. Before we can do that, though, we must deny our *selves*.

Deny Your *Self*, Take Up Your Cross, and Follow Him

We all have been defined by the pains and disappointments we've faced. If we're honest, most of us haven't experienced true healing from those pains and disappointments. We've only learned to live with them and move on because life moves on. But our traumas still scar our hearts and influence our worldviews. When we encounter situations that cause us pain or disappointment again, we know how to handle them. We bury them deep within and continue on because we must.

Every time we swallow our pain or disappointment with how our life has turned out, we build a stronghold of resentment, injustice, and bitterness. The infamous words "You don't know what they did to me" have been carved in stone above the stronghold's door. These words become the *self's* justification for holding on to all the slights and offenses it has suffered. We have suffered greatly at the world's hands—some more than others. No one will deny that. The important thing to remember is that we're all mourning our losses and grieving over the setbacks we've experienced. We put up walls and establish boundaries so no one can harm us again, but people always find a way to breach our walls, cross our borders, and hurt us. It doesn't matter if we look back on some of these events and see that good came from them. Our recognition comes too late. The damage has already been done. The grief we experienced when the setback occurred has influenced our worldview and shaped our identity.

Living with your pain (no matter how well you've managed to cope) is death working in you. If you have any hope of going through the narrow gate and appearing before Christ at the Bema throne with more than wood, hay, and stubble, then you must deny your *self* so you can take up your cross and follow Him. Jesus has unequivocally stated that denying your *self* and taking up your cross is the only way you can follow Him. If you couldn't deny your *self*, Jesus wouldn't have made that a requirement in following Him. But the only way you'll genuinely deny your *self* is if you see yourself standing before Him at the Bema throne, giving an account of the choices you made throughout your life.

That means you must deny the losses you've suffered and the sense of injustice you feel because of those losses. Whether you're entitled to those feelings or not doesn't matter. As the commander of the Syrian army, Naaman thought he was entitled to the respect that came with his position and success. Elisha didn't give him what he felt he had earned, and his resentment of his treatment at the prophet's hands almost caused him to return to Syria instead of being healed.

Most Christians don't believe God is serious about His eternal purpose in transforming us into His image and after His likeness. They think He is good and understands the untenableness of our plight. We are, after all, sinners enslaved to our nature. That's why He winks at our condition and allows us to live any way we choose because He's love, and that's just what love does. There will never be any consequences to our choices as long as we sincerely want to follow Him. We'll stand before Him on that day and explain the situation. He'll understand, and we'll receive our crowns along with everyone else.

That's why we're in the state we're in. Half-in, half-out. Mostly defeated and still living in our past disappointments. We envy what others have and feel as if life hasn't dealt fairly with us. We constantly allow sin against us to produce sin in us. We also allow circumstances and situations to decide who we are.

You must do as He commands if you want more from your life. Deny your *self*, which means you deny the old man, the old ways, the old thoughts, and the old habits. You also deny your pain and the stronghold it's built in your mind. Your *self* isn't allowed to keep its walls and boundaries. You're no longer to choose your way, will, desires, disappointments, and feelings of outrage and offense. You're no longer to govern your life to seek and find what you believe you need to be happy and self-fulfilled. You no longer have schemes for your future. Christ has come. You have a Lord, and He has the only say. You won't be able to come into the fullness He paid for you to have unless you deny your *self*, take up your cross, and follow Him.

That's what being a Christian is all about. You have a Lord. It's not you. That's really good news because most of us make lousy lords. Don't believe me? Take an honest look at your life. Has it turned out the way you always dreamed it would?

The Lord has come to be central and supreme, even in the things you would consider the mundane routine of your life. When you accepted Him as your Savior and Lord, your life was no longer yours. You were bought with a price, and your life belongs to Him. Your *self* gets nothing out of salvation. It receives no gratification. It is to be reckoned dead and denied every single time it wants to have an opinion on what you should be doing.

The Purifying Fire of Christ

At the end of your life, you'll stand before Christ, and He'll judge you on an absolute basis—the measure of His nature in you. If you want His purifying fire to reveal gold, silver, and precious jewels on that day, then you must stop carrying all the pettiness and tyranny of the *self's* wants, needs, and demands. Only what the new man produces in cooperation with the Holy Spirit can withstand the fire.

Jesus is coming and will reward every man according to his work. When He calls your name and you stand before Him, this moment will be the next-to-last chapter written in your life's story. How the final chapter will be written, which will take in all eternity, will be determined by what the fire reveals.

Did it reveal wood, hay, and stubble? Or did it reveal gold, silver, and precious jewels? The fire exposes the difference between your stated motives and your real motives. Nothing will be hidden on that day. Your *self* will no longer be able to deceive you. Will it be a day of regret or a day of celebration? The choice is yours to make. Will you deny your *self*, take up your cross, and follow Him? Will you enter at the narrow gate and find the fullness of life?

Chapter 25
IT'S NOT ABOUT YOU

It is these who follow the Lamb wherever he goes.

Revelation 14:4

OUR LIVES ARE no longer about us. He didn't save us for us. He saved us for Himself. Our old man has been crucified and buried. God raised us up and made us alive, but He won't find His satisfaction in our lives if we keep insisting our lives belong to us. Too often, we're content to incorporate Jesus into our lives to ensure they go as smoothly and comfortably as possible. His will is easily negotiated away if it means the *self* suffers loss.

The *self* along with our worldviews has done us more harm than all the demons in hell, for the *self* convinces us the inward cross isn't necessary for transformation. We can save our lives and still gain the whole world in the process. There doesn't need to be a forfeiture of our souls; God's love would never demand such a price from us.

But the Son of Man will come again with His angels in the glory of His Father (Matthew 16:27). This is a certainty. On that day, what will happen if we have listened to the *self's* justifying lies instead of the Son's truth? We will discover too late that we have nothing to give in exchange for our squandered lives.

Abraham and Isaac

When the Lord tested Abraham and asked him to offer Isaac as a burnt offering on a mountain in the land of Moriah, Abraham didn't hesitate (Genesis 22:1-19). Over the years, two great truths had reshaped his worldview. The first truth: Isaac was a child of resurrection life. Abraham would have no son to offer if the Lord had not intervened on Sarah's behalf and spoken life into her womb. But the Lord had intervened. The second truth: The Lord had promised His covenant would be fulfilled through Isaac. Without Isaac, Abraham couldn't become the father of many nations and a blessing to all the families of the earth. He had seen too much of God's goodness to doubt Him now in this moment of testing.

As Isaac walked to Moriah, his worldview had also been shaped by two great truths. The first truth: He was a child of resurrection life. If the Lord hadn't called those things that did not exist into existence, he wouldn't be on this journey. His birth was an impossibility, yet he had been born. The second truth: He was Abraham's heir, and his children and grandchildren would possess the land of Canaan and become a blessing to all the families of the earth. He had been supernaturally conceived and born for a greater purpose than living for himself. He had been born for God's glory.

Isaac didn't know he was supposed to be the sacrifice offered that day. When father and son arrived on the mountain, Isaac asked Abraham why he hadn't brought a lamb for the burnt offering. Abraham told him God would provide the lamb. The answer satisfied Isaac. He allowed his father to place the bundle of wood needed for the offering on his back. He would carry it up the mountain.

When they reached the place of sacrifice, Abraham prepared the altar. He turned to Isaac and began to bind him. Jewish scholars have differing views about how old Isaac was when this event occurred. He was either twenty-six or thirty-seven years old, depending on which scholar you read. Still, they agree that Isaac was an adult and could have physically stopped his father from binding him and placing him on the altar. Yet, he didn't resist. His worldview and faith in God allowed him to lay his life down on the altar and trust that God would raise him from the dead so he could inherit the covenant.

Abraham took out a long knife and raised it over his son. A brief pause. He thrust the blade downward. An angel of the Lord called out from heaven, "Abraham! Abraham!" He answered immediately, "Here I am." The angel told him not to harm Isaac or do anything to him. Abraham had passed God's test, and had proven he feared God by not withholding Isaac, his only son, from the Lord.

Abraham heard a rustling behind him. He looked in the thicket and saw a ram caught by its horns. He unbound Isaac and helped him off the altar. Then he slaughtered the ram and offered it in his son's place. He called the mountain *Jehovah Jireh*. The translation of the name is "On this mountain God will provide for Himself a Lamb."

Following the Lamb of God

In 2 Samuel 24, David ordered a census of Israel, and God judged David by sending a pestilence into the land. When David saw the angel of death with an outstretched sword over Jerusalem suspended between heaven and earth, he fell on his face and began to cry out in repentance. He had been the one who had sinned, not the people. God sent the prophet Gad to David and instructed him to raise an altar on the threshing floor that belonged to Araunah the Jebusite. This threshing floor was on the same mountain Abraham had received the ram to offer in place of Isaac. David purchased the threshing floor, and Solomon constructed the temple there after David's death.

Golgotha is also on the same mountain. It was there on that mountain that God provided Himself a Lamb to lay down on the altar of His choice. Revelation 13:8 (KJV) reveals that the Lamb had been slain from the foundation of the world. The Father's solution to Adam's rebellion was predetermined long before He spoke creation into existence, for it is through the Lamb that the Father would utterly reverse the nature and constitution of the Fall.

The Lamb's nature is one of meekness, which should never be confused with weakness. Meekness is the laying down of your rights. Meekness is Isaac allowing his father to bind him when he could have escaped and saved his life. Yet, he chose something greater than himself. Meekness is the Son in the garden of Gethsemane after the arresting party had fallen to the ground under the power of His glory. If He wanted to escape the cross, He could have right then. His adversaries were in no condition to stop Him. But He waited until they got back on their feet and allowed them to arrest and bind Him.

The altar God chose to sacrifice the Lamb of His choosing is so powerful that it links the eternities. One arm of the cross reaches back to the point where God decided to create a world in which His image and likeness would fill all and be in all. This arm embraces the immensity of His eternal purpose. The other arm embraces the ages to come and perfectly rectifies what had been lost. It doesn't matter that the Fall corrupted and killed. The cross is much greater than we sometimes allow it to be, for the cross has come from eternity into this present age and the world to come to take hold of God's eternal purpose to fulfill it.

God's purpose for your life far exceeds what you could ever imagine. He's making you His heritage for His satisfaction. Which means your life is not about you. He didn't save you for you. He saved you for Himself. He chose you because He desires something from your life. The question then becomes will you accept the fuller meaning of the cross in order for God to inherit His satisfaction in you? For His satisfaction were you redeemed and not so your life can be blessed with full vats and barns. Your life now serves His greater purpose.

Will you allow God to reconstitute you entirely from the inside out according to the image and likeness of His Son? Will you allow the profound work of the cross to be worked in you? Will you follow the Lamb wherever He goes? Or will you insist on going to places you know He will not go and refuse to follow Him where He desires to lead you?

Where is the Son going? He's going to that place in space and time when the Father sums up all things in Himself and makes His people the fullness of Him that fills all things. He must go there because the Father has given Him the authority to redeem creation from the Fall's destruction. His victory at Calvary was complete, lacking nothing, but as Heir, He governs to secure what He has won. He is also establishing His victory in you, but for Him to do so, you must see your life is no longer about you but His greater purpose.

The first time John the Baptist saw Jesus, he declared to the crowds along the Jordan that Jesus was the Lamb of God who takes away the sin of the world (John 1). When the Baptist beheld Jesus the very next day, the apostle John described it this way: John the Baptist looked upon Jesus as He walked and said to his two disciples (John and Andrew), "Behold the Lamb of God." John chose the word walk to refer to how Jesus lived before God and men.

Both times John the Baptist beheld Jesus, he used similar language to define two aspects of the Lamb's nature and calling. Jesus would become the full expression of a life perfectly surrendered and submitted to God alone, and based on the perfectness of His walk, the Father would offer Him upon the same mountain where He had revealed to Abraham that He would provide for Himself a lamb.

Jesus is God's Lamb before He is ours. As God's Lamb, He fulfilled His calling by honoring all of God's rights. God does have rights, and those rights are defined as His expectation to have creation fulfill the purpose for which He created it. He sees creation, including you, as you ought to be. In the Fall, His rights were lost in man's nature and life, and in the physical creation. God's answer was to send His Lamb who, through His submission to the Father, even to death on a cross, reestablished the Father's rights upon the earth and in the lives of all believers.

God has the right to absolute, unquestioning submission. What interferes with His rights is your *self*. To deal with the *self*, He sent His Heir to reconstitute humanity on another principle—the Lamb, who laid down His *self* and gave God His rights of submission, obedience, and selflessness. The laying down of your *self* is a daily act, and because your *self* was birthed in rebellion, it constantly challenges God's rights. When you decide to give the Lord His rights above your *self's* rights, your *self* will vigorously protest, and your worldview will object to the wisdom of what you're doing.

Jesus laid down His life and was reviled. He suffered the loss of reputation and standing in the community. He endured all the power of hell to tempt Him to rebel against God and act in His self-interest. Satan constantly offered Him an easy way to escape the cross. All He had to do was put His wants and needs above the Father's glory. Jesus refused. His walk before the Father meant repudiating everything that would deny His Father His complete satisfaction. It also meant accepting the cost of His decision to live for God in a hostile world.

How did Jesus endure such temptations when we struggle to do so? The prophet Isaiah described the Lamb's nature as one that even when He was oppressed and afflicted, He opened not His mouth (Isaiah 53:7). He was under constant pressure from all sides to give in to His *self* and preserve His life, but He refused. How unlike us. When we find ourselves in similar situations, our *selves,* influenced by our worldviews, scream, "No!" and seek the first path of escape we can find to preserve our lives.

This is why it's imperative that you change your thinking and deny your *self.* So, when you find yourself in similar situations, you allow the life dwelling in you to have His way and give God His full rights. Do this, and the world will oppose you, but you'll find the Spirit's witness in your spirit. The Father desires such witnesses. Men and women who know Him because they have made it their passion to follow Him at any and every cost.

So don't stop at the first day when John the Baptist proclaimed that Jesus was God's Lamb. Don't just behold the Lamb as the sin-bearer and your ticket to heaven. See Him on the second day, living a life pleasing to the Father. He didn't come to negotiate God's will for His creation. If you stand for God's rights, people will always demand you negotiate His will with them so that they can remain the same. You can't negotiate away what doesn't belong to you. The kingdom of God isn't about you, and it isn't about them. The kingdom is about following the Lamb, so He can secure His victory and present to His Father a creation that the Father can fill with Himself.

The Spiritual Declension of the Seven Churches

Christ has become the temple, and everything that belongs to the temple must serve His revelation. Before the apostle John revealed the glory of the New Jerusalem in the book of Revelation, he introduced us to the seven churches in Asia Minor that Paul either directly or indirectly established. Paul's preaching and letters revealed God's eternal purpose. Believers throughout the region knew all God had done for them in the death and resurrection of His Son. They also knew what He expected of them as His sons and ambassadors of reconciliation. Nothing was left unsaid. Nothing remained hidden.

When the Romans exiled John to Patmos, the Lord appeared to him, standing amid seven golden lampstands, representing the seven churches that were to receive the letter (Revelation 1). Why did the Lord appear to John in such a fashion? Because He had come to judge the churches on how they lived in light of the revelation they had received.

Judgment always begins in the house of the Lord, and the churches in question were in a state of spiritual declension and no longer served their first love. False teaching had infiltrated the congregations, leading to spiritual weakness. Even though the glory of what they had received from Paul was fading, and worldliness was gaining a foothold, Jesus didn't see the believers as thoroughly corrupt. There was something He could commend them for. But on the issue of the revelation they had received, they were severely lacking. They had allowed it to be negotiated and compromised away.

Now He was judging them on this one issue and calling them to overcome the corruption that had set in. He wasn't calling them to overcome certain sins, weaknesses, faults, failures, etc. He was calling them to overcome everything opposing the fullness of the Son's image and likeness in them. An overcomer is one who comes into the value and meaning of God's eternal purpose. They come near to His heart, and He gives them the privilege of living there for eternity.

Living a life where God is satisfied is a love matter. How far will you allow your love to carry you? Will you follow Him for your convenience and ease? Or will you take up the whole issue of image and likeness and follow Him to the measure of unconstrained, uncompelled love? Will you deny your *self*, forget your *self,* and set your *self* aside for Him?

The more you seek the Lord, the deeper He will take you. The deeper He takes you, the more your *self* and worldview will be revealed. His light will shine brightly, exposing your actual condition. You'll despair of your *self* and want to draw back, but the good news of the gospel is that Christ answers to the Father on your behalf even when you want to run away and hide. The Son is enough, and because He is sufficient, you lack nothing.

God is inviting you into His whole counsel. Will you go through the narrow gate or draw back because of the cost? Will you change your thinking about your life and realize that this life you now live by faith in the Son of God is not about you?

When you were saved, that was the last time it was about you. Now, your life has a higher and deeper meaning. It's about the Father finding the full measure of His satisfaction in your life. This is why He created the heavens and the earth and sent His Lamb into the world to redeem His creation. Just as it was with Isaac, who understood that he was born to inherit God's greater purpose, so it is with you. How will you choose to live? For your *self* or His eternal purpose?

Chapter 26
TOBIAH IN THE TEMPLE

Behold, we are slaves. We are in great distress.

Nehemiah 9:36–37

MY CHILDHOOD ABUSE and trauma didn't write the story of my life. The lie that surreptitiously invaded my thinking did, until it became an indomitable stronghold in my mind. The lie could be likened to an invincible warrior who waged war against any truth that came to set me free. The lie became my *self's* identity, and my worldview made sure I remained imprisoned in the stronghold. No matter how badly I wanted to escape, the lie treated me like a dog on a leash and jerked me back to its side if I dared to believe in God's love for me.

The lie poisoned my life in two ways: Fear tormented my every waking moment and self-hatred swallowed me up and strangled Christ's work in me.

Then one night, the Lord unmasked this Tobiah who was ruining my life and threw him and his furniture out of the temple. The heavens opened and flooded my spirit with light. I wasn't worthless with no redeeming qualities as I had always believed. I had infinite value and worth to the Lord, for He had created me in His image and after His likeness.

Tobiah in the Temple

Who is Tobiah? You probably recognize his name as one of the three men (Sanballat and Geshem the Arab being the other two) who worked to prevent Nehemiah and the remnant from building the wall. He was also economically aligned with the leading noblemen and was responsible for robbing the children of Israel of their wealth, homes, farms, and, eventually, their children. He was a great adversary of Israel. When the wall was complete, Sanballat and Geshem the Arab disappeared from the Bible. Not so with Tobiah. He had a more insidious role to play in Israel's history.

When the remnant had finished the wall and set the gates in their places, securing the city from its enemies, Ezra the priest gathered the people in the temple's courtyard and read the law aloud to the assembly. When the crowds heard Ezra's words, they were cut to the heart. They repented in sackcloth and ashes, promised to keep the law, and sealed a covenant pledging themselves to the Lord.

Revival swept through the city. The people vowed to put away their foreign wives, who had introduced the worship of false gods in their households. They would no longer give their children in marriage to the peoples surrounding them. They also assumed responsibility for filling and maintaining the temple's storerooms so the priests and Levites could serve the Lord. As one, the large crowds proclaimed that they wouldn't neglect the house of God.

Artaxerxes had only given Nehemiah a limited time to get Jerusalem's house in order. When that time expired, he had to return to Susa and resume his office as the king's cupbearer. When he first arrived in Jerusalem, the people lived in a perilous state because they had no remembrance of who they were as covenant people. Now they understood that they were a people for the Lord's great name's sake. Nehemiah left Israel hopeful that the remnant would thrive and be blessed by the Lord.

The revival didn't last. The high priest Eliashib ruled over the temple, including the storerooms, now filled with provisions for the Lord's service. Scripture tells us that he was closely associated with Tobiah. What that association was, the Bible doesn't say. It does say that Eliashib emptied the storerooms of their provisions and allowed Tobiah to move in and conduct his business from the temple.

Without provisions, the Levites could no longer remain in Jerusalem. They scattered into the surrounding countryside to cultivate farmland, grow crops, and feed their families. All worship at the temple came to a halt. The people drifted away from the law and forgot their promise to serve the Lord. Corruption crept back into the land, bringing with it dangerous times. The wall stood and the gates remained, but it was as if Nehemiah had never come to the city.

When word reached Nehemiah that the remnant was in trouble, he went to Artaxerxes and asked permission to return to Jerusalem. Artaxerxes agreed, so Nehemiah left immediately. It was only after he saw the Levites working in the fields instead of ministering in the temple did he fully understand Eliashib's betrayal of the covenant the people had signed and sealed just a few years before.

Nehemiah went straight to the temple and threw Tobiah and his furniture from the occupied storerooms. He ordered the Levites to cleanse and refill the empty chambers with provisions. He found the temple's vessels that had been discarded and restored them to their proper place. He gathered Jerusalem's leadership and demanded, "Why is the house of God forsaken?" He dismissed them from their administrative posts and replaced them with men he could trust to uphold the covenant the people had made. He also established new treasurers to oversee the temple's storerooms and distribute food to the priests and Levites.

When Tobiah was able to convince or coerce Eliashib into allowing him to usurp the temple's purpose for his own, there was no one with authority to stop Eliashib from doing so. Tobiah had revealed himself to be the people's enemy while they worked to rebuild the wall, even threatening to murder them if they didn't stop. None of that seemed to matter to Eliashib. He allowed Tobiah to pervert the temple from a place of worship to a place of commerce.

Unfortunately, for many Christians, Tobiah resides in their temple, subverting God's purpose for their lives. They don't recognize him because he secretly took up residence before they were saved. His influence on their *selves* damaged their worldview. If Christians don't understand the importance of changing their thinking, he will remain ensconced in their temples. He is a hireling and a false teacher who robs Christians of their identity. Until he is dealt with, he remains in control.

Tobiah in My Heart

I know Tobiah personally. He lived in my temple for most of my Christian life. He was responsible for the utter chaos that churned inside me. His lie took my *self* captive and poisoned my worldview. I have waited until now to give you my testimony so I could reveal Tobiah as the scoundrel he is and the need for believers to cast him out of their temple.

My childhood was rough. I was caught between two parents who had no affection for each other. As seniors in high school, they had been a couple, but after they graduated they had fought and broken up. Soon after their split my mother discovered she was pregnant, and in the 1950s, if a man got a girl pregnant, he married her. The last thing my father wanted to do was marry. He made plans to enlist in the Navy, but his grandmother (who had raised him) told him he had to do the responsible thing, which he did in October 1958. The union was doomed from the start. It didn't help that they quickly added two children into the mix.

My father wanted the one thing he never had in his young life—control. Now he had two small children he could dominate, which he did through fear and violence. My mother also had a mean streak, but her malice was more covert. When my father was on a rampage, she served my brother and me up on the altar of his temper by deflecting his anger onto something we had done wrong. She saved these infractions until she needed them.

Her strategy worked. His anger zeroed in on a new target, and he would explode in rage. My mother never defended us. She never took our side. She abandoned us to face his anger alone. For as long as I can remember, all her maternal instinct and care were reserved for her many dogs. They were the objects of her love and came first every time. My brother and I were secondary in her thoughts.

I know now that both my parents were dry cups. Who can gain anything of value from a dry cup? They were products of their upbringing and were ill-equipped to deal with the consequences of their behavior. They desperately needed love but didn't know where to find it. So they took their frustrations and disappointments out on their children, who couldn't fight back.

This meant that instead of maturing into a well-adjusted teenager and then a young adult like my friends, I didn't because my self-esteem was severely damaged. Remember when I wrote that your worldview does one of two things? It will either defend or blame you. My worldview held me responsible for the violence happening around me. I, alone, was the reason I was constantly afraid, because I was nothing but a screw-up. No matter how hard I tried not to provoke my father's wrath, I still provoked it, and the beatings were severe.

I was playing outside with my friends during one hot summer evening when I heard him call my name. As I ran up the hill toward home, I saw he was in a great rage. I searched my mind trying to figure out what I had done to deserve the whipping I knew was coming, but I couldn't think of anything. He shoved me into a bedroom, made me lean over the bed, and picked up his wide leather belt. I had on shorts, and my legs were bare. They would feel the full impact of every swing.

My father had some rules when he was spanking us. If we flinched before the belt made contact, we were rewarded with two more swats. Not flinching when I knew what was coming was something I could never master. I tried, but I flinched and flinched every time. The beatings I received that particular time kept increasing. His other rule had to do with my reaction. He would hit me harder if I didn't cry enough, but if I cried too much, he would really give me something to cry about. There was a secret sweet spot that consisted of the right amount of tears and remorse. I had to find it if I had any hope of escaping the bedroom. The quicker, the better.

I blew by the sweet spot that day because my poor little legs were on fire. I heard the front door open. My mother had come home. Perhaps she would save me. I don't know why I entertained that hope. She had never saved me before, but I was desperate. She came to the bedroom door and said with a sneer, "If you're going to hit her that hard, then close the windows so the neighbors don't hear her." Then she disappeared. I was alone. The whipping continued until he ran out of strength. He dismissed me.

I ran out of the house searching for a hiding place. The backs of my legs were on fire, and I could feel the welts the belt had left. The next day, there would be terrible bruising that all my friends would see and ignore. None of my friends' parents ever said anything. I always wondered why they never did. Perhaps it was just a part of that generation's worldview to never interfere with another family's child-rearing.

Sitting in my hiding place, I felt tremendous anger at my father. I never knew what I had done to deserve my punishment. I considered it unfair to be beaten without knowing what I did, but what could I do? The beating would have been more severe if I hadn't come when he called me. I was also angry at my mother's callousness in the face of my suffering, but I believed I had been wrong to expect her to help me.

I reserved my greatest anger for myself. The beating was all my fault. I was responsible for ensuring that I never gave my father cause to be angry with me. It was my fault that I couldn't stop myself from flinching or crying out in pain. It was my fault that I couldn't live without bringing such wrath down on my head. If only I could be perfect. If only I could be who he wanted me to be, there would be peace and security. Peace and security in the house, and peace and security within myself.

As I dried my tears, I realized the beatings would never stop because I couldn't change who I was. I was a failure. Deep down to my toes, I knew this was a truth about me. I deserved the whippings because my flaws and shortcomings provoked my father's anger and my mother's indifference. If my parents ever said anything nice to me (and I'm sure they did), I don't remember. Most of the time, all I heard was that I was a constant disappointment. After that night, I knew I would continually disappoint everyone who came into my life.

I also learned to be afraid that day. A spirit of fear took control of my soul. This fear had nothing to do with what was happening in the house. This fear permeated my worldview, and when I saw the world, I saw people who would soon discover that I was a failure and abandon me for my failings. So I would beat them to the punch. I would hate myself more. That way, when they no longer wanted to be my friends, it wouldn't hurt as much. I believed they were only leaving me because I deserved to be friendless. I deserved every bad thing that came my way because losers never win.

The typical failures young adults go through as they begin to navigate through life threw me into cycles of frustration, despair, and depression. I didn't see my mistakes as learning opportunities. I saw them as proof that I was damaged beyond repair. I couldn't even look at myself in the mirror without wanting to hurt the person looking back. I called myself horrible names and told myself that the one thing I could do to improve this world was kill myself, but I was too afraid to try.

Then one day, when I was in my late teens, my father came home from work. He worked the midnight shift for an automaker, and you could set your clock by his arrival home. I was in my room. I was awake, but I hadn't made an appearance yet. According to the little red cube alarm clock sitting on my nightstand, it was 8:40 a.m.

My father opened the linen closet door right next to my closed bedroom door to grab a towel so he could shower. He asked my mother if I was awake. She said no. I didn't say anything. Then I heard it. These words would seal my identity for the next thirty-nine years: "What a worthless piece of human flesh."

A knife went straight into my soul. His words didn't produce anything new in me. What they did was crystallize and harden what I already believed about myself. I now had words to define my thoughts since that long summer day when I hid from the world and blamed myself for being so terribly beaten. I *was* a worthless piece of human flesh. I didn't know it then, but Tobiah had just set up residence in my soul and took great pleasure in twisting my worldview. When I was saved three years later, he would move his furniture into the temple and subvert God's work in my heart.

When I was saved, I wasn't taught about identity. What I was taught, whether pastors and teachers meant to or not, was that I wasn't good enough for God and never could be because I had this thing called a sin nature that held me captive. This teaching served as just another confirmation that I was worthless. I never learned about justification. I never learned that the old man died in Christ. I never learned that a new creation was a new species. I never learned why I was created. I saw Christianity as a bunch of spoken and unspoken rules that needed to be followed if I was ever going to get God to love me as He loved other Christians.

I was as insecure as Saul and just as tormented. I spent my life ricocheting between two fearful extremes. The first fear: I was so transparent that everyone could see how worthless I was. The second fear: I needed to prove, by any means necessary, that I had value in myself and value to the people I was interacting with. These fears caused me to be unstable in all my ways. Fear poisoned everything. My life became a self-fulfilling prophecy. I constantly overreached my abilities and knowledge, and I fell apart when I was caught out.

My Christian life became a masquerade. I didn't know the Lord. I just knew things about Him. That didn't mean I didn't love Him. Instead of building my house on His Word, I built on a foundation of great fear and self-pity. Sooner or later, He would have no choice but to throw His hands up in despair and finally say those words I dreaded to hear: "You *are* a worthless piece of human flesh." I tried to hold that day at bay by pretending everything was fine. But who can bear a crushed spirit (Proverbs 18:14)?

I knew people who had wonderful calls on their lives. To my warped thinking, a calling meant that God really loved you, and so did other people. To watch these people go into a room, be the center of attention, and be so loved was more than I could stand. I wanted to be loved too. So I called myself to all different types of ministries. I finally wound up in the mission field in Bangkok, Thailand, working with child prostitutes on Patpong Road. I was ill-equipped to deal with the demonic powers that ruled over the country. They chewed me up and spat me out until I retreated to America with my tail between my legs. My worldview poured its vitriol out on me. I was tormented day and night. I believed I was so worthless that I should just kill myself and rid the world of this terrible failure.

I fell into a deep depression. I lay on my couch and ate my weight in birthday cake. I went to work, came home, laid on the couch, and ate my weight in birthday cake for the next five years. Bangkok was the final blow. In heaven, God had finally uttered those dreadful words. I truly was a worthless piece of human flesh. Fourteen years would pass before I would pick up a Bible or utter another prayer.

Fourteen years is a long time for silence, but that was how I lived. During the great recession, I lost my job and couldn't find another one. I had a toothache, but I didn't have any insurance. I didn't know what I was going to do. I had run out of savings, and unemployment wasn't enough to live on. It paid the rent and left enough money to buy some cheap food. My tooth was killing me. I searched the yellow pages for a dentist to treat my tooth for free. I didn't find one, but I kept reading ads for a healthcare credit card that was welcomed in dentists' offices throughout the city. I didn't think a bank would give me a credit card, but I applied anyway.

An hour later, I received an email asking me to call the bank's customer service. I knew they were turning me down, but I called anyway. They informed me that my application had been accepted and they would give me more credit than requested. I hung up the phone, and for the first time in fourteen years, I heard the Lord speak, "I see you. I hear you. I care for you."

You would think those words would have been enough to revolutionize my life. They did for a while, but Tobiah reasserted his authority over my *self* and worldview, which was easy for him to do since I was ignorant of his constant presence in the temple. God may have seen, heard, and cared for me, but Tobiah reminded me that God could never love me.

God Speaks to Me

I was saved in November 1982. In November 2017, I was praying when the atmosphere shifted. I was still in my living room, but at the same time I was standing before the Lord, who was seated on His Bema throne. He spoke only one sentence: "You have squandered your life." I wanted to protest, but my words died in my throat. I knew what He had spoken was true. I had been saved for thirty-five years, and the result of all that I did or didn't do was summed up in the word *squandered*.

For the next seven months, I cried tears of repentance. I withdrew from everything but work. His words offered me a second chance, which I wanted to avail myself of, but I didn't know how. My life was still under Tobiah's influence, but God was at work. I asked the Lord for a teacher to tell me how to stop squandering my life. The next day, my YouTube feed was filled with videos featuring sermons from one teacher. I had never witnessed my feed do that before, so I listened to one sermon, then another, then another. The teacher's grasp of the gospel made my heart burn. I may not have understood all his teachings, but I knew He was speaking the truth. I saw he had also taught at a Bible school, and there were over fifty-two videos available. Each class was almost three hours long, so I had to listen in the morning before work, during lunch, and as soon as I got home from work. I couldn't get enough.

I had listened to this man's sermons for about a month when God unexpectedly turned on His exposure light. Not on me, but on Tobiah, the

206

thief that had stolen from me and was killing and destroying my life. In one clarifying and joyful moment, I saw I was not worthless to Him. I had never been worthless. My father's words were a lie from the pit of hell. My heavenly Father had sent His Son to die for me so I could know just how much I was loved. I wasn't created for my pain and self-loathing. I was made in His image and after His likeness. His purpose wasn't for me to live for myself but for His great name's sake. I was created to be a son of God, and under no circumstance had He ever considered me a worthless piece of human flesh.

It was a miracle. Tobiah had been vanquished from my temple along with his furniture. By the Lord's provision, my temple was cleansed and the vessels restored. I felt as if I had been born again. The Spirit of wisdom and revelation filled my spirit. I repented, but instead of crying tears and remaining the same person I had always been, I changed my thinking about everything. I buried my old man in an unmarked grave. I walked away and left him there, forsaken and abandoned. I put on the new man and consecrated this second chance to the Lord. I saw the Scriptures in a new light. Suddenly, they weren't words Tobiah used to condemn and harass me. They were filled with Spirit and life.

The Lord had work to do in me. I had lived so long for myself that my *self* and worldview still influenced me more than they should. I could feel the sting of rejection. Like Naaman, I didn't like when I was ignored. I still carried a sense of injustice in my soul. But if I was to follow the Lamb wherever He goes, I knew I had to deny my loss, my pain, and any sense of injustice I still harbored. Only what belonged to Christ could go through the narrow gate. It was and still is a process, sometimes a very painful one. Still, with the Holy Spirit exposing why I react the way I do in certain situations and comforting me when I repent, I am continually set free to pursue Him.

Finding My Purpose

I also knew one other thing. I didn't want any other child of God to live as I had. I didn't want anyone else to live with debilitating fear that torments the soul. I didn't want anyone else to be forced to live with Tobiah's lies so he could gain access to God's temple and subvert it for his use. I wanted to go to God's children and tell them all He has done for them so they could throw off their burden of guilt and shame. I wanted to tell them their chains have been broken and their prison doors stand wide open. I wanted them to know that all He accomplished on the cross has completely saved them. They don't have to work for His approval. They are redeemed, justified, and stand before Him holy, blameless, and above reproach. Yes, I know I have used that phrase many times in this book, but I use it because it is a glorious description of who I am in Him.

I implored the Lord to send someone to tell His children this truth. Someone who will love them enough to turn His exposure light on Tobiah and throw him out of their temples. Only Nehemiah had the authority with the people to go against the organized religious spirits of the day. I prayed that He would raise up Nehemiahs in this generation and send them to His children who struggle with disappointment, regret, and grief—send them so His sons could walk in the newness of life Jesus died for them to have.

In response to my prayers, I received this book. Everything the Lord has taught me since the day He set me free from the lies I believed about myself, I have written down in the hopes that it will help you to pursue His eternal purpose for your life. And in your pursuit, you'll come to know and live in the truth that when He sees you, He sees the one He has set His heart upon.

Chapter 27
YEAH, BUT . . .

"No one who puts his hand to the plow and looks back is fit for the kingdom of God."

Luke 9:62

HAVE YOU EVER asked, "Why don't I have the life I want in the Lord?" The answer is simple. You don't have it because you're content to live without that life. But I don't think it's on purpose. I think it's because you haven't understood how your worldview works to keep you from stepping into all the Lord would have for you. For want of discernment on this matter, many of the Lord's people are rendered helpless, impotent, and bewildered. Your worldview and born-again spirit are in a real battle for control of your life.

Revisiting the Consequences of the Fall

By now, you know that your worldview is a product of the Fall and all the harm this world's system has inflicted upon your *self*. Your *self* seeks one thing—love. God created man after His image, and Scripture tells us that God's nature or image is love (1 John 4:16). When man fell, he fell from love to selfishness. Instead of being love as God is love, he found himself in desperate need of love.

Man's idea of love is severely handicapped, for whoever loves him must fulfill all the deep-seated needs within him created by the Fall. This presents a grave problem. For within himself, fallen man cannot meet another person's needs, for he is too needy himself. The moment the object of man's love disappoints him by failing to meet his need to be loved the way he believes he is entitled to be loved, he withdraws his affections and searches for a new person to meet his needs.

One of the Fall's consequences was that the soul (reason, desire, and will) was exalted from its natural place and made to function independently of God. Before the Fall, Adam didn't have to sit down and reason out what God was saying. He didn't have to have committee meetings with his friends to determine what God wanted him to do. His ability to perceive, sense, and intuitively know what God was speaking resided in his spirit. When he fell, his spirit died, leaving him no way to commune deeply with the Lord. He became a man governed and motivated by his *self*. He is a creature of reason, logic, and analysis, which causes him to be easily deceived.

The Desire to Be Loved

The reason you can be so easily deceived is because the *self* is determined to adhere to its opinion on any subject. Since your *self* believes it is the sole authority on what you need to be happy, it doesn't submit its opinions to any court but the court of its judgment. Paul described this lack of submission as carnality, or the natural man. If your natural man (your determination not to submit your opinions to God's Word) rules in you, you'll lack the power to perceive or discern what is of God and what's not of God.

This is the battle. This is where all your "yeah, buts" come from. You don't understand the battle raging in you and this world. You don't make the distinction between what is God's thought against what is your thought. What is God's reasoning against what is your reasoning? In fact, you can be so deceived that you make your reasoning God's reasoning. For example, you may meet someone unsuitable for you, but your *self* tricks you into believing it is God's will that you marry this person because He wants you to be happy.

No, He doesn't want your happiness. He wants your joy. You'll never find true joy, peace, and rest until you realize that your needs come from the Fall, not the new birth. The natural man doesn't receive the things of God, for they are foolishness to him (1 Corinthians 2:14).

Your flesh (the natural or carnal man) and spirit man belong to two different realms. Your flesh belongs to the realm of darkness because of the Fall. It thinks, acts, needs, and wants certain things because it has been taught that they are good and necessary for survival. Again, going back to chapter 1, your worldview has been homeschooled in the wrong home. Your spirit is from heaven and has the destiny of image and likeness written over it. The kingdom of darkness and the kingdom of God are in great conflict. Because you have left one kingdom and have been translated into another, that conflict is now engaged inside of you.

Satan would have you believe that because there is conflict, there must be something wrong. But there's not. God's light, life, and love have come to renew your thinking so that you no longer think destructive thoughts that keep you from your destiny. His light is always positive, but it also means you can't remain neutral. Divine life is not just theology and teaching. It's a menace to the kingdom of darkness. Satan will see it smothered out. His best weapons to do so have already been installed in you: your worldview and the *self's* desperate need for love.

You manifest your need for love in selfishness. It's all about you. "What about what I want? What about what I need? What about me?" You demand someone see you and accept you for who you are. You don't want to change. Not really. You don't want to have to wear the carefully crafted mask you hide behind. You want to be free to have someone love you despite your weaknesses, failures, and faults. You've hidden away so much of your authentic *self.* You desire validation because you exist.

Sometimes you don't see any value or worth in yourself, and that's when you need someone to come alongside you and tell you, "You're okay." That need is an unquenchable thirst. Unfortunately, the current validation only lasts until you run into another person who speaks an unkind word. Then you need someone else to tell you that you have value and worth, which only lasts until someone speaks harshly to you. Off you go to find validation again. "Someone, anyone, tell me I'm okay." You would give everything to love and be loved in return.

Here's why you live with so much disappointment. Because while that's what you're looking for in a person, that person is looking for the same thing from you. Neither of you can meet the demands of the other because of the selfishness in the *self.* You live at the expense of each other, trying to quench that thirst. When you're hurt, your natural inclination is to return the hurt. You live eye for an eye, tooth for a tooth. Someone is rude to you, and it permits you to be rude in return. If you're under pressure or stress, that pressure or stress justifies when you lash out. We withhold or even withdraw our love to punish the one who failed to meet our needs. People weren't put on this earth to meet our needs, because they can't.

So much of Christian preaching today leaves you with the identity of sinners. Forgiven sinners, but sinners nonetheless. That's the beginning and end of your story. It's a wonder the Lord even loves you, considering what a wretch you are. This teaching reinforces your belief that you have no value or worth to the Lord. What an injustice this teaching has done to you.

Finding Your Value in Christ

Your fight is not with sin. You're dead to it. The true fight of faith is believing the Lord knows your value and your worth. That's why when a message that emphasizes your value to the Lord is preached or taught, your *self* cries out, "Yeah, but..." Those "yeah, buts" are the *self* taking its experience and opinions and exalting them above God's Word. The *self* is taking all the rejection it has suffered and letting those rejections determine its value and worth. Your worldview instructs the *self* not to listen because a message of value and worth will only end in more disappointment. There always comes a time when the *self* can't absorb any more disappointments and will choose to live isolated and alone.

You have a created value. The Lord is very clear. You were created in His image and after His likeness. That alone makes you valuable. That alone gives you worth. Now you must do the most challenging part. You must believe that you—even the you that you may not like—has value and worth in Him. You must silence the "yeah, buts" and believe you are who He says you are, even in the face of what life says about you. You're not your past. You're not the sum of all your bad decisions.

You must stop finding your value in other people and the things of this world. You must find your value in Christ crucified and Christ crucified alone. Only Christ can meet the needs of the *self*. Only Christ can teach you how to love and be loved in return. Only Christ can free you from your worldview and give you a kingdom view. Only Christ can finally silence the "yeah, buts" that keep you bound and looking for love in all the wrong places.

If you had no value or worth, why would God send His Son into this world to die such a brutal death? If you had no value or worth, why would God unite you in His Son's death so that you could be freed from your *self* and its worldview? If you had no value or worth, why would God ever adopt you and call you His son? He did all those things because you do have value, and you do have worth. He wanted you. As I have written before, and it bears repeating, you were His choice from the beginning. God has not changed His mind about you. Never once did the thought enter His mind to abandon you because you were unlovable. Never once. Your value and worth were established in heaven before He created the world.

Walking Worthy of Christ

God knows the true you. The you He created you to be. The Fall has been dealt with. The old man has been buried with Christ. The new man is alive. He is saved to the uttermost. He is justified. He is made righteous. He stands in heaven before His Father, holy, blameless, and beyond reproach. He has a new life and an eternal identity of image and likeness.

As early as Genesis 1:26, God told you who you are and your value and worth to Him. Then came all the other voices with a thousand different identities for you. Which identity will you choose—who you were from the beginning, or one of the countless other identities that will always leave you lacking?

The prophet Hosea said that God's people were destroyed for lack of knowledge (Hosea 4:6). That part of the verse gets quoted quite a bit. The next part of the verse doesn't. We are destroyed because we have rejected knowledge. We have rejected what God said about us in Genesis 1:26. We think the Fall changed everything—it permanently changed us from sons to sinners. So we live in the identity of a sinner saved by grace, waiting for the day we finally make it to heaven. Even if that means we live in misery for the rest of our time on earth because this false identity of a sinner being foisted upon us is an ill-fitting garment that will never answer the *self's* need for love.

Yeah, But . . .

It's not God's will that this conflict should go in perpetuity. In the new birth, the Father is developing the mind of Christ in you, so you can know how He thinks, judges, and understands. This new mind must begin with how He views you. You are His temple, His dwelling place, and He paid the highest price to inhabit you.

"Yeah, but..."

"Yeah, but" nothing. This is the truth. And your life will only change when you start believing it. Even after reading this, if you still believe that you're just a sinner, a loser, you will produce the fruit of a sinner and the fruit of a loser. Either make the tree good or make the tree bad. How you see the tree determines the fruit.

You need to take hold of Christ's risen life deliberately. Until you do, you won't understand who you are and the value He placed on you when He created you. You must allow Him to smite your worldview with the cross. You inherited your worldview from Adam, and Adam is the problem.

Once God expelled him from the garden, Adam was lost. He no longer knew who he was and allowed this world's system to tell him. But God remembered. God knew. In the fullness of time, He sent His Son into the world to restore what had been lost: image and likeness. Then came the day when you were saved, and, at that moment, God remembered who you were and the value He has for you.

You must allow Him to break all of Adam's wrong tendencies to keep you insecure about who you are and running to the world to find out. Remember Jacob at Jabbok. All his cunning had brought him to despair. God struck the sinew of his thigh so he would have to look at the condition of his life. When he confessed he was Jacob, God changed his identity and value. No longer was he a usurper, someone who lived by the rightness of his opinions. He was now Israel, a prince with God.

So, don't remain in your allegiance with Adam. Give Christ your allegiance. The choice is ever before you. When you were saved, the Father didn't remove your mind, will, or worldview. He freed you so you can choose the good and reject the evil. In choosing, you are transformed, so there is no longer a mixture of the natural man and spiritual man.

Mixture is abhorrent to God. That's why He crucified the old man in Christ, so the old could be set aside forever. That's why I stand firmly against the teaching that you're *just* a sinner saved by grace, for this

214

teaching allows the Christian to mix the old man and the new man. There was a mixture in Noah's day, and God's judgment on that mixture was the flood.

The law of the Spirit of life demands you are wholly for God or the law cannot operate. His life moves along the lines of what belongs to God. It won't compromise and allow the natural man to mix with the spiritual man. Don't bring Christ down from His throne to make Him less than He is so you can still have what you want and desire. Don't squander your life trying to live in both worlds simultaneously. It won't work, and you're the one being harmed, for your spiritual growth will be arrested and hindered.

"Yeah but…"

Silencing Your Worldview

What does God say? What has He revealed in His Son? What does Christ crucified say about His kind intentions toward you? He paid the highest price so you could enter your destiny and walk worthy of Him. It's not a struggle. It's a daily choice. If you follow Jesus wherever He goes, you must deny your *self* and its needs. You must take up your cross and stop listening to your worldview. You must come after Him and walk the way of the Lamb. It is the way back to the Father. It's the life He predestined for you to inherit. It is the truth of who He is in you and who you are in Him.

Chapter 28
ON EARTH AS IT IS HEAVEN

"The Philistines are upon you, Samson!"

Judges 16:20

PURE GOLD, TRANSPARENT as glass. This descriptive phrase describes the New Jerusalem, a city that is filled with His image and likeness everywhere you look. This is the fullness that has always been His purpose for our lives. Whether we know it or not, how we conduct ourselves in this present age has always been a matter of how it touches the Father's glory. The impression we make on others, what they see in us and about us, must never, for one moment, veil God's glory, hide His glory, or detrimentally affect His glory.

This is our upward calling in Christ Jesus (Philippians 3:14). To reflect well on the Father and the testimony we carry. This is our good fight He has called us to win. If we don't understand the importance of the fight, the kingdom of darkness will see us undone and His testimony sullied and ruined.

Samson

The story of Samson is a cautionary tale from the time of the judges. The people had entered the land but hadn't driven out the former inhabitants as the Lord commanded, so the enemy remained within Israel's borders. Joshua had died and, with him, any form of government over the tribes. The Israelites felt insecure in the land. They witnessed the nations surrounding their cities and towns sacrificing to many gods who protected every aspect of their lives, whether good or bad. The people asked themselves what were the wisdom and benefits of worshiping only one God when you could worship them all. So the people forsook the Lord and served the Baals, the gods of the Canaanites.

God judged the people by giving them into the hands of the nations they had failed to drive out. Their enemies oppressed them on every side, and the people were helpless as the former inhabitants slowly reconquered the territory the people had won under Joshua. Instead of repenting, they settled down into what little the enemy would allow them to have. They could only stand by helplessly and watch as the nations stole their lands, homes, cities, harvests, flocks, and even their children, who became spoils of war and were sold into slavery.

They cried out to God for deliverance only when their misery was too much to bear. In faithfulness and mercy, God raised up judges, mighty warriors anointed for battle. While the judge lived, the people dwelled safely in their borders. Once the judge died, the people began the cycle over again. They would forsake the Lord to worship the Baals.

Of all the nations surrounding Israel, the Philistines were the most oppressive. They ruled over southern Israel for forty years and forbade the Israelites from making weapons of war. The people weren't even permitted to sharpen their farming instruments and had to bring their tools to Philistine blacksmiths to be honed. The Philistines demonstrated great skill in manufacturing iron weapons, which allowed them to create and maintain the strongest standing army in Canaan. At harvest, the Philistines departed their strongholds and raided the surrounding countryside, confiscating all the crops Israel had just reaped, leaving the people starving and destitute.

Samson and the Philistines

During a time of great distress, the angel of the Lord appeared to Manoah's barren wife and promised that she would have a son (Judges 13). He commanded her not to drink wine or strong drink or eat anything unclean. As her son grew up, she wasn't to cut his hair, for he would be a Nazirite for the entirety of his life. A Nazirite was a person who was set apart for the Lord's service (Numbers 6:1–21). The Lord consecrated Samson to provoke and defeat the Philistines. When he went into battle, he wasn't alone. The Spirit of the Lord rushed upon him and gave him supernatural strength.

217

Samson won many victories over the Philistines, but he had a great weakness, which would ultimately be his undoing. He loved and trusted the wrong women. One day, he saw a young Philistine woman and begged his father to arrange a marriage (Judges 14). During the wedding feast, Samson told her kinsmen a riddle and promised if they could solve it before the celebration ended, he would reward them handsomely. When the riddle proved too difficult for the young men, they went to the bride and convinced her to extract the answer from Samson and tell them so they would win the prize.

She begged and cajoled him with tears and sobs to tell her the answer. When he refused, she pouted and refused to talk to him. Samson held out until the seventh day, but he couldn't withstand her tears any longer. He told her the answer, which she promptly told her kinsmen. As the feast was drawing to a close, the Philistines triumphantly solved the riddle. Humiliated by his wife's betrayal, he left the feast in a rage, went down to Ashkelon, a Philistine city, and killed thirty men. He returned and gave their garments to the wedding guests.

Samson and Delilah

Years later, Samson would fall in love again. Delilah lived in the Valley of Sorek (Judges 16). When the village elders heard that Samson was visiting her, they promised her one thousand pieces of silver if she could discover the source of his strength. For three days, she asked him; for three days, he lied; for three days, she betrayed him by binding him in the way he described; and for three days, she called to the Philistines hiding in her room to seize him. Each time, Samson rose and shook himself. The Spirit rushed upon him, and he defeated his would-be captors.

After the first time I was betrayed, I would have probably ended the relationship, but Samson wasn't me. Delilah employed the same tactics his young wife had used to obtain the answer to the riddle. She cried, pouted, and pressed him into revealing his secret. When he couldn't stand her nagging any longer, he told her the truth. If anyone shaved the seven braids from his head, his strength would abandon him because he was a Nazirite.

The following day, Delilah went to the elders and assured them that Samson had told her the truth this time. If they came to her home tonight, they could capture him. After Samson fell asleep with his head on her knees, she summoned a barber to cut off his braids. When the man had finished and safely retreated from her house, she cried, "The Philistines are upon you, Samson!"

Then a great tragedy. The glory had departed, but Samson was unaware. He believed he could rouse himself to battle as he had done countless times before and defeat the enemy. His strength had vanished. The Philistines captured him, clapped him in irons, and imprisoned him. They gouged out his eyes and put him to work as a beast of burden grinding grain.

To celebrate their great victory, the Philistines held a feast in honor of Dagon, their national god. In their merriment, the people called for Samson to be brought out of prison to entertain them. He was led into the arena by a small boy. Samson asked the lad to chain him to one of the pillars underneath the balcony where the people were feasting. The Philistines mocked and scorned him, but they failed to notice his hair had begun to grow out. Samson cried out to God to strengthen him one last time. If the Lord would have mercy on him, he would make such an end to the Philistines and to himself by pulling the porch down on top of him. The Lord granted his prayer. In his last battle against the Philistines, Samson killed more of them than he had in all his previous battles combined.

It is a terrible thing to have the glory go and be unaware. The prophet Ezekiel witnessed the glory depart from Jerusalem. As God's presence lifted from the Mercy Seat, the cloud and brightness of His glory filled the temple and moved to the threshold. There it rested for a moment before moving to the temple's east gate. Once again, the glory waited but only briefly. Then a national tragedy. The glory departed, and no one noticed.

Why? Because the people foolishly believed that God would never abandon Jerusalem. It was the same deception Samson believed. He told Delilah the source of his strength because he believed he could command the Spirit at will. He didn't think his behavior would ever disqualify him.

Israel's Infidelity

Throughout their history, Israel shared Samson's worldview. They worshiped false gods, even bringing their images into the temple. They did so because they believed God's glory could never depart the temple. As long as His presence rested above the Mercy Seat, they were safe from the consequences of their behavior.

But the glory did depart, and they were oblivious. How casual Israel was with the things of God. It's almost too sad to write. God chose Israel from all the world's nations as His chosen people and special treasure. He gave them a land, a city (Jerusalem), and a temple. He was their Father, and they were His sons. He wanted to pour His love out on them with such blessing that the nations would be drawn to Jerusalem to worship this awesome God who loved His people with such a fierce love that the English language can't describe it. The nations would cast aside their false gods to worship the living God because they had discovered He would love them just as fiercely as He did His people.

How did Israel's history end? God sent His prophets to warn the people that unless they repented, God would judge them for their idolatry. They ignored the prophets' warnings, secure in the knowledge that they were Abraham's descendants and the land was their everlasting possession. Therefore, they would live their lives as they saw fit, turning only to the Lord in times of national emergencies. The day came when they did cry out, but it was too late, just as it was with Samson. Their sin had disqualified them. They could only watch helplessly as the Babylonians captured Jerusalem and burned the temple.

The only thing worse than being ignorant of the glory's departure is to be so impervious to spiritual things that you aren't even aware when the glory returns. God's glory did return, as promised, to Jerusalem in the Son of God. What would Jesus find when He went up to the temple? Would He find a repentant people waiting and welcoming Him? Sadly, no. He found a religious leadership that wanted no part of His kingdom because it meant the demise of theirs. The glory demanded fidelity and loyalty, but the priests were only loyal to themselves. So they rejected His claims and lived as if the temple would stand forever.

Jesus lamented their choice, "O Jerusalem, Jerusalem, the city that kills the prophets and stones those who are sent to it! How often would I have gathered your children together as a hen gathers her brood under her wings, and you were not willing!" (Matthew 23:37)

God defines *glory* as the fullness of His nature expressed in His creation. Adam was called to carry His glory into all the world, so God could fill all and be in all. After Adam fell, God didn't change His definition of glory. He sent His Son into the world to show us who we were created to be. We were born again to take up His glory so He can realize His purpose to fill all and be in all.

The Bride and a City Revealed

In Revelation, the apostle John was carried away in the Spirit to a great, holy mountain and shown the Bride, the wife of the Lamb. I wonder if John was surprised that the angel didn't show him a woman but a city. He saw the New Jerusalem coming down out of heaven, having the glory of God. The city carried with it God's blessing because the city expressed the fullness of His nature.

Two things stand out in John's description of the city. The first is that the city shone with the glory of God, and its radiance was like a jasper (Revelation 21:11). When John saw the throne of God in Revelation 4:1, he beheld that the One sitting on the throne had the appearance of a jasper stone. God's throne is the place from whence He governs and judges according to the standard of His nature. The main characteristic of the jasper stone is that it's like a diamond, clear as crystal. When He judges, He does so with a truth that doesn't change over time.

The city shone like a jasper stone, and the walls were also made of jasper. Within the walls, His sons live peacefully with Him, for the city has no temple. God is free to dwell among his people. On the other side of the wall is everything unclean, and anyone who does what is detestable or false (Revelation 21:27).

When Pilate asked Jesus, "What is truth?" (John 18:38), he was confessing that there were many truths in the world. So what is wrong with picking the truth that suits your life and living by it? *Everything* is wrong with that worldview. Men doing what is right in their eyes is responsible for all the terrible tragedies that have occurred in man's history. Right now, creation groans under the weight of subjective truth. Only God's truth can overcome the lie Satan told Adam in the garden.

The second thing that stood out in John's description was the city was pure gold, transparent as glass. When I first read that description, it confused me. How can gold be transparent as glass? I did some research and discovered that the purer gold becomes, the more transparent it becomes. Gold that is one hundred percent purified is clear as glass. Gold in the Bible represents love, and Jesus defined pure love as love that lays down its life for its friends (John 15:13). The New Jerusalem exists because Jesus of Nazareth loved us and gave His life for us.

There's no sun or moon in the city, for the glory of God has become its only light, and the Lamb is the lamp. Christ's nature is pure gold, transparent as glass, and the glory that pours forth from Him has no variation or shadow due to change (James 1:17).

God's Will for Your Life

It is the Lord's will to bring the New Jerusalem's purity into your life so the world can be filled with His glory as He always purposed. He works to refine you until you, too, are pure gold, transparent as glass. This way, His life, truth, and love can shine brightly through you without refraction, distortion, or diminishment. The greatest obstacle He faces in purifying your temple is the *self* and its worldview. Given a choice, the *self* will refuse to lay down its life every time. If you have any hope of shining with His glory, then you must deny your *self*, take up your cross, and follow Him.

The refusal to deny your *self* robs your life of glory. Samson refused to deny his *self*, and the glory left. Israel refused to deny their selves, and the glory departed. God's commandments are not optional. You can't go into the world to find love and fulfillment and expect the Lord to go with you and bless you. You can't keep living the way you've always lived and hope somehow, someway, things will change. Will you hold onto your worldview, or will you change what you see and how you think about what you see? Your spiritual growth from childhood to a mature son depends on it.

It's time to go deeper than you've ever gone before. To go further into the Lord than you've ever gone before. To do so, you must stop thinking about where you've been and what you've done. Those things no longer matter unless you allow them to matter more than what He says.

What do you see when you look in the mirror? What do you see when you look in His Word? Which view is ruling you today? The mirror or the Word? You won't grow spiritually if you don't see His eternal purpose for you. But if you can see and believe all He says about you, you will be transformed, for you're transformed as you behold Him.

The Bride, the wife of the Lamb, has been made so pure that she has no corruption or death left in her. There is not even the taint of the Fall upon her. She didn't do this on her own. She was purified because she allowed the cross to have its perfect work in her. More importantly, as the cross exposed the villainy of her worldview, she didn't draw back into the darkness to hide her deeds. She remained in the light and was cleansed.

So cry your tears if you must. Weep and lament over your condition. When you're done, repent, get up, and continue to follow Him. He is leading you to glory.

All His endless possibilities are before you. Your life is ahead of you and not behind you. It doesn't matter what anyone has said to you in the past. In Him, all their influences die. Those who belittled you and told you that you were worthless and had no value don't know you. You are the son of the Most High God, and He has declared His unfailing love over you. I know you can hear all the other voices. Can you hear His voice? I know you have believed all the other voices. Can you believe His voice? From now on, will you allow His voice to be the only voice you listen to?

Jesus didn't give His life to you so you could remain the same. He gave His life to you so you could walk in the fullness of your destiny. How you see and how you think about what you see will determine the rest of your life. Will you see and think about how you were created in His image and after His likeness and the wonderful blessings and responsibilities that truth brings into your life?

Will you give your life away to grasp God's high calling in Christ Jesus? Will you change your thinking and believe you've been saved to the uttermost, justified, and made righteous in Him? Will you believe that no matter what life brings to you or the situation or circumstance you find yourself in, God has not changed His mind about you? What He spoke in Genesis 1:26 is as true today as it was when He spoke it. Will you walk in the newness of life until you become His Bride, His wife, pure gold, transparent as glass, where the Lord is reflected in your life without shadow or distortion?

On Earth as It Is in Heaven

I've written down everything He has given me to write. But I'd like to write one more thing. God created you in His image and after His likeness, and He will not change His mind about you. Ever!

www.ingramcontent.com/pod-product-compliance
Lightning Source LLC
Chambersburg PA
CBHW062050080426
42734CB00012B/2599